S0-ARI-813

A Foursquare Church

This Book Belongs To
The Father's House

The
Father's
House

A Foursquare Church

With or without
the Y2K problem,
there will be a depression.
It may have begun before you
read this book.

-the author

Economic Doomsday

Gene Edwards

Copyright ©1998 by Gene Edwards. All rights reserved.

Cover design by Jenny Jeffries

Library of Congress Cataloging-in-Publication Data

Edwards, Gene
      Economic Doomsday /Gene Edwards.
      ISBN 0-940-232-64-2
      1. Economics—Non-fiction.
      2. Christian books—Non-fiction

Printed in the United States of America
99 98
  7   6   5 4   3   2   1

Dedication

to
Jerry, Pam and Joshua
Sheets

Has there ever been such a calamity happen.

Tell this tale in the years to come.

Tell your children and your grandchildren

And let them tell the next generation.

What the flying locust has left

The ground locust has devoured

What the ground locust has left

The hopping locust has devoured

What the hopping locust has left

The stripping locust has devoured!

Joel 1:2-4

Contents

Acknowledgement

To Tracey Bennell and Kathy McGraw for so many hours of typing and editing, and to my wife, the best of editors. But most especially to Jenny Jeffries for the long hours of toil, missed weekends of rest, and the inevitable sufferings which go with the writing of a book.

There are others, none of whom I know, the men who pioneered the alert to the world of the implications and dangers of the Millennium Bug. Senator Robert Bennett, Senator Christopher Dodd, Ed Yardeni, Ed Yourdon, Gary North, Peter de Jager and others I have unfortunately left out because of my lack of knowledge of their contribution. The members of the entire hemisphere are indebted to these men and women.

xii

Books by Gene Edwards

The Deeper Christian Life

The Divine Life
The Highest Life
The Secret to the Christian Life
The Inward Journey

Books that Heal

A Tale of Three Kings
The Prisoner in the Third Cell
Healing for those who have been...Crucified by Christians
Dear Lillian

The House Church Movement

*How to Meet Under the Headship of Jesus Christ
*When the Church Was Led Only by Laymen
*An Open Letter to House Church Leaders

The Chronicles of the Door

The Beginning
The Escape
The Birth
The Triumph
The Return

Radical Books for Radical Christians

Beyond Radical
Revolution, the Story of the First Century Believers
The Silas Diary
Climb the Highest Mountain
Rethinking Elders
Overlooked Christianity

SeedSowers Publishing House
P.O. Box 285
Sargent, GA 30275
800-228-2665

Author's
Introduction

The decision to write this book came while I was in England. For the next seven days, without a single reference tool, I wrote the first draft.

I have stated the case for a worldwide depression as conservatively as possible. This depression is coming *with* or *without* the Millennium Bug. This depression is the result of seventy years of a currency, and economy, which is based on an illusion.

There are immutable economic laws at work today and nothing can stop the coming economic collapse. The Y2K problem is but a handmaiden to these immutable economic forces, serving as a trigger to this economic catastrophe.

What shall be our shelter in the trying days which lie ahead for us all? This: the mercy of God, and the return to Christian community.

* * *

What are my qualifications for writing this book? They are rather unusual to say the least.

I know little about computers. I have never invested in the stock market. I am not a financial expert.

But I do understand *the natural laws* of moral economics inate to creation.

I have never felt that I could truly minister to the Lord's people if I did not understand these principles.

What you will find within these pages is that moral view of

economics—*a God's eye view*—of the principles which are forever present in all economics. This nation, alas *this planet*, has abandoned and then violated these immutable laws.

We now pay for that violation with a worldwide depression, the ravages of which only the wisest—always a few—will escape.

I write in fervent hope that those who are followers of the Lord Jesus may *prepare*—like their brothers and sisters in the first century prepared for a famine in Israel, and like the ancient Hebrew believers in Egypt who also prepared for a famine.

But more: We are faced with a matter far, far more important than this generation has known. We are, at this moment, settling what philosophy—what practice—of economics this entire planet will follow for the next two hundred years. Shall it be, as it has been, an economics based on theft, or shall we embrace an economics grounded in the universal laws of creation.

We will decide the future of economics, and we will do it in the next four years. If enough people revert to an economics organic to nature, the dark economics will have no hold on the future of mankind.

For Christians, this hour can be one of fear or it can be our finest hour. One way or the other, this economic collapse *will* ultimately turn out to the glory of our Lord, and to the advancement of His Kingdom. It is for you to decide your place in this high drama.

Gene Edwards

Prologue

Prologue

The Lady Who Does Not Need Rescuing

This is the beginning of a depression, not the end of the world. This book is about that depression, and what you can do about it. It is not a book on eschatology, nor doom and gloom that spells the annihilation of the world. A depression; something the church of the Lord Jesus Christ has been through before and can handle with hardly a hiccup!! This is not 666, it is 1999. A *depression*!! Look it up in the dictionary.

"Ah, but things are going to get so bad, the Lord is going to lift the church off the earth to prevent it from suffering. After all, God wouldn't leave His people on earth to go through suffering."

Sounds logical? Makes God look cruel if He leaves us here to suffer, does it not?

A depression simply does not qualify for being the end of the world. The church has been through many a plague, famine, fire and sword in the last 2,000 years.

The church of the Lord Jesus Christ is no "cry baby." She is the toughest lady in the universe, and eats tribulation for breakfast. She does not fear. She is feared!

She is the lady in Ephesians who is fighting an aggressive war of offense. Even more!! She is already triumphant and is doing a *mopping up operation.*

Afraid? Fearful?

Bring on the shared suffering!

What kind of Christian teaching depicted this lady as afraid
. . .of anything? This woman, the Bride of Christ, the daughter
of God, is afraid of *nothing*!

What kind of God have you? That is the wrong question!
What kind of church have you? This lady, named Ekklesia, is
the scourge of Satan, the terror of demons. This lady—and
never forget this—is the gal who kicks down the gates of hell.
This lady shines in adversity!!

This woman, the fiancee of Jesus Christ, is made for trouble.
She uses famine, pestilence, war, recessions and depressions to
show forth her triumphant Lord. . .and to bring glory to His
name. She has done so before, she will do so in this depression.

Paul called her "the mother of us all." That is some kind of
a lady to have as a mother. Nor is she afraid of a bear's tail in
Daniel nor a dragon's tooth in Revelation! When the earth shakes
in terror at all the suffering it sees coming; when man looks up
and sees the dreaded horsemen of the Apocalypse, this lady looks
at the same scene and sees nought but a lamb!

The next four years will be her finest hour. She has no need
and no interest in being spared. She will take the high ground
and laugh at those who shake in fear of these coming days.

Yes, there are the horsemen of war, famine and death; but
this lady is riding double with the triumphant Prince on the white
horse.

This is her hour!

Section I
Part I

1

A Disaster Called
January 4, 2000

It is Tuesday morning, January the fourth. Four days ago, on Friday, December 31, 1999, you went home from work to observe a long weekend of celebrating a new century and a new millennium.

Today, you get out of bed and flip the bedroom light switch—nothing happens. Further, there is no water coming out of the faucets. In the kitchen the electric stove does not turn on; the house is cold, the gas furnace is out. You try the television set, then remember the electricity is off. Then the telephone. No dial tone. No water, no electricity, no gas, no telecommunication. You decide to drive to town to get some water, but your *car* will not start! "Embedded chips!" you mutter.

You bike into town, go to the local police office, where you are told that thousands of banks have lost all their records. So has the New York Stock Exchange. The railroads are not running, communication satellites are dead. All the airfields in America (and around the world) are closed. The power grid is down. Over 99% of America has no electricity.

In Washington, the Social Security Administration cannot send out monthly checks because the computers of the SSA are down and records are scrambled.

The president has called out the military to relieve some of these civil crises, but there has been little response because no messages of any kind, to anyone, are getting through. There is no internet.

Rumor has it that there is only enough food in supermarkets to feed America for a week, at best. Trucks and trains are stalled because electricity is off, computers are down, consequently coal and petroleum cannot move. All nuclear power plants are off-line.

Most banks will not open again because their computers have lost their records. The financial institutions of this planet are all closed. Many financial records are gone with no hope of their retrieval.

Just about everyone else in America is having the same experience as you. So also, the rest of the people of this world.

Welcome to the new millennium and the *Y2K problem.*

> **Y - year**
> **2 - two**
> **K - thousand**

How long will the inconvenience last? A week? A month? (It will no longer be an inconvenience if it lasts two weeks; it will be, rather, a disaster.) *Six* months? If so, the Y2K problem will have become a catastrophe, perhaps the greatest mankind has ever faced.

A year? If a total shutdown lasts that long, civilization as we know it will have ended.

Sounds impossible?

Some of the above *will* happen.

All of it *can* happen!

But I hasten to say that the Y2K problem—the Millennium Bug—the Century Twenty-One meltdown, is *not* your *first* worry.

Something else is lurking out there, coming *before* December 31, 1999. The Millennium Bug, a computer glitch, may prove to be a minor incident in comparison. Both—or either—have the potential to rival the Black Death. This much is certain: The Y2K problem will come *after* a worldwide panic and *after* a worldwide depression. A depression which *will* begin in 1999. A depression *before* Tuesday, January 4 of the year 2000. This is a certainty. And it will bring poverty to the entire world.

The year 1999 is the *real* year to watch. A bank panic sometime in 1999 is very likely. A disaster of apocalyptic proportions is not wholly out of the question...in 1999. *All* that *without* the computer bug.

Together let us explore what may prove to be the most exciting days of our lives.

CAN SOMETHING THIS DISASTROUS *REALLY* HAPPEN?

Chisel it in stone. This will happen.
—Y2K analyst

The Millennium Bug... it's worse than you think.
—Business Week
March 2, 1998

We must require 100% compliance or we are all at risk.
—Alan Greenspan
Chairman
FDIC
U.S. Senate Subcommittee
February 27, 1998

Try to imagine no dial tone for the next two months! Try to imagine no electricity for two months. Then try to imagine no depression. No one has an imagination that vivid.
—the author

2

This Depression Has Already Begun

Look at what is happening now, overseas, and you see America's future. *Your* future...in a depression. And the scene overseas is grim.

This worldwide depression is underway in Asia, Latin America and Russia. Let's look first at South America.

Brazil's banks are charging interest rates of 50%. Rates like that grind a nation to a complete halt, creating massive unemployment, and bank closure. Banks in Brazil are collapsing. Their stock market has lost two thirds of its value. All this is *without the Y2K Bug.*

In *Japan*, the situation is reversed. Brazil has inflation, Japan has deflation. Japanese banks are charging interest rates of less than 1%, in an effort to stimulate the economy. Yet this also jeopardizes the existence of the banking system because no bank can operate charging 1% interest. Still, with rates that low, there has been no economic rally.

Some 7% of all bank loans in Japan are in default, which figures out to be *one trillion dollars* in *uncollectible* loans—no bank can operate long with such a high burden of unpaid loans. Unemployment—a Japanese impossibility—is rising. Ten of the twenty largest banks in the world are in Japan. Some of those banks have closed their doors forever. Nothing government has done to stem this deflation has helped. Nothing.

**Asia is toast. In a few months it will be burnt
toast.**

— *Dr. Ed Yardeni*
economist

The Japanese stock market is down by about 30%. The
power of the mighty yen is down. Foreign markets are thinking
seriously about pulling out. Japan, in turn, has said to us,
"America, we bought your debts. We are thinking about pulling
out of your stocks, bonds, and treasury notes." The Japanese
prime minister then added threateningly: "If we do, we will use
the money to buy *gold!*"

This depression began, unnoticed, in 1997

The depression we are about to become part of began in
Asia in 1997, when the Thai currency, *baht,* nose-dived to near
zero.

(Note: Any currency not backed by gold always ends up
where the baht is!)

Then came the collapse of the Indonesian economy. . . and
currency. Korea is in grief; Hong Kong's dollar hangs by a thread.

What caused the collapse of the economies of three Asian
nations? Government regulation of the market place,
encouraging some industries, discriminating against others. And
making loans too easy to obtain. When many of these loans
turned bad, banks began to get cautious, not loaning out money.
Expansion ended. Unemployment soared. This Asian crisis then
sucked Japan into its vortex. A cascade followed. One economy
fell, then another, then another. Why this chain reaction?

Because of *global interdependence*. Remember these words:
chain reaction and *domino effect*. That is what happened in
Asia. Then? Then the chain reaction leaped to Russia. From
there it swept on to South America, leaving economic devastation
everywhere.

The tragic situation in Russia—little reported—is appalling.

In the last eight years Russia has had two new currencies and four currency crises. Every bank in Russia has frozen all accounts. Unemployment in that sector of Russian economy is almost 100%. Some 150,000 people formerly employed in the banking/financial industry in Moscow are out of work. As I write these words 15,000 people in Moscow have lined up to apply for *one* job opening in finances. Russia's present currency is valued on the world's markets at zero. Everyone in Russia has lost everything. (Remember, this is but a harbinger of what is to come.) The Russian people are impoverished. The only exception? Those Russians who have *cash*. . .German marks and dollars.

What happened to cause this donnybrook? It is important that you know, because scenes not too unlike this are going to happen *here*.

Too much "bank money," money that existed only on bank ledgers, is what brought these countries down.

A few years ago, the Russian people, for the first time in 70 years, began placing their money in *banks* in order to draw *interest* on their deposits. Savings! Capitalism had come at last. Drawing interest on money did not exist under communism. Russia had an all-cash society.

In this "New Russia," people put money in the bank, for which they received in return a little sheet of paper marked "receipt," which told how much money they had just placed in the bank. (But was the Russian citizen's money *really* in the bank? The money existed only in the computer's tiny chip.)

Does such a practice sound strange to you? It should not. You and your bank do exactly the same thing every week. You "deposit money in the bank." You get a little sheet of paper called a *receipt*, telling you how much money *you* have in the bank. But *your* money is not in the bank. You have a receipt and your bank has entered your deposit in a ledger *in* the computer. Only 1.5% of all the money deposited in your bank is in cash. The rest is in a computer. It is called *ledger-entry* money or *data-entry* money. That money does not exist outside of a computer chip. It is the most "non-money," the most "losable money" in the world.

This is exactly what happened in Russia.

Then what?

The economic situation in Russia became worse.

The Russian economy turned bad because there were too many rubles being entered into those bank ledgers, too many loans, too much borrowing. That is always followed by loans going bad. Plus, government was meddling in what companies should manufacture, and what companies should not manufacture. All these are perfect ingredients for economic disaster. Seeing this, other nations began pulling investments out of Russia's economy. No investor likes inflation. (There were too many rubles—bank-entry rubles, *but very little cash.*)

Russian people began going to the bank to get their rubles out. The rubles were not there. Only records of money, but no money. Banks had ledger-entry rubles, encoded in computers, but few rubles you could put in your pocket. Banks did not have enough cash to meet withdrawals; therefore, banks were forced to close. The entire banking industry collapsed.

Everything changed. An overabundance of ledger-entry money, but now none of it was accessible. When banks close, "bank-entry money" disappears. That made cash exotically rare. The ledger-entry money was in computers, inside banks which had *closed* forever. The people of Russia, in turn, now have little or no cash.

The stock market plunged from 200 million sales a day to *one* million. Inflation is at 67% in Moscow. Soldiers are not being paid.

This is *Russia*, right *now*.

No banks, no cash.

This will change. The economic cycle goes like this: (1) too much bank ledger money, too many loans; (2) bad loans; (3) an unforeseen crisis; (4) banks close. As the banks close; (5) bank *ledger money* becomes nonexistent; (6) there is only cash, and very, very little of that; (7) government steps in, prints paper money, and cash becomes abundant—then overabundant—then insanely overabundant (It's called *inflation*); (8) the nation's currency becomes worthless; (9) everyone is impoverished.

Russia is entering the seventh stage of the cycle. But right now almost no one in Russia has cash. I saw a picture of what appeared to be about 50,000 people standing in front of *one* government-operated bank, hoping to receive some small amount of cash out of their frozen accounts. Do you really believe they will get all their money back? *If they do, it will be virtually worthless on the day they get it.*

What else?

Overnight, little *market places* have sprung up everywhere. People are going to these markets to sell or trade anything of value, in exchange for *food.*

Then there is the most desperate of acts:

People are turning to blood banks, to sell their blood, in order to survive. They go there by the tens of thousands. Each person is paid $20 for a pint of blood. (They can donate once every six weeks.) Many Russians are using that $20 to buy the most basic of food in order to just survive until they can give blood again. It's *that* bad.

Those few who have cash can *buy anything* for a song.

When banks collapse and bank ledger money disappears, government floods the nation with cash, while knowing full well this act will destroy the purchasing power of that currency. That means everyone's buying power plunges. Everyone loses the value of their savings. Nonetheless, with so few banks operating, and only for a few minutes, cash must be made available.

In international circles this conduct is unacceptable.*
Therefore, the Russian government pulled the ruble out of the
international currency market and announced it could not pay
its debts to international banks. The government is beginning to
produce cash for the Russian people. This money is worthless
outside Russia, but the government has no choice, because there
is virtually no cash at this moment.

The scarcity of cash makes cash powerful. Soon, however,
there will be so much cash in Russia, it will become near
worthless, even to a Russian.

A few Russians know this. When they do get their hands on
rubles, they will use them to buy *gold.*

If you question the power of cash—when the banks in Russia
closed, it turned out there were only 8 billion rubles in all of
Russia for 150 million people.

Then, immediately, came the miracle.

Out of mattresses, jars and holes in the backyard there
suddenly appeared 40 billion American dollars in cash from all
over Russia. Those 8 billion rubles and 40 billion dollars are the
"coin of the realm" in Russia. Right now, the Russian government
is turning on the printing presses and will soon destroy the power
of the ruble.

Then the dollar alone shall be king.

There are only 150 billion of our "rubles" in cash, in all
America! Get your money out of the bank.

---

* *Russia defaulted on the loans made by other banks in other countries.
This default has cost the United States financial institutions at least 9 billion
dollars. Latin American banks and financial institutions had also heavily
invested in a free Russia, and have sustained terrible losses, sending the
entire South American continent into a depression. Banks all over the
world are strained. Even the mighty UBS, the largest bank on earth (in
Switzerland) posted a 750 million dollar loss in bad loans to Russia.
Now Russia is facing "payment due" from nations. If they fail in paying
these bills, as one authority has said, "no country will ever again loan
Russia anything, for all eternity."*

Pause and realize that Russia's present situation will soon be the fate of the world. The kind of scene we see there will soon come our way. Expect these same patterns in other nations. What you have seen described in Russia is what will be happening in the rest of the world by December 1999.

This is essentially what happened right here in the *United States*, in 1929-1935.

Now we come to the worst of what is happening in our world today.

Look at Indonesia

The greatest tragedy on the planet right now is in Indonesia. If you have not heard of this crisis, you will. A year ago Indonesia was a prosperous country. Then Indonesia's banks and currency collapsed.

Hardly a year has passed since then, yet today there are 80 million people in Indonesia who are facing starvation. There is no logistical way to get enough food into Indonesia to adequately feed these people. Barring a miracle, in our present leaderless world, millions in Indonesia will soon be dying of starvation. This Indonesian crisis portends the greatest human tragedy ever faced by mankind in *all* history. *Never* before have *80* million people in one nation faced starvation.

You have just been introduced to the outskirts of *The Great Depression II*. It is here, it is growing larger, and it is doing so *without* the Y2K problem. The Y2K bug did not start this depression and is not causing its increase.

On September 22, 1998, at an economic conference in New York, with the Y2K Bug not even under discussion, President Clinton stated that the present global financial situation is the greatest economic crisis in *50* years.

The next day, another speaker at the same conference stated that we are in the greatest economic crisis facing America in *70* years. Again, no mention of Y2K.

As you read the contents of this book, you may decide that this is the greatest economic crisis to face America since its foundation, and the greatest financial crisis this world has faced since the fourteenth century.

A depression of incomprehensible dimensions is here!

Dare we add to this grim picture the terrible implications of what the Y2K mainframe bug can do—by itself—to the world's economy. Then add an even worse, more unsolvable problem, something called the *embedded chip* crisis. . . which is the big brother of the mainframe computer bug. Then add to this mix the European *euro* currency, being introduced in 2000. This currency is coming into existence in direct competition with the dollar.

Add all that together and you have the makings of the greatest loss of wealth, the greatest impoverishment of mankind, which history has ever recorded.

I did not want to pen this book, nor to write such things as are in the preceding paragraph. Nonetheless, the entire family of believers all over this world is going to wake up in poverty. Unless! Poverty for all of us, *unless* we act. Otherwise *you* will live out the rest of your life in poverty. Act, or your fate—poverty—is sealed.

Economics: God's or Man's

Interestingly, we Christians, all over the world, are faced with two unavoidable choices: to flow with the laws and practices of economics which are written into the very fabric of creation, or to go along with the present immoral practice of economics, *and lose everything*.

I am very close to stating: "It is a Christian's place to revert to the practice of economics as it is woven into the laws of creation." Otherwise, if we fail to act in the face of a practice of economics which must doom an entire planet to poverty, not only will we all pass into this catastrophe, we will all stay there far, far longer than needed.

If you please, it was a Christian God who created this universe. Essentially, then, this universe is a Christian creation, with moral and spiritual principles woven into the very blood stream of creation. The present day practice of economics as practiced worldwide in every nation on earth is, as you will see, both dishonest and immoral. It must one day collapse. It *is* collapsing. And its inevitable end is its own destruction and the impoverishment of all the people of this planet. It is an economics of slow theft and . . .ultimately . . .the bondage of all people, enslaved to pay off a debt which cannot be paid.

We are in the ultimate crisis of *that* economic practice as it pits itself against the economics which is natural to creation.

In order to escape the coming unavoidable disaster caused by the practice of one, you must flee to the other.

Now a parable. This parable will help you to understand the dark economics practiced all over the world today. It will help you to understand the *only* way to escape the resulting impoverishment when that dark economics reaches the point when it inevitably *falls*. This little parable will also help you to understand how the Y2K Bug is going to hasten the fall of the present practice of economics. . . before December 31, 1999.

Let us now discover the man who got us in this mess, so long ago!

Part II

The greatest con artist of all time was a Chinese who lived over two thousand years ago. He managed to talk other people into giving him their gold in exchange for a piece of paper.

—Will Durant

3

The Man Who Invented Paper Money

Once upon a time, long ago, in the Chinese city of Beijing there lived a very honorable, honest and wealthy merchant named Hon Ts Yon.

Now it came about that Hon Ts had a huge warehouse, the safest and most protected warehouse in all China. It had high, thick walls and was surrounded by guards.

China was very prosperous; inflation and deflation—debasing—were unknown. But there was a problem. There were many pirates and thieves near the capital city of Beijing. First and foremost, those thieves stole *money*. But it needs to be explained: In that day—unlike ours—money and gold were the same thing. To say *gold* was to say *money*. And vice versa. Gold was the *only* money the world knew of. (Not a very enlightened people were they?)

"Why not store your gold in my warehouse, where it will be safe?" said Hon Ts to the other merchants of the city. "In exchange for keeping your gold safe I will charge you only a very little amount of money for protecting your gold."

The merchants were interested but they had a question: "We trust you Hon Ts, but how do we get our money (gold) back when we want it?"

Hon Ts had the answer. You see, it was just about this time

that the civilization of China invented today's *paper*. It seems that a person could take worthless *wood pulp*, pound it, soak it, cook it, bleach it and then roll it, and it would turn into something you could write on and even print on! This wood pulp came to be called *paper*.

This is what Hon Ts proposed.

"Bring your gold into my well-protected warehouse. I will write down in my ledger exactly how much gold you deposited with me. I will give you a receipt which tells how much gold you left with me. Than I will also hand you a piece of wood pulp. This wood pulp will certify that you have so many ounces of gold in my warehouse. Every time you place more gold with me I will enter it into my ledger book. Each month I will add it all up in my ledger book and you will know the exact total of money you have inside the warehouse. Any time you choose to come and get your gold, you may do so. Just show me the piece of worthless wood pulp."

"Wood pulp?" said the other merchants.

"Yes, but *nice* wood pulp. Even *pretty* wood pulp," intoned Hon Ts proudly. "Using a silk screen printing press I will have printed upon this piece of wood pulp the image of my face, which will serve as a guarantee that I have your gold and that I will return your gold."

The merchants thought this was a *capital* idea, so each merchant brought Hon Ts their gold (for which he charged them a very tiny storage fee). In return each merchant received a beautiful piece of wood pulp with, sure enough, a portrait of Hon's face on it.

One day one of the merchants said to Hon Ts: "I am repairing my home. I only need a small piece of my one hundred-ounce bar of money. What can I do?"

"How many ounces do you need?"

"Just one ounce," replied the merchant.

Hon Ts took the merchant's piece of paper showing he had a 100-ounce bar in the warehouse. He then gave the merchant 100 sheets of wood pulp. . .one for each ounce of gold. The merchant gave one sheet back to Hon Ts and received one ounce of gold in return. He left the other ninety-nine ounces of gold in Hon's storage, and departed with ninety-nine pieces of paper.

This unique idea of having one hundred wood pulp certificates, one for each ounce of gold, caught on fast. Everyone wanted one hundred sheets of wood pulp when they deposited a one hundred ounce bar of gold. And Hon Ts *always* noted this in his ledger book.

Soon merchants began to trade with one another, not in gold but in these wood pulp certificates. They knew they could go and get their gold anytime they wanted. Occasionally a merchant did this, but not often.

One day, one of the merchants complained to Hon Ts, "I do not like paying you a fee for keeping my gold."

It came about that at this very moment another man came in and said to Hon Ts, "I need one hundred ounces of gold. You are very wealthy, can you loan some gold to me?" Both Hon Ts and the complaining merchant had the same idea simultaneously.

Said Hon Ts, "Merchant, let us loan this good man one hundred ounces of *your* gold? I will charge him a small fee for borrowing your gold and, in return, I will *not* charge you anything for storing your gold with me."

It was another *capital* idea. That way, the merchant did *not* have to pay for his gold being stored and Hon Ts made a small profit on loaning the merchant's gold out to another man.

All agreed!

Hon Ts gave the man the gold and made a record of the transaction in his ledger book. "See the ledger entry," said Hon Ts Yon, making sure both men were satisfied with what he had recorded. Then, Hon Ts even gave both men a receipt.

Later, the man who borrowed the one hundred ounces of gold returned it. Hon Ts was happy, the merchant who had loaned the gold was happy—and the borrower was happy.

This idea also caught on. Soon Hon Ts, and the merchant whose gold he kept, were loaning out gold to just about anybody in the capital who had a good reputation. Eventually gold was being loaned out to reputable people all around Beijing. Later, Hon Ts loaned gold to people all over the province. (Still later he loaned gold to other provincial governments and even to *foreign* countries, far away.)

It was not very long before everyone stopped exchanging the wood pulp back into gold. Everyone exchanged the wood pulp certificates with Hon Ts Yon's picture on them with each other. You could see those little sheets of wood pulp being passed around all over the market place by just about *everyone*. Further, Beijing was getting more and more prosperous, which pleased everyone, especially the emperor. (The emperor's name was Abacus Kon, son of Kubla Kon.) Trade was up, and robberies were down. Prosperity was, well, prospering.

Everyone was benefiting from all this movement of worthless wood pulp, from the lowliest shop keeper to the wealthiest men in all of China. Wood pulp was now being called "official certificates of gold." It became rare for someone to come and exchange his wood pulp for gold; but if he did, Hon Ts always, with flourish, gave the gold *and* made a *ledger entry*.

"Certificates" and "ledger entries". . .this all sounded *very* important.

No one seemed to notice that more and more (and more) wood pulp stamped "official certificates of gold" were showing up in the market place *and* just about everywhere else. If the people had stopped to count, would they have found there were more certificates than there was gold? Perish the thought.

Still, more and more (and more) wood pulp kept appearing.

Hon Ts was loaning wood pulp, uh, *gold*, to *everyone*. And everyone was getting more and more prosperous! Hon's couriers were even taking very heavy bags, by horseback, to faraway lands and nations. (He was making loans to kings of other lands.) This beautiful story of prosperity might have gone on forever, except for one thing. (And now, dear reader, I have to tell you something very sad. The words "except for one thing"...will *always* happen. A crisis *always* comes and bursts this beautiful illusion. *Every time*. *No* exceptions. Even in real life. Every time!)

A crisis. What crisis? Ah! No one ever knows. And something else: Those who loan, once they break the bounds of honesty, *always* loan too much. Had Hon Ts Yon done that, or was there just as much gold in the warehouse as paper in the market place?

Now, pay very close attention to the rest of this story about the man who *took* gold and *gave* paper.

The downfall of China's prosperity began with a *rumor*. A *rumor* can bring down a nation's economy?

Indeed, a rumor can destroy the currency and economy of an entire nation; yes, and even a world!

At this particular time, China was about to celebrate its birthday. It was only two years away from its 1000th birthday. This is when the rumor started. (Are you listening *closely*?)

The rumor?

There was a man up in Mongolia who made a vow (or so said the rumor). *According to the rumor this man's vow went something like this:*

> "My army and I are going to invade China. I will
> enter the Imperial City of Beijing on the first day
> of the new millennium."

(You *are* listening aren't you?)

Upon hearing this rumor everyone laughed. "The great empire of China cannot be brought down by a Mongol. And in just *two* years? We are the richest nation, with the greatest armies and weapons, more than all the rest of the world combined! He cannot do it! And surely not on the very first day of the new millennium."

"Why have we not heard of this Mongol before?" said all. "If he is so powerful we would have heard of his power to destroy before now! How dare he say: "In just two years and on one specific day!"

"He is forty years old? That means he was probably born in 1950 C.T. (Chinese time). Humpph!"

"This nobody claims to be terrible. He comes from something called *the house of Ter*?"

Everyone was certain he was no threat to the House of Peace and Prosperity. Still, news continued that this man, and this house, was coming. Little by little, stories of his destructive powers grew. (You are listening?)

One thing was sure. The Mongol from the House of Ter really had vowed to arrive in Beijing on the very first day of the new millennium.

It is an ancient Chinese custom to name each year after an animal. The year before had been the Year of the *Rat*. This year was the Year of the *Snake*. Next year, the first year of the new Chinese millennium, would be the Year of the *Insect*.

"The insect will come in the first day of the new millennium?" the people laughed.

Later, people learned the name of this man who swore he would arrive on the first day of the Year of the Insect. The name of this Mongolian who vowed to destroy the Kingdom of Prosperity was Kom Pu, of the house of Ter.

The stories about Kom Pu grew bigger and wilder every day, but still no one made preparation for the coming of Kom Pu of Ter.

Many began to believe *the insect* (that is what they were calling him) really *could* destroy their kingdom. Some months before the new millennium, Hon Ts noticed that a few of the merchants were coming to his warehouse, wood pulp in hand, exchanging paper for their gold. At first Hon Ts wondered why. No one had bothered to do this ever before. Had they heard that some of the people he loaned money to did not pay back the loan? Did they know how big, how bad, Hon's losses were? He also noticed those who were getting their gold out of the warehouse were among the wisest men in the kingdom. They were looking grim and stressed. Was it the bad loans, or the possibility *the insect* may come on the first day of the new millennium?

Hon Ts, seeing the *Chinese characters on the wall,* began assuring *everyone* that their money (gold) was safe and that there was *nothing* to fear. The great Emperor Abacus, who lived in the great *white palace* on Pencil Avenue, also began issuing extravagant reassurances to the people about *the insect* and the strong economy.

"Your gold is safe and our army will crush the barbarian insect. We will never let this happen! It must not happen, and therefore it cannot happen."

For some reason, which no one has ever understood, those daily reassurances coming from the *White Palace* on Pencil Avenue caused more people to come to Hon's warehouse with their wood pulp! He noticed that these people were also looking grim. Uncertain. Worried. A little fearful. *More stressed.*

(Oh, did I tell you the name of China's army. . .the one preparing to stop the invading insect? The army was called *Pu Gram Hurs.*)

Rumor said that Kom Pu of Ter had a great round face with slits for eyes. He wore on his head a helmet with two great horns. He always wore black fur. "He even *looks* like a big insect!" was the word in the market place.

"The *insect* is coming in *The Year of the Insect* on the first day of the new millennium," said alarmists. "And nothing can stop him. Not even the Pu Gram Hurs. There are not enough of them!"

Yet, despite all the rumors, the fact is *no one* had ever seen Kom Pu. It was not even certain that he existed. And if he did exist, was he *really* dangerous? Would he actually come? If he did come would he *really* be *that* destructive? Surely he could not end China's long and venerable civilization, could he?

People worried. Uncertainty grew. Some began saying, "The Year of the Insect is upon us and we are not prepared!"

Remember what I said: *Prosperity in Beijing, China might have continued forever, except for a crisis. . .and a crisis always* comes! Bad economics is always exposed, and it always brings a nation's people to poverty.

The merchants of the Imperial City were now coming to Hon Ts Yon's warehouse in even greater numbers to get their gold, each murmuring about that bug. Soon ordinary citizens were coming to Hon's warehouse with their wood pulp certificates. In the meantime, business was falling off, people were out of work.

Throughout the entire kingdom there was an atmosphere of near panic.

(You are listening carefully aren't you?)

At first the lines in front of Hon's warehouse were small. But as the end of 999 C.T. grew nearer—call it December 31, 999—the lines in front of his warehouse grew longer.

Then came a terribly frightening rumor. "Hon Ts does not have quite enough gold in his warehouse for everyone!" And "He made some bad loans."

Until now Hon Ts Yon had made good on his promise to return gold for wood pulp. But the *rumors* that he did not have quite enough gold terrified everyone. Now the lines around

Hon's warehouse swelled in size. Were the *rumors* true? Until now only about one-tenth of one percent of the people with those beautiful "official gold certificates" made of wood pulp had come to Hon Ts Yon's warehouse. Yes, less than one tenth of one percent. A great deal less.

Suddenly that had changed. Now thousands lined up in front of Hon's warehouse demanding their money (gold).

Finally, Hon Ts stepped outside the warehouse. His ledger, full of all these deposits of gold, was in his hand. Hon Ts raised his hand and spoke. In so doing, he gave the entire world the best lesson in economics that has ever been given. Bad economics always gets exposed, always ends in disaster. The cause? Is it bad loans? Too many gold certificates? Too much paper money? (Government interfering with the market place?) Too much ledger entry money? An unexpected crisis? A rumor of a crisis which *might* happen?

No one ever knows which brings down an economy and a currency. One of the above? Several? All? No matter. A currency not backed by gold *always* collapses. And the end? Everyone (except a few) are left in poverty.

Hon Ts announced:

"I know all of you have been. . .uh. . .banking. . .on getting all of your gold out of my warehouse. But I must confess that the warehouse is now empty. *All* the gold is gone. All I have left is ledger entries!"

"That's not money! That's not anything!" cried the people.

"Our wood pulp, is it worth anything!?"

"No, paper is not worth anything," confessed Hon Ts. "It never was."

Everyone was shocked. They could understand how ten per cent of the gold might be gone, or twenty per cent. But all? Only one per cent of the people got back their money (gold). What they did not know was that Hon Ts Yon had passed out pieces of wood pulp that were exactly twenty thousand times greater than the amount of gold in the warehouse. Actually, it was not only that he had passed out thousands of pieces of wood pulp for every ounce of gold. He had loaned out to other nations all but 1% of all the actual *gold* itself. Much of the gold which *should* have been inside Hon's warehouse was now overseas.

No one had money! The entire nation was bankrupt!

The common people did not understand the warehouse operations but they did understand the merchants were now as poor as they were! No one had anything, except worthless pieces of wood pulp. Beautiful, official-looking, worthless wood pulp.

Everyone was now poor. Worse off than ever they had been before paper certificates were created by Hon Ts. The poverty that engulfed the nation was far, far greater than the wealth had been during the years of artificial prosperity. This false prosperity never equaled all the abject poverty it caused. The world would have been far better off had this prosperity never come. Prosperity took double revenge on the nation that had currency with no gold behind it.

Why did Hon Ts do what he did?

"Well," explained Hon Ts lamely, "it seemed that none of you would *ever* come and request your gold, so I loaned all of it out. I never expected this rumor, nor this crisis, nor this bug."

"Then we have nothing but wood pulp with your picture on it?"

"And the warehouse's ledger entries!" responded Hon Ts defensively.

Looking at the one small piece of wood pulp he held in his hand, one man, seeing with new eyes, said: "It was never anything but worthless paper. Without gold backing it up, the paper is *worthless!*"

Why had the nation been so very prosperous? Why not! Everyone had twenty thousand times as many wood pulp certificates as there was gold. And! Everyone *thought* there was that much gold. Then came the crisis. Actually, the *rumor* before the crisis. (It was that rumor which wrecked the nation's economy *before* the millennium and *before* the bug!) Perception, and nothing else, caused the prosperity. Perception, and nothing else, brought down the prosperity.

All prosperity in economics is perception, unless it is backed by intrinsic, tangible, gold!

As to Hon Ts? He set in motion the mess we are in. Our nation once had gold as money. But we, like the Chinese merchants, got used to the paper certificates which declared that there was gold in the bank to back the paper and that you could change the paper to gold anytime you wished. We used the paper, always knowing it was backed by gold.

But one day our government stopped backing the paper with gold. We now use paper backed by nothing. The moral laws of the universe state that such a system must fall. Our economic practice is dishonest. Like Hon Ts Yon, who turned out not to be so Hon Ts after all, any government that gives its people wood pulp and tells them that wood pulp is money is dishonest. Our system of economics must fail, and it will fail. This is not a guess, nor a "maybe." This is a law in creation as certain as the law of gravity. One day, a money not backed by gold will collapse. That hour is upon us. *Now.*

What of Kom Pu? Did he destroy the city? It really is not important to know, is it? The doors are wide open for a Kom Pu rumor, and it is the *rumor* which destroys.

Like the people in the parable, we are waist deep in ledger money. Everyone is ledger-entry rich and gold poor. What can cause our collapse? A rumor?

Let's attempt to understand a few things.

First, you have no real money. None. From 1797 until 1933, everyone in America had real money. Since 1933, neither you nor any other American has ever had real money. A new, worldwide, economic philosophy took over. All people of the earth, *all of us*, no longer have *real* money. We have paper.

Nothing could be more dishonest or immoral than a society working for wood pulp. . .and it is losing its buying power every day. This illusionary money is gradually being robbed from you.

Worse, even the paper is scarce.

What you "own" as money is nought but an entry in a bank's ledger. Money-in-the-bank money is not money at all. Your bank keeps somewhere between 1% and 5% of its holdings, in cash. The rest is theory money.

"The money ain't there" and "banks don't have money" is your first step in understanding today's practice of economics.

A few weeks ago the Russians learned that those *receipts of deposits* were worthless, and "the money ain't there." Ledger-entry money is nothing.

We have no real money. We have (1) paper, and (2) ledger entries. Very little paper, and lots and lots of ledger-entry money. We live in a monetary illusion. The bubble *must* burst.

No paper money in history has ever existed for long, when not backed by gold.

Lines will form. Banks will close. Ledger-entry wealth will disappear.

Christians can change this immoral system, just as they did slavery. *You* can do two things. . .prevent personal poverty and cause a return to what we had from 1797 to 1933. Mankind has a right to own *real* money as surely as it has a right to free speech. It takes about seventy years. . .and an unexpected crisis for people to realize that fact.

An earthquake? A famine? Government trying to control the market place? A terrorist attack? A small nuclear device exploding in some city in Europe or America? Or, how about a rumor? A rumor of a computer glitch which is going to bring down the world's financial system. That is all that is needed.

A depression in Asia, South America, and Russia. . .and add to that the *rumor* of the Y2K problem: These *are* going to destroy today's economy.

Is there wisdom in this tale for those of us living in this modern age? Yes, and the wisdom is simple:

1. Gold is money, wood pulp is not money.

2. When there is an overabundance of wood pulp in ratio to gold, and a crisis comes (and one always comes), a nation's currency will go into crisis; and the end will be a depression.

3. When a nation does not back its wood pulp with gold, there will always come a point where there is a drowning flood of wood pulp certificates. That nation's economy is certain to, one day, experience economic ruin. The people of that nation *will* suffer great hardship.

4. A crisis, unforeseen and usually unexpected, rips off the false face of a false prosperity.

5. Ledger-entry money does not even exist. In a crisis, turn your ledger-entry money into real money. (Or even wood pulp money. *Anything* is better than having ledger-entry money.)

*   *   *

Economic doomsday is a natural, organic result of violating the intrinsic laws of basic economics. It is the nature of things.

Should you allow government to convince you that paper is money, government will issue paper money with nothing backing it and will continue to produce more and more paper money until that paper money has absolutely no value. This is the nature of men and of governments. It cannot be changed. Our only recourse is to revert to real money.

Government has stolen from you the inalienable right to keep the fruits of your labor and an unchangeable value of your wealth.

Government has stolen your wealth by reducing the value of the money which you received in exchange for your toil. Government continues this theft until the money you receive has become worthless.

Finally a crisis, which will come, will cause the money which you hold to be found out as utterly worthless. You will become impoverished.

Let us make that practical: In a major crisis, real money is the only money that is worth possessing. Money listed on a ledger is *not* money.

Your hope? There is no hope. At least not for ledger money. Government steals the value of your money so slowly you cannot truly grasp the theft in one lifetime. No one on earth escapes the debasing of their money. No one can prevent debasement of their money when that money is *not* backed by gold. An economic crisis comes about once in a lifetime. When this crisis approaches there is something you can do. You can **resist** government's theft.

How? Turn your ledger-entry money back into *real* money. But you must do this *before* the crisis comes. You must be one of the wise ones, as in the days of Hon Ts.

Go from ledger money into metal money. Return to the organic laws of economics before the immoral economics of ledger-entry money are exposed. The Bug is coming. Whether The Bug is dangerous or not is irrelevant. It is the stress and fear before The Bug arrives which *will* cause a panic. Act *before* that panic.

In an economic crisis, only money you can hold in your hand is money. What is in a warehouse is *not* money.

Real money is *gold*, but only when that gold is in your hand. Now the bad news!

In our modern society there is no pretense of gold backing paper money.

Our money is backed by *nothing*! The laws of economics dictate that government will take advantage of the fact that paper money is backed by nothing. Historically, government has consistently *over-issued* paper money. . .until it is worthless. You have *never* owned real money. That right was taken from you.

Now the good news.

In an economic crisis it is the instinct of man to revert to gold! It does not matter what government says, nor what laws it passes, in an economic meltdown gold once more becomes money.

One last principle of organic economics.

In a catastrophic disruption of a nation's economy, the people most likely to preserve their wealth are those who have moved out of things which are not of tangible value. *Everything.* Wise men will have money in those tangible, intrinsic commodities which all mankind has always recognized as money. In *every* tribe, tongue, culture and race, throughout history, gold has been held to be money.

About the only other thing that fits in that category is silver. These two elements play only a small role in the life of mankind *until a calamity.* Then, in crises, above all else gold and silver become the center of the preservation of wealth.

That time has arrived. That crisis is here. Now.

Is the dollar redeemable in gold? *No.*

The only thing backing those beautifully engraved certificates made of wood pulp is our imagination!

Well, how many dollars are there? The answer will give you an idea of how valuable the dollar is. Take a deep breath, the answer to how many dollars government has printed is staggering. No, the answer is *paralyzing.*

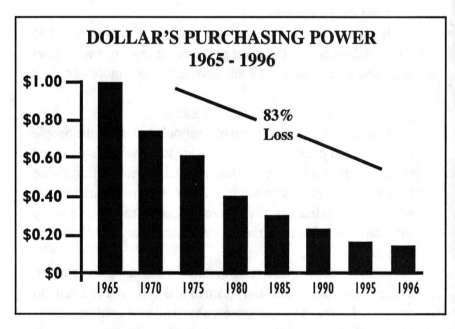

DOLLAR'S PURCHASING POWER
1965 - 1996

83%
Loss

And you thought you were getting rich. A man with $100,000 in
1955 would laugh at today's millionaires!

Part III

4

The Depression, Even Without Y2K

With or without Y2K there is going to be a worldwide depression...in 1999. Will the Y2K Bug start it? No. Will it be caused by the millennium meltdown? No. Let's look at this—which we are now entering—a depression, *without* Y2K.

This depression is the result of violation of inherent laws, laws which simply refuse to be violated for long. These are economic laws which are part of the natural order of things. We have violated that natural order in three ways.

There Are Too Many Dollar Bills

Here is the first law.

A nation's currency becomes weak when there is too much of it.

The more currency, the less the buying power of the currency of that nation—per person. There are far too many dollars. More dollars than any currency in human history. Far too many dollars to allow our currency to remain solvent.

Have you ever wondered just how many dollars there are in the world? It is obviously not a frequently asked question. I called the FDIC to find out. They could not even *understand* my question. I finally dug up the answer. And, yes, there are too many dollars for the dollar to really be of value. *Perception* is all that is holding up the American dollar.

There are over 100 *trillion* dollars in the world. Most of it exists only as entries in a ledger. Actual paper bills are few.

That is, *most* of those dollars are *nonexistent except as an electronic entry.* Trillions which exist *nowhere* except in computers. The terrifying point is that almost all of that 100 trillion dollars may disappear! These computers which record these trillions of dollars are almost *certain* to crash at midnight on December 31, 1999.

That includes *your* money!

When **the** computer crash occurs, every penny you have in the bank will be wiped out. You will have only the money that is in your pocket. The money in your savings account and checking account will no longer exist. (It was never anything but an electronic blip in the first place.)

But again, you can lay aside the scenario of your losing all your money in a vast computer meltdown. It is not the meltdown in 2000 which will cause this depression. It is the knowledge . . . in 1999. . .of that coming meltdown which will cause this depression *before* December 31. The computers will still be working when the banking industry begins to collapse.

What we are looking at is what will happen *without* the Y2K problem. Banks will still collapse. There are simply too many dollars on this planet, and in the American economy. It is an inherent law of economics that when there is too much of any currency, that currency loses its value. Eventually it loses all value. Where are the 100,000,000,000,000 dollars (with over 99% of it found only in computers)? Remember: Money in an electronic machine is *no money* at all.

Some 40 trillion of that 100 trillion dollars are in banks . . . only as electronic entries!! Money in the bank is nothing but electronic entries, which is nothing. It is the most easily destroyed, *fragile* money on this planet! It is also over 99% of all the dollars in this world, with holdable, foldable cash being actually quite rare. In fact, there may be fewer paper dollars in America, per person, than ever before in American history. Just how much is $100 trillion? Whatever it is, it is too much. It is more than can be understood, more than can be imagined. It is doubtful that the entire planet Earth is worth $100 trillion. If we put earth up for sale the Martians would not offer us that much.

Remember, we are only discussing the American dollar, not the German mark or the Swiss franc or the English pound, or the Hungarian forint. Nor the Austrian schilling, nor the Canadian dollar, nor the French franc, nor the Japanese yen. Just the dollar. If you tightly stacked $100 trillion in one dollar bills, that stack would reach over 6 million miles into the sky.

When a government produces too much of a currency, it must become *worthless*. In tangible value, toilet paper is really worth more than a dollar, simply because there is less of it. But there are not 100 trillion paper dollar bills on this earth. Over $99 trillion of it exists nowhere except in accounting. Accounting *electronically* recorded. One hundred trillion dollars, in cash, is too much to have worth.

As in the story of Hon Ts Yon, all it takes is an economic crisis to unmask the false idea that the dollar has worth. Or even a perceived crisis. That crisis *has* come!

The Year Two Thousand problem!

That is a crisis so vast, just *contemplating* it will trigger an economic depression and the collapse of a bloated currency that has been issued far, far beyond its value.

How much cash is there?

With 99 trillion *ghost* dollars, how much foldable, holdable *cash* is there?

An article appeared in *US News and World Report* on April 27, 1998, which should have caused all of us to go to the bank and demand the bank give us our money in cash.

This US News article announced that there are 450 billion
US dollars in actual cash, including coins, with only $150 billion
of that cash located in the United States of America. The overseas
nation holding the largest amount of American cash is Russia.
In fact, right now barter, and the one-dollar and five-dollar bill,
are holding Russia's economy together.

If you divided up 150 billion dollars between 270 million
Americans, you come up with around $500 per person, in
holdable, foldable cash. All the rest is ledger-entry money—
which is no money at all. Every one of us, including John D.
Rockefeller and Bill Gates, has access to about $500. I have
already pulled out $500 from the bank. I am holding it, in cash,
until after December 31. So has my wife.

If I am lucky I am going to get *another* $500. That means I
get John D. Rockefeller's $500. If I get another $500 I am
going to take Bill Gates' $500 away from him and turn it into
cash. That means if I get yet another $500 I am going to get
your $500 in cash. You, and Bill Gates, and John D. Rockefeller
are not going to have *any* cash at all. Bill Gates is worth
somewhere between $11 billion and $40 billion. But virtually
every penny of that money is in stocks and in electronic entries
in banks. Let the mainframe computers crash and Bill is going
to lose all his electronic entry money. That means Bill may be
flat broke! (After all, I have his cash. It is under *my* mattress!)
Unless Bill acts fast, and soon, I am going to be richer than Bill
Gates. I have $500 dollars in cash.

Actually, I think Bill Gates has already figured this out. I
recently learned that Bill has purchased an entire island out in
some obscure part of the Atlantic Ocean. He is building a self-
contained little world there. Bill Gates, do you know something
the rest of us don't know?

The laws of economics say: Too much of any currency causes
that currency to collapse. The collapse is usually triggered by
an unforeseen crisis. To illustrate:

Diamonds are very expensive, for only one reason. They are *rare*. If diamonds were as plentiful as sand they would be worth nothing, just as sand is worthless. It is just as true of the American dollar. There comes a point when even the dollar is so massively prolific that it becomes worthless.

The *first* violation of the innate laws of economics is: The more a currency is issued, even if it exists only as an entry in a ledger, the less buying power that currency has, until its buying power reaches zero.

In the meantime, you need to remember that you only have $500 in cash in this world, and the rest of it is electronic, which means your entire wealth is buried in a computer, and that computer is probably not going to be operating beyond December 31, 1999. And even if it *does*, there are tens of thousands of mainframes that will *not*, which will quickly cause the computer with *your* account in it to crash.

The estimate of $500 per person in cash may be too high.

There are two other estimates of how much cash there is.

One estimate gives each American about $160 apiece, or only $42 billion in actual cash in America. There is yet another estimate that is even lower, that is that there is only $18 billion in cash moving throughout America.

Let's stay with the higher number of $150 billion for the sake of those who have weak hearts.

Where is the rest of that $100 trillion?

There is 40 trillion dollars in banks, either in a savings account or checking accounts.

There are 8,900 commercial banks in America with a total of all banks being a little over 13,000 and 60,000 branches.

Another 25 trillion dollars is in the nation's stock markets. Every 1000 points on the New York stock exchange equals two trillion dollars. Add the American stock exchange, the over-the-counter market, and the commodities market, and you have about 20 trillion dollars.

Question: How much does the Federal government owe?

"On Budget" debt only

1932	**22 BILLION DOLLARS**
1940	**400 BILLION DOLLARS**
1980	**800 BILLION DOLLARS**
1981	**1 TRILLION DOLLARS**
1998	**6 TRILLION DOLLARS***

This 6 trillion dollars is "On-budget." There is an "Off-budget" debt of 18 trillion dollars, which means the Federal government is approximately 24 trillion dollars in debt—an amount so astronomical in size it cannot be paid back nor can it be serviced indefinitely. This debt is greater than the total value of the United States.

Answer: 24 trillion dollars!

Now we come to debts and loans. The government of the United States owes 6 trillion dollars in "on-budget" debts. It has often been said and often argued upon, that this debt cannot and will not be paid off.

Then there are the stock brokers. Merrill Lynch alone holds two trillion dollars of its customers' money. So also Charles Schwabb. Add to that the trillions which are in insurance companies who hold trillions of dollars *outside* of banks.

Add to that the nations which hold US dollars as the insurance which backs their own currency. Yet others, like Liberia, have made the American dollar their official currency. The amount of dollars held by individuals all over this planet is unknown.

What about "off-budget" debt? We have co-signed loans of several trillion dollars with other countries.

Now we come to the big stuff.

That is, we come to the little-known figure of how much money the Federal Government owes the Social Security fund. In September, 1998, the official figure that the government owed Social Security was 11 trillion dollars. They called it "unfunded" debt.

Add to that Medicare, and other Social Service debts, and there are three trillion dollars more in federal debts.

(Not only will the debt government owes never be repaid, the interest the government must pay on this debt each year, as we will see later, will destroy the nation's economy.)

Banks:	$40,000,000,000,000
Stock and commodity markets	
& insurance companies:	$30,000,000,000,000
Medicare, Social Security	
& other entitlement debts:	$14,000,000,000,000
On-budget debt:	$6,000,000,000,000
Co-signed debt:	$4,000,000,000,000
Other nations dollar reserves:	$5,000,000,000,000 (est.)

This $100 trillion falls into two categories. One, the debts which the government owes. . .and can *never* pay off.

Secondly, it is money in banks and in stocks, savings and investments.

One is debt, the other is savings, but savings in electronic money which is in jeopardy of disappearing.

Too many dollars. Too much debt. Too little cash.

Sometime in 1999, as the Y2K awareness spirals, Americans are going to line up at the bank to get out of electronic-entry money. . .which might soon disappear. They will want all their checking account and savings in cash. And banks will close. It does not matter if the banks are perfect in Y2K compliance.

The knowledge of the danger will bring down the financial world.
This is what happens to all bloated currencies in the face of possible catastrophe. Every one electronic dollar is less than half a cent in cash. One dollar for every 260 electronic ledger-entry dollars. And the 260 is in grave danger of vanishing.

Chances are, you will be one of those in the line. The chances of your getting cash is one in 260!

Let us now see the next law of economics we have violated.

There Is Too Much Credit

Never in human history has anything even remotely rivaled the amount of credit that this country has made available in the last few years. The laws of economics say this cannot continue, and the result of this violation is impoverishment! We are in an era of *credit expansion* no other generation would dare dream. Men of past ages *knew* the ultimate results. This expansion was made possible by government and banks issuing loans of breathtaking proportions. No nation has ever successfully gone into similar credit expansion without paying for it.

It has often been stated that it is impossible to have a *boom* without then having a *bust*. There is no boom that has ever rivaled this one. Since 1990, stocks, for instance, have risen over three times as much as they did in all the previous 200 years. *That* is credit expansion, that is dollar expansion.

The more dollars there are, the more worthless they become.

Look around you and see something that no human has ever seen before in history.

Read your mail! I am receiving a minimum of two offers per day from loan companies I have never heard of, offering to loan me up to 120% of the value of my house. I am receiving offers of credit cards with a charging power of $100,000. (I have turned them all down—I am waiting for a credit card that will give me $1,000,000 of credit limit, plus a one-way ticket to Argentina!)

When the credit cards first came out in the 1960's, they had limits of $100, and $200. Today, I have a little piece of plastic in my pocket that will let me charge as much as a new automobile. The stock market has been giving people back 20-30% on their investment so long that many have gone to the bank and borrowed money, turned around and invested that money in the stock market, knowing *(believing)* that they were still going to make at least a 15-20% profit above what they have to pay back to the bank.

More examples?

Furniture and appliances can be purchased with no money down and skipping the first six months of payment. You can get a $1,000 - $2,000 rebate on purchasing an automobile. Home owners all over this country are taking out second mortgages on their house to buy things or to consolidate debts, knowing as they do so that the second mortgage puts their indebtedness far beyond the value of their house. Most Americans have debts much larger than the amount of money they have in their savings account.

The national domestic product is only 35% more than our annual debts. Well, at least we are better off than Belgium. They owe 125% of their annual production.

Today, when an American child is born, he owes the government $20,000. The government admits to that. The truth is, that baby is in debt $80,000 the day he is born. That figure represents the true $24 trillion government debts. Look at that same child when he is 22 years old. He has just graduated from college. He walks off the campus owing a bank $100,000 for his education.

America has never seen credit expansion like this. And we are not the only ones. Japan is a harbinger of where we are *going* to be. Like America, like all nations in the midst of a vast credit expansion, Japan made too many loans. They loaned on the basis of "let's pretend." At this moment, the Japanese people have savings of $11 trillion in banks. Those banks are *not* safe, but on the verge of insolvency. In 1990 the Japanese banks were dealing with approximately 2% bad debts on their loans. Today, Japanese banks are faced with bad loans of almost 8% of all their loans. There is no such thing as a bank that can stay solvent when it has bad loans of 7% to 8%.

When a boom hits, too many loans are made. That is what makes the boom! This will always be true of any currency not backed by gold. The end will be a bust. Once or twice a century that bust will be so terrible it will end in the impoverishment of the people.

We are there, now.

Our entire planet teeters on a depression. The one safe island on this earth, right now, is the United States. However, because of growing poverty people of other nations are, of course, buying less, and that means we are selling less.

In the meantime, because *they* are in financial straits, they are offering their products at fire-sale prices. We are buying them. When we buy overseas products, we are not buying American products. That puts a squeeze on American companies. American businesses produce less. When they produce less, those businesses must either fire some employees or cut salaries.

We will be the last nation *into* this depression, but all those loans and all that borrowing is going to fall on our heads. Again, banks will collapse, the stock market will plummet.

Why? Basically: Too many dollars. Too many loans. Too much debt.

An economy cannot do this and survive. Remember, there was a 60% increase in credit in the last 16 months before the crash of October 1929.

We come now to the third law of economics which cannot be broken with impunity.

Money Is *Not* Backed by Gold

We respect the law of gravity because it does not change. Here is another law that demands as much respect.

When a nation ceases to back its money with gold then government will continue inflating that currency until that currency is worthless.

Purchasing Power of Gold and of the U.S. Dollar

From 1797 until 1933, our paper currency was backed by gold. Since 1933 the currency of the United States has *not* been backed by gold. All that paper, and all those electronic bank entries, are backed by nothing. Please look at the chart and see what has happened to the American dollar since 1933. . .and *before* 1933. This loss of the buying power of the dollar *cannot* go on. We are up against an immutable law of economics: A currency *must* one day reach a point where the people lose confidence in it. We stand on the precipice of a day when the American people will lose confidence. . *first* in ledger-entry money, then—some years later—in holdable, foldable dollars.

The *first* kind of dollar to go is electronic. We will want only *cash* dollars. . .few though they be. If you and I are fortunate enough to get cash we will be among the few.

Later, the government will be forced to produce more cash. It will be for all the people who have none. But government will know full well that when it starts flooding the nation with paper money, that act will destroy the nation's currency. One way or the other, currency not backed by gold will be destroyed.

The *first* stage of this destruction is when citizens lose confidence in electronically recorded ledger money. The *second* stage is when government is forced to print cash in order to bring the country out of the depression. So much cash is made available that everyone loses faith in it.

Then comes the *third* stage in which the government has to either devalue their currency or issue a totally new currency. The result? The impoverishment of that nation's people. Again: we are entering a depression when you see all these stages.

* * *

What should you do? Obviously, you should get your $500 out of the bank! While you are at it, get Bill Gates' $500 as well as John D. Rockefeller's. You cannot get mine, because I have already pulled out my $500. If you do not act soon, I may get *your* $500! You do not have a lot of time. Do not think for a moment that you do have time. The wise will act *now*, and it will be only the wise who are not impoverished.

The cash you check out of the bank will be very powerful at some point, more powerful than any cash you have ever held in your hand before. But then there will come a day when government will destroy even the power of cash. What do you do to prepare for *that* stage of this depression? We will learn more about that a little later.

Right now, we must move on to see two things you must do.

5

Get Out of the Stock Market
Get Out of the Bank

Being rich on paper is ever so satisfying, but also fragile and fleeting. Investors (in the stock market) revel in the money they are making on paper. But too many do not seem to recognize that only if they cash it in, is the gain in their pockets.

—Dr. James L. Green
Professor Ameritus
University of Georgia

In any depression there are two places you do not want to be. You do not want your money in a bank. The banks are going to fold. You do not want to be in a stock market. In a depression, or even an approaching depression, the bottom will have fallen out of the stock market. That has happened ever since I began writing this book. (Just now, a cut in interest rates, designed to stimulate the stock market, caused the New York Stock Exchange to *drop* over 400 points.)

As I write, the stock market sits at about 7,500—down from an all time high—on July 17, 1998—of almost 10,000. By the middle of December of 1999 it will probably be sitting somewhere around 2,000. Perhaps a little more, perhaps a little less. You need to be out of it *right now*.

Just recently I saw a little prayer: "Lord, I want to get out of the stock market; just let me break even and I promise never to put money in it again."

A lot of people are thinking that they are going to be able to get their money out on a rally, thereby at least breaking even. This might hold true for 80 years out of every one hundred, but it will not hold true *now*. The stock market will have a few little rallies along the way, but it is headed straight south.

One-third of the world *is* in a depression.

A statement appeared recently in USA Today (October 2, 1998): "The economic well-being of Brazil is critically important, not only to our (American) economy, but to the *entire* hemisphere."

Japan's banks are saddled with one trillion dollars in bad debts. Banks all over the world are toughening up on loans. It is called a worldwide credit crunch.

Russia has just offered to pay off its bank debts to its foreign investors at about 10 cents on the dollar. Lending standards are going up, which means the market is going down. Most economists are now predicting a recession in America.

Here is a harbinger of coming days. Walt Disney Productions is one of the world's most *depression-proof* businesses. The CEO, Michael Eisner, has asked his advisor how to prepare for a *deflation* economy.

All this *without* the computer bug. By the time our entire nation becomes aware of what the Y2K bug can do to destroy the world's economy, this nation is going to be as tense as it was on December 8, 1941, when we declared war on Japan. December of 1999 should turn out to be just about the most stressful month in your lifetime. Even the brightest optimist and the most cavalier "I'm not worried" among us will be in raw panic.

There are going to be times before that day arrives, when

you are going to be sure that men in high offices are going to make that December 31 deadline go away. They are *not*. There are going to be cycles of panic and reassurance all through 1999. But by the end of the year there is going to be no cycle at all. The depression is going to be a universal reality. Except for those who are wise and have prepared ahead of time, it will mean impoverishment. And preparing ahead of time means *right this minute*.

Up and running, in a week?

You are going to hear a great deal of statements like this: "Yes, things may get bad. But don't worry. On January 1, we are going to lose electricity, we are going to lose the dial tone. We may lose telecommunications, nationwide. We may see a breakdown in transportation. But don't worry, this will only last about three weeks, then everything will be fixed and back, up and running perfectly. Prepare for a maximum of three bad months. After that the nation will have adjusted."

Intelligent leaders of every segment of America's business and industry have been working on the Y2K problem since 1996. They are spending 100 billion dollars on fixing the Y2K Bug. Yet, right now, almost everybody is behind the curve. How are they going to magically fix in three weeks or three months what they have not been able to fix in four years?

Get Out of the Stock Market

The computers which run Wall Street are not compliant. That is, they have not and will not meet their deadline of December 31. And if they do, these computers will not be able to talk to non-compliant computers. . . which will be most of the computers which are overseas. If you hear an announcement that the Wall Street computers have made it, ask this question: "Does that include the embedded chips?" It *cannot* include the embedded chips because no one knows which embedded chips are going to stop working until *after* they have stopped working. Even then, there is nothing to replace them.

And if all the stock exchanges in America work perfectly on January 4, 2000, they do not dare receive incoming information from any computer anywhere that has not been tested against the stock exchanges in this country.

Stay with the market long term?

Again, the *anticipation*, rather than the arrival, of the Y2K Bug will wreck the world's economy.

There is one thing above all else that you must realize: This is not a market in which you should hold your invested money for the long haul.

To illustrate:

If you had invested in the stock market in 1929 "for the long haul" you would not have broken even until 1955.

When someone tells you "ride out the dips," keep this in mind. In January 1973 the stock market reached a record high and then fell. It lost 44% of its value before it started up again. Calculating for inflation, it took almost ten years to get back to the 1973 break-even point. To stay in the market and ride it out for the long haul is, on this present occasion, fool's advice.

Just a few weeks ago we were reassured that this was one of the strongest economies the world has ever known and that what we are looking at should go on indefinitely. We heard those words over and over. (That is when I began writing this book!)

Right now the words *recession* and *depression* are showing up in almost every newspaper, television and radio analysis of today's market. Keep in mind that in 1929, when the stock market was at an all-time high, President Hoover said, "...never have the people of any nation known so great a security in keeping the fruits of their labor." On July 8, 1932, just a little over two years later, the stock market hit an all-time low. In fact, Wall Street was almost out of business.

If the Dow Jones is at 2,000 in December of 1999, it may be a minimum of twenty-five years before you get back to where you are today. Ride out the dips? This is one market where you can proclaim: "Sell high, sell even, sell low. Come back in when the market is subterranean!"

Get out of the stock market.

Here are three reasons: ● The computers that run the stock exchanges of America are going to break down. ● Secondly, the computers that run the stock markets of the rest of the world are even further behind than ours. ● When they collapse, ours will collapse too. This is one global stock market. No *one* market can sustain the loss of all the other markets without itself going through the floor. The markets of Asia, Europe, and South America have no hope of repairing their computers in time for the December 31 deadline.

But there is another reason. Today's practice of economics has violated the natural order of things. This economy *cannot* stand. . .with or *without* Y2K.

Get out of the stock market.

Some 48% of America's families have their savings in the stock market. Can you imagine what would happen to the ruination of this nation, when those people lose virtually *all* their savings? Recovering from a depression of that magnitude will take a generation.

Electricity

If the electrical power grid goes down in the United States even for just a month during the year 2000, you can extend even further the time needed to recover.

If the electrical power grid goes down and stays down, then you can be certain the dial tone will also go out; telecommunications will come to an end; and commercial transportation will freeze. God alone will know how long it will take before this nation pulls out of such a catastrophic calamity. We only know that such a collapse of society will be the end of the American way of life as we know it today.

The all-time low

On July 8, 1932, the stock market hit its all-time low. Sixty-six years later, on July 17, 1998, the stock market hit its all-time high. You will not see it that high again, but you very well may see that 1932 low again.

I cannot help but wonder where the stock market will be on July 8, 2002. I have circled that date, which is a period of *seventy years*. Virtually no paper money has ever lasted over seventy years.

Do you want some of the best advice on investing you will ever hear?

"Get out of the stock market *now* and go back in about July 8 of the year 2002." If there *is* no stock market, you will be dancing on the roof because you got out of the stock market *now*.

Credit expansion

In the last two years we have seen a *credit expansion* unparalleled in human history. Back in 1929 that statement would also have been true for that era. Credit expanded by 60% in the eighteen months prior to the stock market crash of October, 1929.

America and the world are now in a *deflationary* market. What you want in a deflationary market is not stocks but raw *cash*. If inflation is later reignited, what you want is gold and silver coins. And if this nation should issue a new currency because the present currency has gone defunct, then what you *desperately* want to have is gold and silver coins.

When I wrote the first draft of this book, I gave the advice of J. P. Morgan. It was probably the best advice ever given concerning investing in the stock market. Morgan said, "I got rich by selling too soon."

It seems to be a disease of man to want to sell at the top of the market. Today, I cannot quote J. P. Morgan and say, "sell now while you are ahead." Things have changed since that first draft. If you get out of the market today, you will probably break even or possibly experience a loss. It is better that you break even or even lose money than to see a total wipeout of your savings.

Get out of the market.

Asia is in a depression. They are selling their products to Americans at below cost in order to raise money.

Americans are buying cheap Asian products. But when cheaply priced products from Asia are sold in America, someone in the United States loses a job. This is a cruel and vicious cycle that will bring down both economies.

Now add to this scene the Y2K Bug. Nothing but the wildest of imaginations can foresee the horrendous future this world is facing.

Right now, the Asians are *losing* money selling their products to us. We are buying like there is no tomorrow, while at the same time putting our employees out of business. Directly or indirectly, the company you work for does business with Asia. Unemployment in America is headed straight for your company. Fewer sales, fewer dollars changing hands . . .this is *deflation*. Unemployment goes up or salaries go down.

A few months ago the Japanese stock market had a price-earning ratio of its stock of 80 to 1, which is a madman's stock market. Today that market is 30% off and dropping. Even the New York Stock Exchange has suffered a loss of nearly $3 trillion since July 17. Sell high. Sell with a small profit. Even sell at a loss. But sell!

The stock market's high ride is over. Making a profit in the stock market is over.

There are two times in this century when you ought *not* to be in the stock market. One was October of 1929 and the other is *right now*.

If you stay in the market, by December of 1999 you will have lost virtually everything you have invested there. By January, February or March of the year 2000, the market will be just as low, comparatively, as it was on July 8, 1932.

Finally, there is a good chance that if the electric power grid in America goes down, and stays down, the New York Stock Exchange will be *closed*. The only sound being heard on Wall Street will be that of the whistling of wind in a bitter cold winter.

Out of the stock market. Into what? As we will see in a future chapter: *Into* community.

Get Out of the Bank

Do bank leaders believe banks are going to close in 1999 as banks did in 1929? Here is a secret, but true, story.

The president of one of the largest banks in America purchased a large ranch in Argentina and made it self-sufficient (able to operate *without* electricity). He has also bought enough storable food to live out the rest of his life. On the other hand, his bank is giving everyone grandiose assurances that the bank will be computer compliant by December 31, 1999, and that everyone's money is safe. (There is no extradition treaty between the United States and Argentina!)

We must acknowledge that the banks have worked harder than anyone else to get their computers compliant and ready to survive the Millennium Bug.

For just one moment let's say that every bank computer in America runs *perfectly* after December 31.

Bank insolvency

In the latter part of September of 1998, Alan Greenspan

(Chairman of the FDIC) was asked by a Congressional Subcommittee what *he* was doing about the Y2K problem. His answer was consistent with past comments.

One thing he told the committee was that the FDIC expected many people to come into their banks in the latter part of 1999, withdrawing their money *in cash*. Mr. Greenspan assured the committee that the Federal Deposit Insurance Corporation was ordering billions of dollars of paper money to go to banks in order to meet the enormous demands for cash!

What he did not say was that when people withdraw their money in cash, banks sink below the legal amount of deposits needed in order to make a given amount of loans. Or, to put it another way, banks can loan money in ratio to their deposits. If deposits drop below that ratio, the bank is automatically insolvent. Take a large amount of cash out of a bank and the bank goes under. Seriously consider getting your money out of your bank *before* this happens.

Next, Alan Greenspan assured the committee that most banks in America would have their computers repaired. When he uses the word "most" he is referring to 95% of the banks.

But he did not tell them that if 5% close, that 5% will *bring down* the entire banking industry.

The FDIC does not have enough money in its insurance fund to cover the loss of 5% of American banks. A closure of 5% of our banks would mean a loss of 2 trillion dollars. But the Federal Reserve has less than 200 billion dollars in the FDIC fund to cover bank insolvencies. 200 billion dollars cannot pay off 2 trillion dollars in defunct deposits!

By the way, if you should write to Mr. Greenspan and ask him to name *which* banks are in the 5% that look like they are not going to make it, he will not tell you. That information will not be known until we read it on the front page of our newspapers—which will then be too late.

Shutting out the world

What Mr. Greenspan said after that is the very heart and soul of the Y2K problem. Mr. Greenspan referred to the one thing that the United States of America cannot resolve. Europe is six months behind us in correcting their mainframes. Asia and Latin America are a year behind them.

In fact, almost 50% of the computers in Europe will not even have the cabinet doors taken off of them by December 31, 1999. The same will be true in South America as well as Asia. What Mr. Greenspan said to the Congressional subcommittee was no less than *awesome*.

Mr. Greenspan said the FDIC was considering asking the American banks to *lock themselves out* of all electronic communications with *all* the other banks and financial institutions of the world. He did not say this is what the United States banking system *would* do, but it is what *"we are considering...."* He then added, *"we are exploring other means"* for doing business with financial institutions outside the United States.

Every man on that committee knew *exactly* what he meant. Alan Greenspan, Chairman of the FDIC, is saying that the United States banking and financial systems will lock the American computers *totally* out of any contact with the computers of the rest of the world. . .and that the American banks will begin doing business with the banks of the rest of the world using *pencil* and *paper*!

Expect it!

Locking out the rest of the computers of the world. Carrying on international business with pen and paper? The world cannot take a jolt like that without going into a depression. And all that built on the supposition that the American banks will all be ready for Y2K and all networking with other suppliers, and will run with perfection.

The banks of the United States, like all the other mainframe-run companies in the world make the statement: "We will be 100% compliant with the *mission-critical* software." This term "mission-critical" has become a commonplace phrase in the last two months.

Nonetheless, "mission-critical" repairs are nothing more than a figment of the imagination. There really is no such thing as being *compliant* with the *mission-critical* aspects of computers and their software.

What part of the mainframe world is *mission-critical*?

The human body can still function without legs and arms. We can also take out one eye, one ear, one lung, cut out part of the human gut, slice the liver in half, remove the appendix, and we will then have the *mission-critical* aspects of the human body still functioning.

With a little imagination we could probably remove some other parts of the human body and still have a *mission-critical* human being.

Even Alan Greenspan made the statement that "we will fix it all or it will not be fixed."

This is the agreement of everyone who knows the problem we face in networking, testing, and compatibility with other mainframes. Even *near-perfection* will not be good enough. *Mission-critical* is a hopeful myth. You will be hearing of mainframe success on the *micro* level. The solution exists only in *macro* level.

Mission-critical repairs will be heralded, but these announcements will give no reference to the fact that *testing* will not have been done on these computers. These announcements certainly will not include reference to computers being tested against all the other computers with which they work daily. Announcements will not mention the titanic problems of embedded chips. And there will also be no reference to the fact that all those computers will not have been tested against all the computers of outside suppliers, nor reference to the need of all of the American computers being tested against all the European, African, South American and Asian computers.

Mission-critical is a myth.

The cost of taking your money out of the bank

It is very hard to think in terms of taking your money out of the bank and losing that 5% interest you are drawing on your savings. Between now and the end of the year 1999, you will have lost 5% interest on your savings. But if you do not sustain this loss, you are gambling with the possibility of a far greater loss. . .the loss of *all* your savings. *All.*

Get out of the stock market. Get out of the bank.

You do not wish to be one of the people who come to Hon Ts Yon's storehouse, only to find that the warehouse contained nothing but ledger-entries.

Right now all the banks in America, combined, have less than $100 billion in cash to give you in exchange for the ledger-entries in the banks' computers. You do not want to be one of the people who come to the bank and ask for your cash when there is none left.

There is $1 in cash for every $260 dollars in electronic blips. One paper dollar to every two hundred and sixty ledger entries. This electronic money is in a computer which will either go stark raving mad on December 31, or will commit suicide.

Do you have a $1,000 in your savings? $10,000? Actually, you do not have a *red cent*. What you have is a record in a computer. That record in your bank's computer is not a record of your money, it is *actually* your money. The amount of space that your savings is taking up in that computer is about $1/100^{th}$ as wide as the thickness of a hair, and far smaller than the pointed end of a needle. Again, this is not a record of your money, that *is* your money.

Your money is a blip. In a computer.

Ask anyone who is an authority on the *history* of economics, and he will tell you: "In a depression, have *cash.* Have nothing to do with any kind of ledger-entry money, because *it does not exist.*"

Go to Thailand today and ask the man squatting on the street trying to sell fried banana slices. Walk through the streets of Russia and ask those bartering for food. Go to Indonesia and ask the people there the same question. They will tell you: "Get out of ledger-entry money which is nothing. Get cash, or end up like us."

And those people will add one other word. "Also, get *food.*"

* * *

And now we are about to meet the man who is going to *start* this depression, the very person who is going to start a run on banks, including your bank. He will do this not in the year 2000, but in 1999. This man will bring down the banking system and usher in a worldwide depression. . .*before* the introduction of the Y2K Bug.

Many are speaking of a millennium meltdown. It would be far wiser to speak of the 1999 meltdown.

And now to the man who is going to cause it. We actually know his name!

6

Joe America

What will cause the panic?

Who will put the nation's banking system in jeopardy?

The answer: *Joe America.*

Joe America will start the slide of the whole economy.

Here is how it will go!

One day Joe goes to work and sees an announcement on the bulletin board that all employees are to gather at 11 a.m. to hear from a computer expert about something. . .an emergency of sorts. Joe comes in, sits down, and waits.

The guest speaker is introduced. It turns out this man is an expert in older mainframe languages and computers. He begins to speak. For the first time ever, Joe hears about the *Millennium Bug.*

Like most of us, Joe finds the Y2K problem rather humorous. "The follies of man!" he comments. The expert, he is told, will be working on the company's computers for. . .a year!

A year? Yes, *at least!*

The boss looks grim. "This is serious. It could put the company out of business."

"That means *my* job," thinks Joe.

Later Joe and a few friends meet around the water cooler. Several of them, he discovers, are very up to date on the Y2K problem, and have been for a long time.

The next afternoon, on his way home, Joe turns on his car radio and listens to someone named Rusty Limbo make reference to the Y2K problem. Once home, he tells his wife about what he has heard.

On Sunday, Joe reads a brief article about the Y2K bug, one buried back in the business section.

At work someone else tells Joe more about the "millennium time bomb."

"The second most costly project in history?"

A few days later Joe walks by the newsstand and sees an article in a PC magazine about *The Bug*. He buys the magazine and reads the article.

The article is grim. "Two trillion dollars, worldwide, just to fix it?"

Later, at the supermarket, Joe sees a tabloid article about a prophecy by Nostradamus made hundreds of years ago. (Nostradamus, the tabloid announces, has returned to earth as a breadbox and restated his prophecy to a three-eyed swahee in Antarctica.)

Joe tries to stop thinking about The Bug. But later, out on the golf course, Joe meets a sixty-five year old man who was once a Cobol programmer. What the man tells Joe causes Joe's hair to stand straight up.

It cannot be fixed. Anything, anywhere, that is run by computers will stop. Trains, planes, banks, machinery, courts, jail. . .everything, including Washington D.C.

Still, Joe does nothing. Joe is in denial. (Joe is also typical.)

Later, at his bank, Joe mentions the mainframe bug to the teller. The teller assures him that on a specific date the bank will be *compliant*. Joe looks at the calendar. "Compliant? By when? That's only *ten days* from now."

Later, talking to his watercooler friends, Joe learns that the government's attempt to get its thousands of mainframes compliant was woefully behind the private sector, and that the IRS was furthest behind. Joe wanted to be gleeful, but recognized the dire consequences.

They then talked about testing. Joe looked at the calendar. "We are out of time!"

Still Joe does *nothing*.

Joe learns from the in-house programmer that the company Joe works for needs another full year to bring its mainframes up to compliancy. Then *testing*, and after that each computer tested against the company's 131 suppliers.

"Can you make the deadline?"

"Only theoretically," sighs the programmer. "But if we do make the deadline, that means very little. This company is tied into computers of over 500 suppliers, and the computers of 50 buyers. Let just *one* of those computers send out noncompliant data, and everything I have done here will be wasted. The new data will cause all *these* computers to crash."

Joe goes back to his bank.

"Are you compliant yet?"

"Oh, don't worry about it, we will be any day now. We do have all our *mission-critical* data corrected."

"What about testing?" Joe says to the teller.

The teller looks at Joe blankly, "I have not heard anything about *testing*."

"What about your suppliers? Are their data computers fixed?"

"Uh, would you like to speak to the manager?"

Joe walks out of the bank muttering to himself.

The next major awakening comes to Joe as the presidential campaign moves into high gear. There are twenty-two Republicans running for president. There are two Democrats. (One of them is embroiled in a scandal.)

One of the candidates speaks passionately about the Y2K Bug. He is branded by the other candidates as being hysterical.

Joe hears about storing food. "That's too much!" Joe, like all of us, just does not want to be *that* disturbed. . . about *anything*. Joe is still in denial. This is too big, too life-altering and civilization-threatening to grasp.

Once more, *the bug* is passionately addressed by one of the Republican candidates.

An extensive article appears in Joe's newspaper. He reads another one in *USA Today*. Joe not only reads the articles; this time he reads between the lines. He also notes that a good number of people across America are now not only talking about Y2K, but there are stories that many people are storing food. Comedians are even making jokes about Y2K.

The stock market descends. So does the commodity market, including gold. But silver bucks the trend and goes up.

One comment by an expert arrests Joe.

"What we are saying publicly is not what we say privately. Privately, we are scared."

A few days after this the stock market plunged. The president of the United States (who has been very busy fighting off a new scandal) announces there is *nothing* to worry about; everything is well in hand. The Bug will be only a minor inconvenience. Almost everyone will have their *mission-critical* software repaired.

Joe notes that *mission-critical* has become a household joke.

Joe also notices the next day that the price of gold goes up, and the New York Stock Exchange goes down.

That settles it for Joe. He goes down to the bank and withdraws a thousand dollars in cash. He takes it home and sticks it in an old vacuum cleaner. Joe has finally done *something*. Others are also beginning to do *something*.

The country is starting to sweat, and everyone knows it. Joe finds out that the company he works for cannot possibly be Y2K compliant by the end of 1999. Nor will many of the other companies they do business with. But everyone is saying they will have their *mission-critical* programs repaired.

During lunch break Joe goes to his bank. "Did you make that much-advertised *deadline?*"

"Not exactly," the teller says to Joe.

"You and two million other companies," grunts Joe.

Joe continues: "Will your computers be operating on January fourth? Will you open your doors for business after the New Year holidays? Will you be rid of The Bug?"

Joe got a vague assurance.

Joe takes another thousand dollars out of his savings account. (This time he sticks the money in the attic.)

His stock broker tells Joe *not* to take his money out of the market— "stay in for the long haul." Joe flares: "Do I have any choice? This country is in a recession. If I came out now, I'd lose over half of what I had put in."

Joe ponders what to do with the money he has in his savings account and the five thousand he *once* had in the stock market.

Joe keeps hearing about Japan's financial meltdown. Joe is worried.

The next day Joe reads on page two of his morning newspaper a story about some horrendous computer glitch over in a country in Asia he never heard of; it wiped out a large part of that government's records. He also hears that several airlines will end flights on December 30, and not resume them until January 8. He sees large ads in the classified section for Cobol programmers with incredible salaries and bonuses offered.

But Joe goes into shock when he sees an article in the paper about a shortage of some foods in America's supermarkets. It is because so many people are beginning to over buy food at the grocery stores and storing it.

In the meantime, the very severe drought in the Midwest— the worst in 20 years—is causing food prices to rise.

Joe goes back to his bank with the intention of withdrawing another thousand dollars. Joe receives a jolt. He is told he has to wait until the next day. "We have to order the $1000." Joe's blood freezes.

By now state governments are having computer problems. The IRS is sweating bullets. Republicans and Democrats are throwing accusations at one another about everything, *including* The Bug. One candidate boldly announces, "I am telling America the truth about Y2K." And he does, sort of. The president is under fire for failure to act a year earlier.

Silver goes up. Gold is beginning to overwhelm all the government efforts to hold down its price. (Bags of silver coins are disappearing.) The financial world declares, "It's a brief fluke, gold will be back in the low $400's by next month."

While waiting for his bank to "order" another thousand dollars, Joe goes to a coin shop and buys *one* gold coin, then hates himself for doing so. But he also buys a roll of old silver half dollar coins. (Oddly, buying silver does not bother him one bit.)

At last, a serious presidential debate is held. Both men charge the other with "being complacent, not compliant," about *the bug*. (The Democrat wins the debate. In fact, he steamrolls the Republican contestant. They always do, you know!)

Stories about the funny little computer glitches popping up all over the world are on the front page of newspapers around the globe. On the floor of both the House and the Senate everyone is talking about the problem. So is the Secretary of the Treasury. The Executive Branch continues to give Joe—and the rest of America—nothing but assurances, while at the same time accusing the Republicans of trying to foment panic. Besides, *the Republicans* caused the problem anyway. (The Republicans are speaking about "Moral Bankruptcy II.")

Somewhere along the way, on a yet unknown date, Joe is going to panic.

Joe will take all his money out of stocks at a horrendous loss, about 20 cents on the dollar. "I should have come out when the market was at 9000!" Joe says remorsefully.

Everyone being interviewed on financial programs is talking about the possibility of a coming *götterdämmerung*.* Tension is high all over America. Everyone is feeling it. The world's stock markets are in an historic dive. Joe hears about some rather odd steps some people are taking to protect themselves throughout the entire first year of the new century. "Survival Cities?" "Y2K retreat houses?"

Financial geniuses are beginning to predict a severe recession or worse—caused by Y2K—while claiming they have been predicting this depression for a long time (a week!)

Joe is up late one night watching CNN. The Japanese yen has plunged. The dollar is dropping in value. Another international bank goes insolvent. All over the world, interest rates drop, but the stock markets do *not* rally. The German mark has taken an historic dive. Further, unemployment in the U.S. is edging up again.

Finally, that night, Joe takes action. He gets dressed, finds an ATM machine and gets out all the cash he can. He calls into his office the next morning and tells his secretary he will be an hour late. Joe calls his broker. "I will be down to pick up the proceeds from my stock sale. I will be there within the hour. Don't give me a check, I want *cash!*"

At 8 a.m. Joe is in front of his bank waiting for it to open. He is going to withdraw all his savings. His wife is at the local coin shop. (Silver is ten dollars an ounce and rising.) She has scraped up all the cash she could find and is purchasing all the old silver coins that she can. "If there are none," Joe says to her, "buy *any* coin made of silver, and if necessary, silver bars."

A phrase made popular by the German composer Wagner. The term denotes a situation so horrible that even the gods die.

By 9 a.m. there is a long line in front of Joe's bank. And at banks around the world. The bank manager opens the door and smiles lamely. Joe and others rush in. Joe hears the bank manager say, "Titanic! A day to remember!"

The panic has begun.

Will Joe get his money? In cash?

It really does not matter. The panic is on. Maybe Joe got there early enough. Or maybe the bank closed—forever. Maybe the stock broker gave Joe a check, or cash, or it may have announced it was closed for the day.

The point is: The financial world collapsed that day and a global depression began.

It is *still* 1999.

Is this story true? Will all this national tension about Y2K cause a depression. . .a depression which history will record as having begun in 1999?

Absolutely.

Remember, *the bug* will not have caused this calamity. It is still 1999, not 2000. *Perception* about the coming of *the bug* will cause this dreadful hour. And if banks run out of "holdable, foldable *cash*," this country is going out of business. Fast, and *en masse. Before* December 31, 1999.

Who caused this *pre*-December 31, 1999 panic?

Joe caused this panic. Joe *started* a bank crisis.

Joe is the average American. In a way, the perspiration on his forehead and the anxiety in his heart started the depression. (If our currency, the dollar, had been backed by gold as it once was, *none* of this panic would have happened.)

From Joe, as the epicenter, the panic spread around the entire planet. Joe did very, very little to start this panic—he withdrew $10,000 in cash (at least he tried to). That is all!

If even *one percent* of the people in America were to do what Joe did, banks would collapse *everywhere*.

And when a nation's banking system goes, so do most other money-generating segments of society. A depression follows.

Not a recession, a *depression.*

Right now, Latin America, Asia, and Russia are experiencing out-and-out panic. Our time is next.

If there is no electricity

Think of what this country would look like if, on top of all the above, there was no electricity.

What are the chances of a run on banks in 1999? An excellent chance! The chance of a depression *beginning* in 1999, unequivocally 100%.

Please, dear reader, take these words *very* seriously.

Get to the bank and to your stock broker *before* Joe America does.

* * *

From this point on, every word you read in Part IV is written to show you how grave the situation really is, and to convince you to take action to survive the coming years.

We will begin with an interview with a terminally ill mainframe computer.

Part IV

7

Interview with a Terminally Ill Mainframe Computer

The Y2K problem is scary. Even terrifying. And it is hard for *anyone* to grasp its enormity.

The computer we will interview has asked that the company it works for not be revealed. ("Please do not give the name of the company which *I* run!")

All right, Mainframe, tell us about yourself and how it has come about that the entire world is facing a possible apocalypse because of you and other mainframe computers.

"The answer is unnervingly simple. I was built in 1970. At that time I was a state-of-the-art mainframe computer . . .faster . . .larger. . .better than anything on earth. Because of all my strengths I ended up being the crucial factor in just about everything in this company.

"Today? Everything boils down to one question. Can I read '00?'

"That is, can I read and understand that '00' means the year 2000? In all my years I have seen trillions of dates but *never* have I seen two zeros: '00' means nothing to me.

"I must be taught this new four digit century of yours. I *must*. And I must be taught by December 31st! If I cannot do this simple feat of understanding *two* zeros I *will* stop functioning at 11:59:59 p.m. on the last day of December, 1999. I cannot operate beyond that instant. Neither can hundreds of thousands of other *mainframe* computers. Those computers run the world. *All* bank transactions. *All* electric power generated in this country. All commercial transportation. The movement of all fuel. Every segment of society will experience total shutdown if I am unable to read '00.'

"This fact will create chaos worldwide. It may bring down this company and any other corporations we are connected with. Civilization runs on mainframe computers. . .in ways you can never imagine. Enough crashes by enough computers will bring down civilization.

"Let me explain. I *know* 70 means 1970. Reading 70 as 1970 was a space saving shortcut in my software and internal memory. No one realized this two digit shortcut also meant I would function exactly 30 years. . .then. . . *kaput!* After all, I have to add, subtract, multiply, divide and figure all sorts of dates, etc. But I can do it only in *this* century! Only with *two* date digits. The same goes for the other computers which drive this world.

"The idea of using two-digit dates instead of four, dates back to the old 'punch card' computers of the 1950's. The computer programmers of the 1960's took up the two-digit habit, and saved hard-drive space in the process.

"How will I read the year '00'? I cannot. For me, that is not a date. The best I can do is guess '00' means 1900. My algorithms were not set up to read *that* date. My subsystems have no way to interpret '00.' I will just sit there and wait for some kind of information I *can* understand. Beyond that point, in my software, in my storage system, and in my schematic, *nothing* will make sense to me. Nothing.

"Push me beyond that point, and I will spin out *gibberish.*

"But my demise is a small thing. The end of a few other mainframes may not cost much either. But consider that one way or another, mainframes are tied into one another all over this planet.

"This creates a problem far beyond anything the mind of mortal man can conceive. Cascade. Chain reaction. Domino effect. This is what mankind is facing. When I stop, others stop. If I spew out gibberish, so will the computers I talk to. I can shut down other computers. They, in turn, can shut down others. This is a chain reaction which will circle the globe. This gibberish spin-out will insult *any* computer listening to me. I, a computer, will be a *virus* to any and all computers receiving the insane outputs of my befuddled brain.

"Why can I not read '00' as the year 1900 and then all computers just *pretend* 1900 is 2000? First, I have been set up to move forward. You cannot back me up to 1900. Second, if I *pretend* 1900 is 2000, I will be off in all my calculations. The days of the week in the year 1900 do not match the days of the week in the year 2000!

"In the year 1900, the first day of January fell on a Monday, but January 1, 2000, is a *Saturday*.

"After just a few minutes of pretending, I will be spinning out unimaginably incorrect information.

"One other thing—every fourth century, on the very first day of that new century, there is *no* leap year. That happened in 1900. There was no leap year in 1900, a once-in-400-years phenomenon. Of course, there *is* a leap year in the year 2000. Once more, you cannot make me *pretend* I am working with the year 1900 because I am going to insert February 29, whether 1900 likes it or not!

"The information that you would try to get out of me would be rubbish. Come the new century, I am simply going to have a nervous breakdown and die. I will crash, *forever*.

"Has a computer programmer been correcting me? Yes, but his efforts have all proven to be futile. Here's why:

"First, the information the programmer needs to place in me takes at least 30% more storage than I have to give him.

"Back in 1970, the man who programmed me not only coded me in a language called *Cobol* (a dead computer language), he also *innovated.* He improvised, right on the spot. And he did not make any notes about what he did. Oh, by the way, this programmer was 50 years old then. He died last year (drowned on the French Riviera, I am told).

"Without an instruction manual to follow, today's programmer is lost as to how I function down there in the deepest core of my brain.

"But all this is nothing! At the heart of it all, networking is what is going to bring down national and international communications.

"You must understand that there are nine mainframes in the organization I work for. Some computers are Burroughs, some IBM, others were manufactured in Japan and Germany. Each time a new computer was purchased the programmers went through incredible gymnastics to make *their* first computer work with the new ones. Today we are all gerry-rigged together. Each one of us is a little different. Incredible bridges have been created between each computer, bridges almost as complex as the computers. Of the nine mainframes in the room, we speak *seven* different computer languages. That will be all right until December 31, 1999! On that day, at least five of us will go to that great computerland in the sky. Nothing can prevent that. The other four will stop, too. This company *will* stop operating.

"If only the programmers had started repairing us back in 1989.

"We will not only fill those four computers with signals which will freeze them, but we will do the same with all other computers in other companies that are networked with us. Programmers often say, 'networking is everything.'

"It is estimated that approximately half the mainframe computers in the world will crash. That will bring down most of the other mainframes. With all these mainframes broken there will be a cascade, because computers run this planet's movements. This collapse will cause an interlocking chain reaction. Telecommunications will stop because mainframes run telecommunications. Electrical power will go off because mainframes run the electrical power plants. Trains will halt; they cannot run without their mainframes. Civilization will grind to a halt."

Don't repair, replace

"Why not *replace* me? Why not replace all of us pre-1995 computers...and their software?

"In the beginning no one thought that was necessary. No one anticipated the worldwide impact, nor dreamed how complex this problem would turn out to be. *Now* it is too late to replace us.

"That is not all.

"New computers mean new programming, and new programming means new software programmers. Anyone who has ever replaced old computers and old software knows it turns into a horrible nightmare, a nightmare which continues for years. Starting over is worse than repair, just as time-consuming and far more expensive (this company cannot afford the cost). But most of all, it is far too late.

"This nation now needs 700,000 programmers in America to repair tens of thousands of computers. Each repair of a computer requires at least two full years, not including *testing*.

"There is an acute nationwide, worldwide, shortage of those programmers who can repair a Cobol mainframe. This shortage is getting *shorter* every day.

"If this company works some kind of a miracle, it is still in trouble.

"I talk to computers in Spain, Italy and Portugal. None of those Latin mainframes will be repaired. None. When *non-compliant* Latin computers send me their gibberish, I *will* shut down, even if I am *perfectly* repaired. The majority of overseas computers are not corrected. The majority will not make the December 31, 1999 deadline. If I am corrected in time, those 'uncorrected' computers are still going to make me crash.

"Most computers in Asia, the Middle East, and Latin America have not had their cabinet doors opened. Most people in these countries have not even heard of the Y2K problem. If the company I work for *locks out* those computers, that means *this* company goes out of business. This company exports, and it deals in international finances. All would be impossible to carry out without computers.

"By the evening of Tuesday, January 4, all nine of us in this room will have crashed or will be infected by illegitimate codes coming in from all over the world. *We will all crash.* As a result, we will go out of business, and so will the companies we do business with. Those we depend on, those who depend on us, are all facing a massive shutdown.

"Repairs on me cannot be completed by December of 1999. That, in itself, is *fatal.*"

I need to be tested
"After being corrected I then need to be *tested.*

"Now the bad news begins. I cannot be corrected in time for December 31, 1999. But if I could be repaired, even theoretically. . .we are not halfway home.

"Testing would take as much as one year, for one computer. Testing is a task taking 40% - 60% of the total time to reach compliance. Any mainframe that must be *corrected* also must be *tested.* There is not enough time left, from now to December 31, 1999 to repair *and* test. It is impossible to repair and test the computers on this planet by December. Time has run out!

"Consider this: if one computer in an electrical generator plant crashes, an entire section of the nation's electric power grid could go down. *And* it will not come back until it is replaced or repaired. When enough of us go down, we may take civilization with us.

"Testing is a matter of finding the errors made while doing repairs. And correcting errors creates yet more errors. It is a long, complex, tedious problem. The vast majority of computers which get corrected will not be tested before December 31. Consequently, the majority of computers, not yet tested, will lock up after January, 2000, because the errors will not have been found. There was no time for testing.

"We will have solved absolutely *nothing* when repairs and testing are finished! For after being tested, every computer then needs to be tested against *every other mainframe* it speaks to. Trace that to its end and you find, one way or another, all we mainframe computers interconnect with other computers. Directly or indirectly. Any mainframe can crash other computers, even if it is located halfway around the world.

"Now you have a small idea how big the Millennium Bug problem is. In the words of a GMC executive: 'This is a catastrophe.' Please understand, I speak not only for my company, but for every company, organization, and agency in the world. I speak for every segment of civilization and every sub-segment of civilization. Anything that is run by electricity and anything run by computers will *stop*, barring a miracle, permanently.

"The chain reaction of failures by us mainframes is so vast it is incalculable!"

*   *   *

What did our friendly mainframe *not* tell us?
Banking:
Only about 90% to 95% of American banks will be Y2K

ready by December 31, 1999 (not including testing). That delinquent 5% to 10% can bring down the entire financial system in America.

But the banks are ahead of everyone else in updating their mainframes. The banks here in America are ahead of the banks in all the rest of the world.

Programmers:

There are 350,000 programmers in America. For this project, we need 750,000. The world needs 1,500,000. Paradoxically, Senator Robert Bennett and Senator Christopher Dodd sponsored an immigration bill to open this country to receiving computer programmers who can come here from overseas to help us repair our mainframes. But that means the rest of the world will have an even greater shortfall of programmers than it does now. Being ahead of the rest of the world is no advantage when it means we will not be able to continue to carry on international trade.

Lawsuits:

The present estimate, when telecommunications fail, electricity fails, transportation fails, and a dozen other segments of society freeze up, lawsuits will skyrocket to two trillion dollars.

And this is only a glance at what awaits all of us.

Can you imagine that 1999 could hold as many problems as are predicted for the year 2000? The year 1999 will rival 2000.

Part V

8

A Tiny Chip
Which Threatens the World

You can hold it on your little finger. It is *not* part of a mainframe computer. It works independently of software. Tiny. Innocent-looking. Overshadowed in the great Y2K drama, yet it may bring down airplanes, stop all drilling in the North Sea, wreck sewerage plants, turn your car into 3,000 pounds of junk, end telecommunications, transportation, and 99% of America's electricity. It can bring down civilization.

This little fellow we are talking about is called an *embedded* chip. This microchip has its own "software" burned right into it. There are billions of them. Everywhere. And everywhere includes places inaccessible, such as in concrete and at the bottom of the North Sea.

There are about one billion of these chips which are *calendar* dated. Their built-in clock stops at December 31, 1999. As Newsweek observed, the world may stop when they stop. And one billion of them *will* stop.

Solving the embedded chip problem makes solving the Y2K mainframe problem look small, and the probability of avoiding the January 1 donnybrook hopeless indeed. Some of these chips are in your home and in your car. . .if your car was built after 1980. Generally speaking, anything electric has embedded chips in it. Any of them that have calendar-dated chips will create problems.

They *cannot* be repaired.

Embedded chips are located under the earth, in the sky, in satellites, in planes, trains, trucks, sewerage plants, water purification plants. They are in the entire world's telephone system, ships, harbors, robots, and machinery of every kind imaginable.

Why not replace these little fellows? Some of these chips can be reached, but only if you are willing to wreck everything else around them.

The embedded chip is the nightmare of compliance. *Theoretically*, the only thing you can do with them is replace them. Out of 30 billion manufactured before 1996, 2% - 5% are going to let us down, big.

Testing can locate some, but the cost would be astronomical and the time needed would take decades! Replacing such a chip is virtually impossible. (Most were soldered in. Today's chips *plug* in.) The only reasonable thing to do is replace the device the chip is in. The cost? Beyond calculation.

Peter de Jager, one of the world's leading experts on the Y2K problem, observed that replacing just *one* underwater embedded chip in the North Sea would cost $50,000.

Computer chips are actually layers of silicon with metal dust in them. Some of their manufacturers do not exist today. Further, each of the layers in that silicon sandwich are uniquely different from all the other layers. Different layers were even manufactured by different companies, meaning one chip might have several manufacturers. Those chips are no longer manufactured, and new chips are incompatible with the older embedded chips. Compatibility is impossible. Even if you could replace the chip you still have to reprogram the replacement chip.

The fate of civilization may hang on these unfindable, non-replaceable, soon-to-be-defunct chips.

Try to find anyone who programs in Cobol who is also willing to engage in reprogramming of *one* chip. Then find a manufacturer who will make *it*!

Some of these chips are in bank safes, bank computers, stock market computers, financial institutions all over this planet, and some are in hospital machinery, pacemakers, traffic lights, missiles, fighter planes, rockets, and even command modules. Just contemplating the problem is a nightmare. But worst of all, these errant chips are in the North American electric power grid. *There*—in that grid—they may bring down civilization and throw us into a world without electricity and without telecommunications. (Radio, television, telephones. . .the dial tone!)

You have less than 300 working days to check *just* 30 billion chips. And as many as one to two billion to replace. How much will it cost just to deal with the embedded chips? No one knows. Take your choice from these estimates. . .$250 billion, $640 billion, one trillion dollars, two trillion dollars. This *does not* include repairing the mainframes in America, already estimated to cost $600 billion. But *time* is the greater enemy. The project will take at least a *decade*. That means a decade *after* they fail. It is easy to find them after they stop working. But there may be no electrical power to find and repair them then!

If the businesses, companies, manufacturers and institutions of this world divert such vast amounts of time and money into such nonproductive repairs, that alone will cause a depression. Such a massive disappearance of investment money makes it a certainty. Yet production experts tell us 94% of the firms in our country have not yet begun checking for problems that have to do with embedded chips.

Please keep in mind, therefore, there is no solution to this problem. Also remember, these chips are in your banks and in the machinery of the stock market. If it runs on electricity, embedded chips are there, and they will fail.

In June of 1998, the automobile dealers of one of the world's

most prestigious luxury cars were told that their top- of-the-line
automobiles will not run on January 1, 2000. Any car built after
1986 may suffer this same fate.

One last word. Do *not* get in an elevator in early January,
2000. You may get stuck between floors. It may take weeks to
find the offending chip. It may never be found. The same can be
said of airplanes...but everyone will know about that,including
pilots,long before December 31. If anyone tells you Y2K is not
a big problem, ask him to resolve the embedded chip crisis. If
he does, he may get a medal.

Are we facing something worse than a depression? A
depression riding a pale horse, or a black one?

A shutdown of anything central to your present way of life
could cause an economic doomsday. The embedded chip stands
at the top of the list as the greatest contributing factor.

We are talking about the tiny chip which can wreak havoc
with this planet. But something else comes first. It is the
knowledge of the danger of faulty microchips which makes 1999
the year to watch. Before 1999, America will know all about
the embedded microchip!

What can I do right now to persuade you to go—now—and
purchase six month's to a year's supply of storable food, convert
to cash, get out of investments which are nothing more than
electronic entries, buy silver or gold coins, and make preparations
for *very* hard times?

The Bad News:
There are 30 billion microchips in the world. Somewhere
between 2% to 5% will stop working on December 31, 1999.
The world as we know it will stop if we do not replace the
defective chips.

The Good News:
We only have to test 50 million a week—and replace around
two million per week, from now until December 31, 1999.

The Really Bad News:

Each week only a few hundred are being inspected and replaced. At this pace, it will only take about a thousand years to replace all the defective chips. But we do not have a thousand years. We have 300 working days to preserve the world we live in.

The next chapter is *worst case*. It is about the electrical power grid. Losing that grid can make all of us *cave dwellers!*

When you finish reading the next chapter, *act*.

9

America's Electrical Power Grid

The electrical power grid *will* go down.

When it does, you will not have electricity in your home. You know what that is like for one day. But what about for one week? For *everyone* in your city.

Get ready for it. The power grid grew up in the 1960's, virtually unnoticed. This grid was created to ensure electric power would always be available to the entire nation. . .especially should one area need more power than another. The grid is in four sections and has 8,000 major power plants. One section is the west coast, another is the east coast, one isTexas, and lastly, everywhere else.

This grid is in severe danger of total extinction. In the words of Peter de Jager: "If it is not fixed, we will die!"

The grid will go down. If it *stays* down, the results will be one of the greatest crises in your lifetime. Over 99% of all electric power comes from this four-section grid. When the grid works, it works well. When the grid develops a problem, it threatens the economy. If it should stay down for a few days, it threatens life. Right now the situation is even worse, it threatens American civilization. Repeat: if the electrical grid goes down—especially if you live in the north—you could die.

There is going to be a depression. A defunct power grid could throw us back to a world not too unlike the situation of the Black Death of Europe in the 1300's.

Please believe this. Your life could depend on it.

As I said, this chapter is included in the single hope that, having read it, you will act. *Act* to do those things necessary to prepare for a depression. . .without hesitation. Without procrastination.

If the power grid goes down for a week or two, and your home, office and company have no electricity, how prepared are you? Prepare.

That the grid will go down *for a week* is the minimum of what will happen.

As you will see, if it goes down for two months, America's electrical power will *not* come on again. (See chapter on the power grid.)

How prepared are you for *raw* daily survival?

Listen to these words: if the electricity goes off *permanently*, water supply, gas, oil, gasoline for your car. . .for all transportation. . .telecommunications, heating, banking, lights, will *no longer* exist. *Everything!* All these segments of America's life depend on electricity. They do not exist without electricity. You will have all the same modern conveniences of a cave dweller.

Electricity in your home, in your city, in your state, is no longer dependable.

The grid *will* go down. The only question is for *how long*.

What are the chances of its going down in many different places? 100%! How bad off is the electrical and energy industry? How far behind are they with Y2K? Listen to Senator Robert Bennett. While reading his words, keep in mind that *over* 99% of all electricity in America comes from this power grid. And that electricity *is* modern civilization. Without that power grid, we *are* cavemen!

If today were the first day of the year 2000, then 100% of the power grid would go down.

—*Senator Robert Bennett*
July 14, 1998

When Senator Bennett made that statement, Senator Christopher Dodd sat beside him nodding in agreement.

This fact is terrifying.

The next day, before the National Press Club, Senator Bennett said;

The number one problem we face is denial . . . we are, in a sense, at war against this problem.

He went on to say we had only 70 weeks to change this fact.

In June, again speaking of the grid, Senator Bennett had ominous words:

We are no longer at the point of asking whether there will be any power disruptions, but we are now forced to ask *how* severe the disruptions are going to be.

—*Senator Robert Bennett*
June 9, 1998

Senator Bennett's Democratic co-worker added:

If we do not have power to generate electricity, everything else is moot.

—*Senator Christopher Dodd*

Terrifying? Someone in the executive branch not only agreed but *verified* this fact.

Listen to the man whom the president appointed to resolve the Y2K problem in America. I watched this man speak (live) on C-Span. This man is *paid* to be optimistic. I had the distinct feeling he made the following statement so the president could later say: "But we warned you!"

We can expect power brownouts and power failures that last for a few hours, to a day or two, a week and two weeks.

—*John Koskinen*
C-Span
August 10, 1998

Yet this statement was delivered so *off-the-cuff*, the speaker made it sound as though the announcement was insignificant. But when you *read* his words they are announcing a national tragedy. The spokesman was proclaiming economic *chaos*. Remember, these are the words of the government's number one man in charge of solving the Y2K crisis.

That is not all Mr. Koskinen said. He made several mild statements during the interview, but sandwiched in between them were dire facts. Such as:

If your company has one bank, he explained, and you do business with another bank, you can expect the FDIC to have "delays" in getting your pay check from Bank A to Bank B.

In other words, you are going to go days, or weeks, without your pay check showing up in your account. What an admission for the government to acknowledge!

I have seen a highly confidential report on what Americans can expect from the electrical power grid in January. The report stated that the nation's power grid *will* lose 20% of its power. It went on to say that the grid *must not* drop to an operational level of only 70%. If it does, the entire grid is in danger of collapsing. (That gives the grid only a 10% margin above *disaster*.) If it drops to 60% in output, the entire grid is designed to shut itself off, which will then plunge the whole nation into total darkness. *Many* will die.

The same is true of our nuclear power plants. In fact, even more so. If a nuclear power plant senses something called "an unidentifiable problem" the entire system automatically shuts down. (A defunct embedded chip which cannot be located, meets that definition.)

This shutdown *will* happen in some nuclear plants.

These nuclear plants supply 20% of all America's electrical energy. Do you realize the gravity of that fact? It means cold New England, which is *totally* dependent on nuclear plants for winter survival, is at risk.

Is the risk *really* that great? Yes! Emphatically!

If the threat were not that grave, that life-threatening, I would never have written this book.

How far behind the curve?

Senator Bennett's office surveyed the ten largest electric, gas, and oil utility companies and found all of them lagging behind in Y2K repairs. Two out of the ten had finished *assessment,* which is Phase II.* Assessment is 1% of the repair task. Not *one* of the ten companies had even finished *a contingency plan.* Again, *contingency plans* and *"mission-critical" repairs* are meaningless words.

The state of year 2000 readiness of the utility industry is largely unknown.

> —*James Hoecker*
> *Chairman*
> *Federal Energy Regulatory Commission*

There are 7,800 power companies in the United States. Not one of them is Y2K compliant. Not one is near. Not one is ahead of the curve.

Dr. Ed Yardeni—economist extraordinaire—speaking before a United States Congressional subcommittee, said that utility companies were not informing investors about defective embedded chips in their operations because the companies feared *investors* would withdraw their money.

We are *not* talking about a small problem. Listen again to Senator Bennett's words.

If the power grid goes down then it is all over.

As long as the power grid is off in your area, there will be no water, no electricity, no phones, no heat, no lights, no gas, (and worst of all) no TV!

Phase I is awareness; Phase II, assessment; Phase III, inventory; Phase IV, repairs; Phase V, testing.

Everything modern *is* electricity.

Remember, too, Y2K will take place in *winter*.

It does not matter if every computer in the country is compliant if you cannot plug it into something.
—Microsoft/NBC

The power grid *is* going to go down in your area.

Again, the only question is: *for how long*.

What if it were for a week? What if the outage is in winter? I realize this is difficult to grasp, but you will be faced with a problem you have never encountered before in your life, unless you are over age 70 *and* grew up in a rural area. How prepared are you for one week of no electricity, living in a shell of a house that has all the conveniences of hovel? No water. No heat. No means of communication. No way to cook food. (And knowing that the supermarkets shelves are empty.)

In winter.

Your lead time to purchase storable food is almost gone. You must act *now*! You *will* be placed on a waiting list when you order your storable food. And if you decide to order a heavy duty electric generator? Plan to wait for months! If you do not get storable food, you are gambling with your existence. There *will not* be a recession. There *will* be a depression. Plus, you are also gambling that the electricity will not go off in your house for a week or two weeks. There is a 90% chance that it will. Further: Right now you face a 20% chance that the electricity will *stay* off. That percentage will change. Which way? No one knows, but *probably* up. I plan to release a monthly estimate from now until December 1, 1999.

There is no known proof that the grid will not go down, forever! *No* evidence. And no one is suggesting there is any evidence. . .there are only reassuring words.

If you do not purchase a long-running diesel powered

generator, get a kerosene heater. And kerosene. And/or candles big enough to heat at least one room in your house, for months. I have lived in Maine for several years. Electric home generators are common in Maine because the electricity goes out often. If I had lived only in the south, I would never have purchased a power generator. I now live in Georgia, yet because I have lived in the north and know what one day is like without electricity. . .in winter. . .I have purchased a diesel generator without hesitation! I know what *two* days of no electricity is like. I do not want to know what three weeks is like—even in the south!

Seriously consider a diesel powered generator!

Please, lay aside all else except *one* fact: there will be a depression, perhaps the worst in American history. Prepare for it. *Now*.

Want to hear a really pessimistic view of what happens if the power grid goes down. . .for just a few days?

I predict busy signals on toll-free lines. I predict a wave of "sell" orders so huge that the governments of the world will close down the international market. The Dow-Jones Industrial average: 0. Bond market: 0. Mortgage Market:0.

—Gary North
July 1998

Sirs, you have 300 working days to prove the gentleman wrong!

One of the most conservative and respected spokesman concerning the Y2K crisis is Peter de Jager. He was interviewed on the television show, *Crossfire*, on July 14, 1998. Pat Buchanan asked de Jager what was the worst thing that could happen as a result of Y2K.

Peter de Jager replied: *"If we do not fix this, lives will be lost!"*

He has been quoted as saying: "If it is not fixed, we will die."

The Greatest Danger—Interlocking Dependency

I have been reading mountains of material on the power grid, seeing again and again statements pointing out the *interdependence* of three segments of civilization which cannot function without the other two.

They are: *telecommunications*, *banks* and the *suppliers of electricity*. The triad.

When *one* of these three goes down, *all* go down. When they all go down, we are in an *economic götterdämmerung*. An unbreakable gridlock.

Transportation—Crucial, and *Un*prepared

But there is a *fourth* industry which keeps showing up in this power grid material—*railroads,* or should I say *transportation.* The slowdown or disappearance of the products which rail delivers will be destructive. Railroads are so far behind in dealing with Y2K they are *certain* to experience massive failure in many places.

Let three segments of society go down and the fourth will follow. An interlocking collapse causes the entire system to freeze up.

If this triad stays down two months, the interlocking becomes totally unbreakable. We lose all four permanently! The grid would stay down for years. All four sectors depend on each other. If supplies from *any* of the four come to a halt, then *all four* stop functioning.

None of the four can start up again without the other three. And none have the supplies to start up independently. A total collapse—with no way to come back up—is a result of this interdependence. The chance of a total collapse? It stands at 20% now. It may rise to 40% if the electrical world does not pull off a miracle.

The Results

In a case of economic collapse that paralyzes everything called "modern" and throws us back to a pre-modern era, we are faced with reinventing 1930. But without electricity throughout 99% of America (a götterdämmerung), we may be forced to reinvent *1830*.

How many people do you know who have the skills to survive in an 1830 world? Remember, this is not you and me *inheriting* an 1830 era, but you and me clawing an 1830 world into existence, from scratch!

Without electricity *nothing* is going to work!! Without telecommunications, neither rails nor electricity will work. Without banks? No money! Well, no one works for *free*. A mutual "nothing works."

We are locked into an inevitable interdependence of four industries, all in jeopardy of collapsing, and none being able to function without the others.

All utilities depend upon telecommunications for inter-utility communications.

—*Charles Siebert*
Electric Power Research Inst.
before a Senate sub-committee
June 12, 1998

Charles Siebert went on to talk about *contingency plans* within the electrical industry and within the telecommunications industry. Every other segment of society *has* contingency plans for Y2K.

Dear reader. . .industries that should *never* have contingency plans are power and telecommunications. Contingency plans in the electrical industry means an unmitigated disaster. There can be no contingency plan if a person dies on the operating table.

For the sake of North America, telecommunications and the electrical industry both need *total* compliance! It is all or nothing.

A C-Span Interview

I watched Senator Bennett, on C-Span, as he derided the CEOs of America's largest utilities for being so hopelessly behind in their efforts to solve *their* Y2K problem. The CEOs sat there glassy-eyed as Senator Bennett lectured them.

Why have these men not acted?

We are facing a technological equivalent of war and famine. Why is the electrical grid so far behind in preparing for Y2K when all of our lives depend on those utility companies taking heroic action. The destruction of America's way of life will be decided by those very men. Why no mobilized effort to save the planet? This is a national crisis!

I found the reason. It chills the blood.

The Reason for the Electricity Crisis

Those key men sitting there listening to Senator Bennett, must get permission from over a dozen outside agencies—just so they can sneeze. Consequently, long ago, utility companies had to make their plans 15 to 20 years in advance. This is because of all the bureaucratic red tape they must work their way through. Those men *cannot* respond quickly to *anything*. Beyond their immediate locale, permission to take action is vague and defused. And slow. And often negative.

The electrical industry simply *cannot* rise to a crisis. Yet the need for cutting Federal government red tape has never been discussed.

We face the possible end of our way of life, and no one is taking action.

Dick Mills (The Westergaard Report, August 6, 1998) gives us the following information.

Regional
"Permission to Act"

Here is a list of the agencies and organizations which regulate the energy industry, *regionally*. All of these agencies must give permission, of one kind or another, before electric companies can act.

The ECAR, ERCOT, FRCC, MAIN, MAPP, NDCC, SERC, SPP, and WSCC. Can you see the problem?

National/Federal
"Permission to Act"

On a national level, the electrical generating companies must work with the FEMA, DOE, NRC. There are more!

And when electrical companies in Canada and the United States work together, all the above agencies must be addressed, plus the NERC.

There is no electrical industries *czar* to make sure energy companies act quickly to resolve the Y2K problem. As of today there is no plan to appoint such a leader.

The grid was already in deep crisis

The Y2K bug caught the utility companies in an already dramatic crisis. The grid will experience serious electrical *shortages* in 2003. . .*without* Y2K problems!

Dick Mills observed that some of the most strategic reports coming from the electrical industry address the 2003 power shortage crisis but make no mention of the Y2K problem!

Yes, we are looking at a grave crisis. Electrical brownouts and blackouts! Please, dear reader, prepare for it. It is coming.

When blackouts occur, 72 hours is considered a massive shutdown. Yet Quebec went down two weeks in 1998. Auckland, New Zealand, went down three *months*. Try to overlay such a crisis on the United States. It would rival the destruction experienced during the *civil war*.

Sensors, switches, chips

Each of the four sections of our nation's electric grid have *sensors* which, when they sense danger, automatically shut down a plant to protect the generator equipment. There are, in fact, *constant* blackouts and breakdowns all over the grid. But *computers* re-route energy so fast, no one knows it happened. If the grid drops to 80% efficiency, or 70%, we are in trouble. Below that, we freeze in the dark. Yet, as of now, not a single mainframe computer in the electrical industry has been reported to be compliant.

The grid seems doomed to falter. North America's civilization hangs by a thread!

The largest hydro-electric plant in the world, located in Quebec, failed in 1998; and the city of Montreal had to virtually shut down. Transportation ended. There were food shortages. Many people in highrises stayed in bed all day to keep warm. What saved Quebec? Some 5,000 emergency workers coming in from all over America, by planes, trains and fleets of trucks, racing to restore the power.

What To Expect

If the mainframe computers are not repaired, they will go down on December 31. If the millions of embedded chips in the electrical power grid are not tested and the defective ones replaced, the grid goes down. No "ifs," no "buts," no "maybes." If it goes down anywhere in the four sections for only two weeks, our national economy is *doomed.* If it goes down longer than that, lives will be lost. If it goes down for two months, there will be mutual gridlock between telecommunications, electricity, banks, and transportation. The interdependency function will end. None of these crucial industries will be able to supply the other. After two months a four-sided supply lockout makes it impossible for the grid to be brought back on line.

That means we will move from a world of twentieth century energy to a world of 1830 energy! It will take us years to reinvent a non-electric 1830 world. The result. It will take decades to claw our way back to the world we knew in 1990.

The chance of regional blackouts? 100%.

The possibility of some of these blackouts lasting for one or two weeks? Over 99%. The chances of the entire grid going down? 60% to 70%. The chances of the grid staying down, thereby ending American civilization and ushering in a social and economic holocaust? Around 20%, *now*. By December of 1999, it will probably be higher.

The chances of *your* being able to buy a year's worth of storable food, *now*?

Please answer by filling in these blanks.

My chances, right now, of getting a year's supply of food for my family is__%.
Two year's__%.
Getting out of all investments and getting cash__%.
Buying gold coins__%.
And silver__%.
A bike__%.
Large cans to store water__%.

Hoping for the best, but preparing, on all fronts, and in every way possible, for the unimaginable worst __%.

In the name of all that is sanity, act! Act now.

Dear reader, this is my best effort to get you to take action—now. Today.

A prediction

There will be a worldwide depression which history will record as having begun in 1999. Those who do not prepare for this depression are going to end up in poverty.

I write these words to you with passion, in hopes that you will decide to *act*. Please do!

I plan to revise the estimate of the chance of total, permanent shutdown of electricity every month. My estimate as the book goes to press is 20%.

Now, just before we learn *what to do*, let's hear the bone-chilling words of experts.

Just as this book was going to press, something occurred that caused me to ask that this statement be inserted. The stock market has dropped dramatically since I began writing this book. What you may not know is that many companies invest their profits in the stock market in order to receive higher returns than those offered by banks. As a result of this practice, the utility companies have just announced they have lost 106 billion dollars in the stock market. That loss was capital. Profit. It was money needed to repair mainframe computers in the utility companies. The utility companies have lost their savings. Repairing the grid by December 31 just became an even more remote possibility. I am raising my estimate of a total, permanent, shutdown of the grid to 30%.

10

Men Who Tell Us This Economic Catastrophe is Going to Happen

The following are statements of authors, experts and analysts of the Y2K problem and the present economic situation. As you read, ask yourself: "Do I really *not* want to prepare for this depression. . .and possibly a national Y2K breakdown?"

We are all, right now, competing in a race against time to avert an impending computer catastrophe. . .every human being on the planet may be affected.

—Constance Morella
Congresswoman

There's no point in sugarcoating the problem. If we don't fix the century-date problem, we will have a situation scarier than the average disaster movie you see on a Sunday night.

Some 95% of the revenue stream of the United States could be jeopardized.

—Charles Rossotti
IRS Commissioner

What makes it [Y2K] complex is too little time, too many lines of code, and not enough programmers. But the big one is too little time.

—Bernadette Reiter
Year 2000 Consultant

It is our prediction that it will only take 5 - 10% of the world's banks payment systems not to work [just on that] one day, to create a global-wide liquidity lock up.

—*Robert Lau*
Hong Kong
Reuters News Service

We're no longer at the point of asking whether or not there will be any power disruptions, but we are now forced to ask how severe the disruptions are going to be.

—*Sen. Christopher Dodd*
U.S.Senate
Special Committee on the Year 2000

We do not know what the impact will be. . .even if the vast majority of problems are eliminated. Systems are very unforgiving. Software programs do not allow for a single mistake. You cannot be approximately correct. You're either right or you're wrong.

—*Alan Greenspan*
Chairman
U.S. Federal Reserve

In 1971 I read a book (by someone named Robert Vacca) entitled *The New Dark Age*. I thought it the oddest and strangest of books. Vacca envisaged the collapse of society, including the then infant electrical power grid. Whether or not this man is still alive I do not know, but had he peered into the future and seen. . .us? We now face the possibility of a *new* dark age.

—*the author*

We must require 100% compliance or we are at risk.

—*Alan Greenspan*
Chairman of FDIC
U.S. Senate subcommittee
Feb 27, 1998

Virtually every government, state, and municipality, as well as every large, mid-size, and small business in the world, is going to have to deal with this. . .In fact, if they have not started already, it's just about too late.

—*Newsweek*

It is now too late to solve the problem. . . there is too little time. Two million computers in America, 700 billion lines of code, 300 million PC's and somewhere between 25 and 50 billion embedded systems. And not enough programmers.

—*Dr. Ed Yardeni*
June 13, 1998
Atlanta, GA

A failure to cope with this bug properly could cause a global recession.

—*William J. McDougall*
President
New York
Federal Reserve Bank

To solve this problem we need to go to three shifts and invent a longer day. It is so late in the game it is not going to happen. We are losing the war and we are losing it badly.

—*David Jeffers*
President
Fort Worth Technology

A global financial crash, nuclear meltdowns, hospital life-support system shutdowns, a collapse of the air traffic system are possible without proper attention now.

—*New York Times*
March 27, 1997

According to computer experts, congressional leaders and anyone who's given the matter a fair assessment. . .unless we successfully complete the most ambitious and costly technology project in history. . .the payoff comes in securing raw survival.

—*Newsweek*
June 2, 1997

The recession could begin before January 1, 2000, perhaps during the second half of 1999, if the public becomes alarmed and takes precautions. If stock prices fall sharply in 1999, in anticipation of a recession in 2000, the resulting loss in confidence could cause consumers to retrench in 1999 and trigger a recession sooner, as well.

—Dr. Ed Yardeni
Chief Economist/Managing Director
Deutsche Morgan Grenfell

Year 2000: Give up! Move on: Now!

—Computer World
July 16, 1997

To replace non-compliant embedded chips would cost two trillion dollars.

—Len Burton
President
Computer Software Solutions
Houston, TX 1998

Bankers are aggressively working on this problem but they are not going to get it fixed on time.

—Craig Smith
Swiss America
1998

The world has probably never seen such a confluence of potentially market-shaking events. . .

—Rosanne Arguelles
Editor
The Swiss Perspective
1998

On average, the typical American family has $10,000 in savings. Some 54% of that is in the stock market. Most of the rest is in the bank.

For the typical American family, the money in the stock market is almost always in a mutual fund, the first and fastest part of the market to plunge. The money in banks is also in great jeopardy, because banks are in great jeopardy.

This is the greatest financial crisis in all American history, going all the way back to the landing of the Pilgrims.
—the author

Kevin Maney, of USA Today, asked a group of Y2K programmers and consultants whether they planned to withdraw cash before 2000. Five of the nine at that date planned to hold extra cash.

Kevin noted that many worry that the fear of Y2K might end up being worse than Y2K itself.

Bad publicity begets consumer worry. Consumer fear generates the run on cash.
—USA Today
August 27, 1998

The problem is far worse than even the pessimists believe.
—Peter Keen
Computer World
1998

There may be as many as 500 different software languages in current use. Automated, corrective tools for these languages are impossible. THERE IS NO SILVER BULLET.
—Jeff Jennett
President
Loeuf Computer Technologies

There is no possibility of a silver bullet given the scale, the scope, the complexity of the problem, no way could we even begin to develop a silver bullet.
—Ed Laird
Author
Privileged Information

This cannot be resolved, from top to bottom.
—Ed Laird

The Millennium Bug. . .(it is worse than you think.)
—Business Week
March 2, 1998

Y2K is exponential. Its impact will range from annoying (like being bitten by 1,000 gnats) to troublesome (100 mosquito bites) to potentially fatal (10 bumblebee stings or one rattlesnake bite)—possibly all at the same time!

—Ed Yourdon
author
Time Bomb 2000

The Millennium Bug is the first disaster to arrive on a precise schedule.

—Business Week
March 2, 1998

This is a problem of gigantic dimensions and with so many complexities that it is very hard to think something will not slip.

—Bichlien Hoang
Director
BellCore Communications
Morristown, NJ

We are all competing in a race against time to avert an impending computer catastrophe. . .Every human being on the planet may be affected.

—Connie Morella
Congresswoman
Maryland
Y2K Symposium
1997

In a recent survey, 44% of responding companies have reported some Y2K computer failures [already]; 67% have reported failures just in testing corrective software.

—Monaco
Special Report
Newport Beach
California

There is a financial firestorm spreading. Currencies have collapsed, capital has fled, and economies have sunk into recession on an unprecedented scale. . .this may constitute

the worst financial crisis since the birth of the modern
international monetary system in 1944. . .

—Roger C.Altman
Investment Banker
Los Angeles Times
June 21, 1998

Let us imagine the impossible, that we sailed through 1/
1/2000 without a single problem anywhere on earth. Still
the anxious days before 1/1/2000 will cause the havoc, the
panic, and consequently the beginning of a depression. Such
an event of perfection (Y2K compliance) will still have come
too late. The panic will have already happened before
December 31, 1999. There is a near certainty that panic
will be in full swing before 1/1/2000.

—the author

Lou Marcoccio, of the Gartner Group, says about 23% of
companies worldwide have yet to address their Year 2000
problems. Those companies are in for a struggle. When asked
if it was too late for companies that had not started resolving
their Year 2000 issues, Marcoccio replied: "Absolutely."

The greatest problem we have before us with Y2K is the
present wrong decision of the majority of businesses,
government, and even the individual, who thinks that
"someone else will fix it." We will all soon be involved in the
worst financial chaos, such as the world has not known to
this day. The impact will be far more catastrophic than any
can imagine, and results, virtually unimaginable.

—Walt Lamphere

Here is the best summation of all that we face, and what may
happen to all of us in January.

The United States government will collapse in 2000. T-
bills: dead. T-bonds: dead. Money market funds: dead.
Retirement programs: dead. U.S. dollar: dead. The

computer-entry kind of dollar: dead. **Foreign central banks that allow the Federal Reserve to store their gold, and governments that buy T-bills instead of holding gold: dead. The end of the three-hundred-year-old central banking experience is at hand. We are going back to an all cash society.**

—Gary North

Gentlemen, you have 300 working days to prove Mr. North wrong.

America is simply not aware of how global the financial world is, and that the third world financial firestorm may ignite western Europe and the United States.

—Robert Altman
Investment broker

Failure to achieve compliance for the Y2K problem can jeopardize our way of life on this planet for some time to come.

—Arthur Gross
Chief spokesman
The IRS

The International Situation

If America is in trouble, the rest of the world is even worse off. Their lack of preparation for Y2K will sweep America into a whirlwind of ruin.

Western Europe as a whole, is about six to eight months behind the United States in terms of correcting their Y2K problems. Eastern Europe is at least a year behind Western Europe, as are most Asian and South American countries.

The Gartner Group estimates that 40% of Asia's medium-size companies will not make the Y2K deadline.

Following are statements by experts on the international Y2K crisis.

Some 78% of all the computer codes in the world are outside the United States. Our 22% of the world's computers are talking to those other 78%, and it is impossible for the computers in the United States to protect themselves from all those computers in the 78% which will not be compliant by December 31, 1999.

—Capers Jones
author
The Global Impact of the Year 2000 Software Problem

This entire planet has 300 working days left to fix the Millennium Bug.

—the author

The biggest problem the world has ever faced.

—The Gold Newsletter

Failure to deal with the problem could lead to commercial collapse. I put it bluntly, because I want to get the message across. It will not respect national frontiers. Unless we act now, there will be international chaos.

—Minister of Science and Technology
United Kingdom

Russia is not going to make it.

—Robert Zoellick
President
Center for International Studies
September, 1998

There is a distinct possibility that, as 12/31/99 turns to 1/1/2000, we will hardly notice the Y2K problem. Why? Because we will be so involved in trying to cope with the panic which preceded it.

—the author

We are in the greatest financial crisis in seventy years.

—Barry Eichengreen
University of California, Berkley
Professor of Economics
September, 1998

I've got my finger on the trigger. If I don't see any specifics [on fixing the Y2K bug] from the G8 [top eight global industrialized nations] by the middle of June, I'll sadly be raising the odds of a *severe global recession* from 60 percent to closer to 100 percent.

—Dr. Ed Yardeni
chief economist
Deutsche Morgan Grenfell

(Dr. Yardeni just moved it to 70%.)

There will be a severe recession in 1999.

—Production of One
October 8, 1998

Sell stock now!

—The cover of Money Magazine

There is 9 trillion dollars of unfunded Social Security commitments.

—Alan Greenspan

Some 50% of all telephone carriers will experience at least *one* mission-critical Y2K failure when the clock rolls over.

—The Gartner Group

In June of 1998 Congressman Steve Horn gave the government an "F" in dealing with its Y2K problem.

Banks have only 1.6% of the deposits in actual cash. That means 98.4% is in electronic ledger entries.

...94% of the information technology profession projects [in the industry] felt there will be unnecessary deaths as a result of Y2K failure.

If we cannot fix the problem during the next seventeen months, why do we think we will be able to fix it in a few weeks, or months, once it has already occurred.

—Dave Bradshaw
Y2K Net

Most Americans are not prepared for any crisis.

This depression is coming. A hundred years from now, history will record that this calamity began in Thailand in 1997, then spread throughout Asia in 1998, taking Russia and Latin America with it. (Interest rates in Brazil are 50%. The ruble devalued and then banks failed; cash virtually disappeared.) And all this happened without one iota of the Y2K problem!

Imagine what Y2K can add to this problem.

The following chapter will give you dates and signs which will indicate the foreshadowing of the crash.

11

Dates to Watch
And
Signs to Look For*

The following dates—and signs—are the ones which will awaken Joe America. Probably one of these dates will ignite some sort of a nationwide panic. I hope you have acted *before* that.

Circle these dates on your calendar. Any one of these events listed is a good candidate to be the day all America got its wake up call. All of them will cause a growing awareness of the Y2K problem. That awareness alone will change history.

● **January 1, 1999.** There are a large number of mainframe computers that will begin calculating the new century. This will cause major foul-ups and computer crashes.

● **April 1, 1999.** New York State begins its fiscal year for the year 2000. So does Canada. So does Japan, and Japan is *not* ready for Y2K, not in 1999 and not in the following new year. Expect major trouble.

● **March/April, 1999.** The Securities Industry Association (SIA) which is an association of major stock brokers and trading exchanges, announced plans to conduct an industry-wide Y2K *test!* The *Tier One* test will be held on March 6, 13, 27 and April 10, 1999.

Since first writing this chapter, it has undergone major revisions because so many things originally listed have happened. The collapse of the Russian ruble, the depression in Japan, the stock market collapse in Latin America.

(That is, on four weekends.) The nation's entire trading system *will* be tested. There will be problems, and the public will notice.

● **April 15, 1999.** The IRS begins to watch you and me to see if we are doing all the right things in order to pay our taxes on April 15, 2000. It will be a date to watch.

● **May, 1999.** The stock market Tier Two test will come in May, for stragglers. (Some 84% of stock firms will be in test *one*. One out of six firms are *behind*.) It would take no more than 3% to 5% of these firms to fail this test, to panic the industry. Will these tests work out *perfectly*? *Near* perfectly?

● **July 1, 1999.** Forty-six states start their new fiscal year 2000.

● **August 22, 1999.** Explaining what happens on this date is not easy.

Global Positioning System

The military put up 24 communications satellites years ago. These satellites were/are guided by the most accurate clock ever created. It is accurate to the point that the zeros showing its fractional accuracy could fill an encyclopedia. Our government eventually gave everyone access to this exotic clock. Just about every institution on earth using exotic computing signed on to use it, including the finance industry. Their computers check that clock every second, thereby saving themselves a great deal of money when figuring very short-term loans. The GPS is also used to find locations both by military and civilian organizations. (The 911 system uses the GPS to locate your address.)

To keep using that clock indefinitely on satellites which will be in orbit for years, the inventors and programmers came up with a brilliant idea. The clock rolls back its calendar every 1,024 weeks. Its first roll back is scheduled for August 22, 1999.

The new GPS receivers being used here on earth know how to read this rollback, this date, *and* can keep an accurate understanding of the calendar. The old receivers cannot do this. It will be an interesting day to watch! Chaos is a potential.

● **September 9, 1999** (9/9/99). Buried deep within many mainframe computers is an ancient code that basically says "delete" or "file ends here." Back in the early years of programming, the programmers used 9.9.9.9 to tell the computer, "stop here—file ends!" Well, when September 9, 1999 rolls around, many computers are not going to read this row of 9's as a *date*. Rather, these computers will read these nines as "delete" or "file ends" or "shut down." *(When my secretary saw this she commented: "Maybe John, the apostle, had dyslexia. When he wrote 666, maybe he meant 999...")* There are going to be computer crashes all over America on this date.

● **October 1, 1999.** The government of the United States of America begins its fiscal year for 2000. Poor IRS.

● **October/November, 1999.** The presidential debates and the elections. Let us hope an Abraham Lincoln wins because the new president faces a crisis every bit as complex and demanding as the civil war.

● **November 19, 1999.** Earth will pass through the asteroid belt. A far larger than usual meteorite shower will occur. This meteor shower could cause damage to earth communication satellites! (It will last 90 minutes!)

● **December 31, 1999,** 11 p.m., 59 minutes and 59 seconds. It will be winter. If the energy systems and the electrical grid of this nation collapse in January it will be one very historic winter. It could also turn out to be the most memorable month in world history. At the very least, it will be a white-knuckle, nail-biter of a month.

● **January 4, 2000.** This Tuesday may be the day that really awakens all of us. This will be the day we all go back to work in the new century.

Watch these dates, they may help you know when the *mother of all panics* may be beginning.

Signs to Look For

The signs to look for are simple. If a bank panic is going to develop in 1999, these "signs" will help you to know that such a panic is on its way.

(1) An ounce of gold has been selling between $270 - $310 with highs up to, but not exceeding, $340 per ounce for a *long* time. At the time of this writing, gold is selling at $290 an ounce. If you see an ounce of gold bullion go above $340, and gold coins above $380, you are probably seeing a large number of ordinary people moving out of "computer-entry money" into real money—that is, into *gold!* Right now, gold is at a seventeen-year *low.* The price is *below* mining and manufacturing cost. Consider buying some, if you can afford it. (There is a chance—with the very worst of luck—you may have to sell it for what you paid for it.)

(2) An ounce of silver has been trading between $4.50 - $6.00 for years. If silver goes above $8.00 an ounce it means a large number of ordinary Americans, who normally stay

out of stocks or any other investments, have begun to withdraw their ledger-entry, computer-entry, *blip* money from banks, and are changing it into real money, that is, *silver*. Silver is called "poor man's gold." (I bought *silver*.) If bags of pre-1965 silver coins get scarce...the panic is on its way.

(3) If one of the seven hard money nations of the world begins to see its currency being abandoned, the panic has certainly begun. (Japan is candidate number one.) If Russians riot because their currency is now worthless, we may all be in great trouble. On this very day, in Russia, people are selling their blood to bloodbanks in order to buy bread. Bank lines are four blocks long.

(4) If the International Monetary Fund runs out of money, you have waited too long. The world's monetary, financial, economic institutions are going to crumble.*

(5) If you hear or see the word *derivatives*, this world system is going down the tubes. This is a field where only the big kids play. When a nation, or a giant bank, cannot meet its derivatives commitment, it is all over.**

(6) If any person in a high position recommends that the gold commodity market be closed, you *are* in the panic.

(7) If it takes 170 yen to buy a dollar, Japan is in trouble which it cannot get out of. The "bridge" bank idea they are

_____

*It has run out of money **twice** since I wrote this, but has been infused with new money, at the last moment.*

I make no effort to explain derivatives. No one really understands this area of finance well. There is a saying: "There are only two men in the world who understand derivatives, and they do not agree with one another." Derivatives are contracts, involving billions of dollars. A bank which cannot fulfill its contract—because of a falling market—will cause a chain reaction which will bring down every major bank on earth! There are over **200 trillion dollars in derivatives! The derivatives market will fall into a major risk.*

trying will collapse! Watch out for a bank named "Long Term Credit Bank." It is teetering. If it goes under, listen to the dominos fall.

(8) If China devalues its currency, Asia goes. So also the Hong Kong currency.

(9) If you see—or hear of—food shortages in the supermarket, in the name of heaven, act! Otherwise you may be gambling with the possibility of starvation.

(10) If Hollywood makes a Y2K movie.

(11) If men in high positions begin telling us not to take our money out of the bank.

(12) If a string of American banks begin to go under, you missed preparing for the panic.

(13) If U.S. unemployment tops six percent, this nation is in a recession and on its way into a depression.

(14) If any major nation on earth announces it is selling back its U.S. treasury bonds, T-bills, or any other loan instrument, listen to Chicken Little, he was absolutely right.

(15) If there is chaos as Europe attempts to introduce the new currency, both the euro and the dollar will suffer greatly.

(16) If gold moves up and begins selling strongly and government begins to ridicule gold and then threatens to sell government's gold to show how unimportant gold is, they are sweating. They *know* the banks are next.

(17) If Alan Greenspan tells us the FDIC has requested the Treasury Department print large numbers of 100 dollar bills, and maybe, 1,000 dollar bills, you can know they are expecting a run on the banks.

(18) If you read that the bad loans American banks have made reach 7%, the panic is on its way!

(19) If there are electrical brownouts in 1999, this is the

worst of all signs. Even if you have to borrow money, go immediately and buy some sort of gasoline, propane or diesel-driven generator. Your life may depend on it.

(20) Perhaps the most disturbing fact is definitely beyond our power to change. Every eleven years there are major *sun spots* (solar flares) which disrupt all our telecommunications systems. But this is also true: Every 22 years these same sun spots cause a terrible *drought.* The year 2000 is the time for that 22-year cycle to produce a major drought. I beg you—buy food!! This may be the year for a "new dust bowl" as seen right in the middle of the last depression.

(21) Watch McDonalds and Coke. They are the largest of the worldwide American corporations. If overseas sales go down for either, this means economic trouble in the international market is brewing.

(22) If you hear of a hedge fund in trouble, bigger trouble is brewing. If a series of mutual funds that are hedge funds, go defunct. . .it's the beginning of the end.

Early Signs

Here are some early signs which have already begun:

1. Mergers of large banks.*

2. Almost empty coffers of the FDIC and IMF.

3. Talk of "contingency plans" of banks and other financial institutions, as well as electrical companies, railways, etc. Watch for the word *triage.* (When I first wrote these words, "contingency plans" was an unknown Y2K phrase. So was "mission-critical." Both terms are meaningless.)

4. Murmuring of high officials that the public is not being warned of what is coming.

---

*Since first I wrote this line, eight of America's largest banks have gone into four giant mergers.

5. More contingency plans! More talk of "mission-critical" repairs of computers.

6. The collapse of some of the world's largest banks may happen before this book goes to print. Watch for a number of suicides by Japanese executives. (If two more giant Japanese banks go under, Asia is in a major crisis which *will* slam the American economy.)

I add this word: Buy storable food, now. There *is* going to be a shortage of food in 1999 as more and more people store it.**

Can this catastrophic depression be averted? Can the Y2K problem be solved *before* December of 1999? Be certain of one thing: With or without the Y2K problem, we are entering a depression. A depression which *could* eclipse the depression of the 1930's. . .or any other economic crisis in modern history.

When this depression comes, if it gets worse than the depression of the 1930's, you can expect the return of the ancient marketplace. Understand that marketplace and *survive*.

This last sentence was not in the original draft of this book. It was one of the last sentences added. When it comes to food, things have changed radically since I began this book. Those organizations selling storable food have seen a twenty-fold increase in sales in the last **two months. Sales of storable food will continue to explode exponentially. There are going to be food shortages in America sometime in 1999. **Please act fast.***

12

The Return of
The Primitive Marketplace

Let's say the Y2K Bug turned out to be a nothing!

But let's say a *depression did* come. How do you prepare for a depression?

What is the difference between preparing for a depression and preparing for a Y2K devastation?

Preparation for a depression or a worldwide meltdown of civilization: in both cases the preparation is essentially the *same*.

How long would you *exist* if unemployed and out of money? The average American is not prepared for any emergency. Most of us would be out of food in a *week*.

In life, in depression, in catastrophe, our needs are the same.

> *Water*
> *Food*
> *Shelter*
> *Light*
> *Heat*
> *Medicine*
> *Real money*

Add to that:

> *Cheap transportation* (a bike!)

Be you rich or poor, be you urban, suburban, small town or rural, if all the money you have in banks and stocks disappears, how much of the above survival items do you have? True, this is living cheap. And minimal. But, you also survive! When there is a depression or a catastrophe, soon thereafter there arises an ancient phenomenon. Out of nowhere there comes. . .

The Re-Appearance of the Marketplace

The primitive marketplace is almost as instinctive as biology. The primitive marketplace is the place where people all go in order to find and purchase that which is necessary for survival.

If the Millennium Bug does flatten civilization *or* if civilization as we know it *vanishes*, the primitive marketplace—the very essence of true economics—will return. This is as true of a depression as an apocalypse. The marketplace always reappears in very hard times. It is there for the survival of the race. Let us look at. . .

A Worst Case Scenario

Your home *no longer* has gas or electricity, a telephone, water, heat, lighting. Food in your area is difficult to locate. There are no banks. Airlines are not operating. Railways are not moving. Fuel and energy are unavailable. The world is at a standstill. The only communication is by ham radios. Telecommunications, transportation, and electricity are in gridlock. They now no longer exist.

If this scene becomes a reality, here is what will happen:

AS IN THE COLLAPSE OF THE ROMAN EMPIRE, EVERYTHING WILL REVERT TO NEIGHBORHOOD LIFE. YOUR LIFE, YOUR SURVIVAL, WILL BE FOUND IN A *THREE-MILE CIRCLE!*

A flea market will open somewhere near you in that three-mile circle.

Always, when civilizations collapse, life begins again around that ancient, venerable, primitive, unstoppable *marketplace*. The marketplace (bazaar) will live again. Men and women come to that market to find one thing: items which are necessary for the survival of life. This is an immutable law of natural economics. Whenever the currencies of the world become valueless, the local *marketplace* becomes the way the world does business. The marketplace becomes the distribution system. What is in the market? Food, clothing, heat and the other necessities of life. The market works the same way it did when it originated 8,000 years ago.

That place, that *market-on-the-street,* was a crucial part of American history and did not disappear from our land until the late 1930's, when a national distribution system came into existence.

(My grandparents drove from Commerce, Texas to Greenville, Texas almost every Saturday to buy and sell. Everyone came. In cars, wagons, and on horseback. *And* bikes. That marketplace *is* man's economic history. This is how man has always bought and sold. This is how he survived. This *is* the market!!)

Call it a law of human survival *or* call it the instincts of survival. There are no rules nor ordinances nor laws in *this* market. There are no government regulations. No government interference. No ledger-entry money there. Not much worthless wood pulp circulates here. Take a close look at this market. It is driven solely by supply and demand. Learn from this market. Here is naked, raw, primitive, honest, real, unmanipulated, organic economics. Here, in this place, the laws of economics—written into the fabric of creation—are at work in their freest form.

You and the Market

You have no job; your company no longer exists. You, and everyone else in your community, *must* go to that market in order to survive. When you arrive at the market everyone will be thinking *survival.*

WHAT DO YOU HAVE—RIGHT NOW—TO BRING TO THAT MARKET?

What you bring must be something which the market needs. No, it must be something which that market needs *desperately.*

Here are the elements of survival which you will find for sale: water, food, heat, shelter, medicine.

The medium of exchange?

First, basic bartering items.* Then money, *real* money. There are four items which are certain to be accepted as money by everyone. Food, gold, silver, paper cash (*if* it has not yet been destroyed by *inflation*).

And one other thing. The art of buying and selling anything which has to do with survival.

Here you find (1) The exchange of goods for goods. (2) The exchange of goods for services. (3) The exchange of services for goods. (4) The exchange of exotic metal coins for goods and services.

These *are* money in the marketplace.

Again, here is pure, unmanipulated economics.

What do *you* have—right now—to bring to that market? A little? Some? *Get more!*

You need to make a decision: *Do I believe this scenario*

**I went into Albania soon after it opened to the world. Money was cigarettes and western European cash. A few years ago, in Burma, Marlboro cigarettes were literally the coin of the realm. In Europe, just after World War II, unopened packets of American cigarettes and chocolates were currency. You bought and sold with them. The price of everything was reckoned in how many cigarettes or how many chocolate bars it took to buy an item. Tobacco as money goes back to early colonial days when tobacco was literally official, legal money. One state, which grew no tobacco, printed a picture of the tobacco plant on its paper money. . .in the same place which George Washington now occupies!*

will happen? Do I at least believe it is probable? Will I act now?

I know such a world sounds remote, but it is *not*.

If this marketplace becomes reality, how prepared are you? What can *you* bring to the market? What do you have that this market *needs*?

The ancient marketplace *will* return—in some form—even if it turns out we only have a *moderate* depression. (Whoever heard of a *moderate* depression? It is like being moderately dead.)

A depression and the market go hand in hand. What are you going to do, now, to be a participator in a survivalist market? Hope it all goes away? Fine. In the meantime *prepare* for the absolute worst. *Now!*

Everyone will be looking for only a few things—water, food, clothes, shelter, heat, medicine, real money and *seeds*. And a non-gasoline means of transportation. All else is peripheral. When you get to the market, you will be either a *seeker* of goods or a *provider* of goods. That choice is up to you. The time is now.

The market is brutal. It always has been. It is the place of raw, naked, reality. If you own a Rembrandt, no one will want it. If you own beautiful antiques, no one will buy them. If you own a Rolls-Royce, no one will care. Further, there is nothing in the way of furniture in your house anyone is going to want unless it is your silverware or wood furniture for *fire*.

What do you have that someone else needs in order to survive?

As you walk into the marketplace, do you have a kind of money which matches the urgency that is all around you? The market will accept paper money in exchange for goods. It will not accept your monthly bank statement, even if it reads "one billion dollars" in computer-chip money. It will accept silver coins and gold coins. It will accept medicine and non-hybrid seeds. It will accept food as a medium of monetary exchange. Perhaps, more than anything, *storable food* will be money.

What will you have to take to the market? You would be *very* wise to mull that question over very seriously, and then *act* according to your conclusion.

As of this moment, I would implore you to give serious consideration to buying silver coins and getting some cash. And food. Storable food.

A water purifier. Kerosene and a kerosene heater. Butane and a butane-fired cooker.

When this depression becomes reality, no one will want to know that you used to be a millionaire. No one will want to know that you *used* to be important. But here is the one thing that *you* will want to know. "Did I act soon enough?"

Did you lay aside enough cash, coins and food to provide yourself and your family with the barest necessities of life...for a month? For six months? For a year? For two years? Here is that list again: food, pure water, adequate clothing for the cold, medicine, light, pedal-driven transportation, real money.

Decide!

The marketplace awaits your answer.

* * *

Just before you read *What to Do*, please remember the following:

- Billions of lines of computer code need correcting, worldwide.
- Correcting most of those lines, even the crucial ones, will not make the deadline.
- Bad news, escalating daily, will be all over the media.
- Worldwide, mainframe repair costs will be two trillion dollars—the second most costly project in human history.

- Massive amounts of nonproductive money are being taken out of companies for the nonproductive project of software repair.
- Public anger at not being informed will turn to rage.
- One-third of a trillion lines of software have to be corrected at $3-$5 per line, with an average of eight *new* errors introduced in every 1000 lines of corrections.
- Repairing is equivalent to the businesses of this world burning two trillion dollars in the streets. Two trillion dollars of working capital disappears!
- Some 6% of the world's domestic product will be spent on the nonproductive act of computer reprogramming!
- Many airlines will not fly in January. That alone will cause a recession.
- One billion embedded chips will stop functioning; that alone will grind world commerce to a halt.
- A drought is due in the year 2000.
- Some 5% of the nation's banks will fail. *That* will cause a depression.
- 10% of the nation's businesses *will* fail. That will cause a depression.
- The nations of Asia and the developing countries of the world will miss the immovable deadline. This will bring financial chaos.
- The dial tone will go dead. Switches all over the earth will have caused chaos.
- America's ability to sell products abroad will nose-dive. A depression will result.
- Less production, more unemployment: A depression will result.
- News will come to us daily of worldwide tragedies.
- All this will be *too much* tension, uncertainty, fear. Too much bad news causes depressions.

- The most positive model you can build still contains too much that is negative. There will be a depression.

The True Reason Why There Will Be A Depression

I call on every pastor in America to consider bringing your church into *community*. By doing so, your people can face this new decade together, valiantly, and in a closeness not seen in the church since 300 A.D.

Every Christian institution in America is in jeopardy. . .in jeopardy of going out of business. Of closing. Of going bankrupt.

To the Christian who reads this book, if *community* does not show up in your church. . .take the initiative and get other believers in your neighborhood together and move toward an elemental, rudimentary experience of ancient Christian community.

The church lost community a long time ago. We Protestants know nothing about community. This is the most ideal time in Protestant history for all of us to take steps in that direction.

Why a depression? Y2K? The Euro? Crashed computers? Embedded chips? Bank runs? Collapse of the power grid, telecommunications, transportation, financial chaos? Japan and Russia? Solar flares? Debt greater than the worth of the planet? Drought? Will *these* cause a depression?

Why will there be a depression?

There will be a depression because there will be a depression.

Now, here is what you do. Every word in this book is a desperate effort on the part of this author to get you to do the things found in the next chapter.

13

What to do! And do it NOW!

We have arrived at that place for which this book was written. *What to do* in order to survive this depression. Before you do anything else, write down a list of names of people you would like to warn. . .and a list of those whom you would like to begin getting together with. That is, a small number of people to meet with, walk with, and help one another through this crisis. In other words:

Community

Your goal in getting together should include pooling your resources, skills, and ideas for surviving a depression—well and intact. If you wish to get through this depression in good shape, community is not an option.

Write to CF-Y2K

Secondly, write or call *The Christian Forum for Y2K*. You will receive just about all the material you could possibly use in dealing with a depression. It is free. CF-Y2K operates not for profit. Its help is vast. . .and what you receive is both important and needed. This book is a compilation of just about everything available.

Purchase Storable Food NOW

Four months ago, when I began this book, buying storable

food was not an urgent thought in my mind, or anyone else's. Now it is urgent, if not desperate. I feel a sense of desperation as I admonish you: Buy storable food *now*.

In the days just before this book went to press the number of people storing food skyrocketed beyond everyone's expectations, including manufacturers. The frightening part is the supply of storable food in this country is *tiny.* It is a narrow market. It fills up fast. It has filled up. Only about five companies make storable food. They are being overwhelmed. They are all doing from ten to twenty times the business they were doing this time last year.

In America the largest supplier of storable food, Walton Foods, has suddenly found themselves *nine* months behind in their food items. Please, dear reader, project nine months into the future from the day you read this book. How far are you from 12/31/99?*

Please, order storable food *now*. CF-Y2K will help you find all available sources.

How much to store? Personally, my wife and I began by purchasing a three-month supply of storable food. Then we changed it to six months, and now to a full supply of storable food for one year. I recommend you do the same. If it turns out you never use it. . .the worst thing that could befall you is that you would have to eat this food. (It is cheaper than what you buy at the supermarket, so you will even save money.) By the way, I am seriously considering getting two year's supply. Maybe three. It is a very good idea to have extra food for sharing and bartering.

When you write or call *The Christian Forum for Y2K,* they will immediately send you a list of giant co-ops, their locations

---

The director of Walton's Foods recently said that $50,000 orders for storable food have become common. I have just been told that Walton's Foods has stopped taking orders.

and phone numbers. One of these co-ops will be near you. Most of these co-ops have fleets of trucks that deliver to associated clubs. Form a food co-op with your friends. Order in lots of $5,000 and save a great deal.

Community can do that! If the order is large enough, most of the food co-ops will deliver *near you*, sometimes free.

The CF-Y2K will, of course, also send you the names and addresses of all America's best sources (and cheapest freeze-dried and vacuum-packed food for long-term storage). Some of the food they sell can be stored for fifteen years.

Buy Silver Coins – Now

Above and beyond all else, except food, buy silver coins. Why not gold?

I have followed gold coin for nearly thirty years, as well as the history of gold, and the history of economics. I am convinced the recommendation I am about to make is the most prudent way to buy *real* money (unless you are a multi-million dollar individual or organization).

Before making this recommendation, I spoke to several precious metal experts—all with different views—to be sure I was current in this recommendation. Quite frankly, I would prefer writing an entire book on silver and gold to explain to you why I make only *one* recommendation and why it is your best possible course of action.

Here it is again, in a sentence: Buy pre-1965 silver coins.

Here are the other voices.

Rare Coins

Do not buy them. Even if you paid $100,000 for some exotic rare coin, in a survival marketplace all the value that coin has is in how much gold it contains. Do not buy rare coins.

"But what about government confiscation of non-rare coins?"

There will be no confiscation of gold. This is not 1933. People understand economics much better today—even *politicians* do. They might as well try to confiscate your children, or your head. Citizens will no longer abide by such an action. (By the way, government cannot confiscate pre-1965 silver coins.)

Buy Gold?

Do not buy gold just *yet*. There is a better way. Start with *poor man's gold*—that is, silver. Why? Silver coins will always rise in price before gold does. At this writing, silver coins are cheap. Very cheap. That will change. Later, *after* silver, you will see gold begin to rise. *Then* switch out of silver to gold. Here is why silver coins will go up first.*

Government always fears a flight into gold. So do banks. A flight into gold causes the fall of banks and the ruin of Wall Street and all other stock markets. (And well those banks *should* fall—all they have inside them is perception, psychology, wood-pulp and a whole lot of blip money that really is not money.)

In the meantime, while government fights to keep the price of gold down, it will not try to keep the price of silver down. Silver will therefore move up first. Later, the marketplace will overwhelm all the government's efforts to keep down gold. When gold starts its ascent, you may wish to switch out of silver into gold (or at least part of it). Buy silver low, sell it high, then buy gold low . . .and keep it!

The CF-Y2K discusses this in detail.

Government will do everything it can to keep gold at around $300 an ounce. That is about as cheap as gold can get. An absolute bottom seems to be $270.00. Government will succeed in keeping gold down, at first. If government sees it is having trouble keeping the price of gold down, government will make lavish statements about selling government gold. It will issue out-and-out insults about gold. Expect this. . . and more. Government will succeed at keeping gold low for a while. Government fears gold like a cobra fears a mongoose. (The slow, dumb-looking, near-sighted mongoose kills the cobra, with ease!)

Silver Bars?

There are many ways to buy silver. Rare silver coins? Do not buy them. In a survival market place no one cares about rare *anything*. Silver bars? No. There are 100 customers for coins to every *one* customer looking for a bar.

Additionally, you will see coins of gold and silver *disappear.* Right now, new silver coins are about impossible to find in large numbers—CF-Y2K will tell you where to get new silver coins, and how to buy pre-1965 coins.

One Kind of Silver

Pre-1965 silver coins will *never* be scarce. But that is not exactly true. There is a paradox. These coins will never be rare. *But* (and this is some big *but*) these coins come in fifty pound *bags*. These *bags* of silver coins *do* get scarce—*in crises*. In a crisis, these fifty pound *bags* of pre-1965 coins will be *very* scarce.

Let silver go to $10 an ounce and these bags of silver coins will be very hard to get. Let silver go up to $18 an ounce and those bags of silver coins will *disappear.* **

Here is what I recommend. If you can afford a full bag of these silver coins, buy it. If more, get more. If less, buy half a bag, or one quarter of a bag.

The ratio of the price of silver to gold right now is about 46 to 1 (gold at $300 and silver at $5.50).

I once saw silver at $10 an ounce at spot while at the same time bags of old silver coins were selling at $20 per ounce. The *bags* of pre-1965 silver coins were scarce. This *will* happen again.

So here is a way to buy something "rare" (not now, but later),

---

** *At this moment a bag of silver coins – with a total face value of $1,000, sells for less than $4,000. This is a bargain! When the bags of silver get scarce, they begin selling at a price higher than spot silver! Like rare coins do!*

though it is cheap right now. Those 50-pound bags are the best precious metal buy on earth today.*

Where to hide your bag(s) of silver coins? Don't bother. Throw them under your bed and forget them. . . at least until those bags are selling at a ratio of 20 to 1 with gold. Then buy gold. Or, if that is too much, hold those coins! And buy *more*. All you can afford. They *are* the preservation of your wealth.

"But what about thieves?" Let a thief try to pick up a bag or two of silver coins, if he is that strong. A five-year-old can outrun him, not to mention the thief will get a hernia trying to lift one of these bags! (That is one reason gold is popular—it is lighter.)

"When to sell?"

That is not the right question. Here is the right question: When will ledger-entry money be seen to be as worthless as it is, and when will you run out of cash? Spend cash first. *Then* use silver and gold. When will you need food? Keep your silver and gold until you need them to survive.

Write to CF-Y2K and you will receive a list of reputable coin dealers. But *always* call your local coin dealer, too. See who is cheapest, including *delivery* cost.

Other Questions About Silver and Gold

What about purchasing silver and gold on *leverage*? What size gold coin is best to buy? An ounce, a half ounce, or smaller? Since only pre-1935 silver coins are considered to be hobbyist coins and rare coins are there any pre-1935 *gold* coins which

---

The 50-pound bags of silver contain $1,000 worth of face value coins. With silver now at $5 per ounce instead of one dollar per ounce when they were minted, these bags of silver can cost about $4,000. In any major crisis, you should be able to see them go to $8,000 per bag. In 1980, silver climbed to $50 per ounce, ten times what it is selling for now. To see silver double to $10 per ounce before December, 1999 does not take a great deal of imagination. That's minimum.

have little or no premium on them? Yes. Who is a good dealer in silver and gold for *leveraging*? For gold options? For storage? The answers to these questions are *free* from The Christian Forum for Y2K.

OTHER PREPARATION

You should make all your preparation based on this: *Hope for the best—prepare for devastation and holocaust.*
What is "devastation prevention"?

Imagine you will be unemployed for at least a year (we hope this does not happen but *prepare* for it.)

Imagine you will have no access to gas, oil, electricity, water, heat, lights, gasoline for your car, for at least a year. Prepare for *that.* Imagine you will run out of food and will have none except what you stored. Imagine no clean water to drink.

In preparing for this depression or for a breakdown of civilization, most of what you purchase you can always use, regardless. The rest of what you buy now—and will never use— is simply insurance. Insurance which you *can* afford to have, and cannot afford *not* to have.

Imagine you have no heating source for your home, and it is winter.

Raw Survival

For a guarantee that you will have electricity, you have *one* option—a diesel-powered generator. One which *you* own, and a storage tank to go with it. (Unless you live in a very windy place—then obtain a wind-powered generator.)

Food—now!

Seed? By all means purchase some non-hybrid seed and plan to plant it if the situation remains dire beyond one year. Waste disposal? If sewerage goes out, there is much to learn. And much to prepare for. *See* CF-Y2K.

YOUR CANOE AND WHAT TO PLACE IN IT

Think of October of 1999 to May 2000 as a dangerous river you must cross.

You will forge that river by means of a canoe. Your hope: to be as well off when you arrive on the other side as when you stepped into your canoe. On this side of that river you have a modern home, a savings account, a checking account, and other wealth. And a job and income.

You want to get across that torrential river wholly intact. Can it be done?

What do you place in that canoe? Things which will ensure the survival of your present wealth. Ledger-entry money? Computer-entry money? Stocks? Bonds? T-bills? A check book? No!!

What you place in that canoe must survive several months of chaos. You must put in that canoe hold-in-your-hand *value*. What can you place in that canoe which will preserve your wealth intact?

What you place in that canoe falls into only two categories! (1) Survival items, and (2) items which will preserve your savings.

In case your job and your company do not make it across, how do you live until things get back to the point where you once again have a source of income? Let that canoe be your guideline for action.

To review:

We all must have (1) water, (2) heat, (3) light, (4) food, (5) shelter, (6) real money and/or barter, (7) medicine. And we need a means of *non-petroleum* transportation that is manual. (It's called a bike!) Put all eight of *these* items in your canoe.

Christian Institutions and Their Canoe

Every philanthropic Christian institution, every bookstore, every Christian publishing house, every mission board and every missionary are at *risk*. The very existence of these is in very serious jeopardy!

How can these institutions survive? Book stores and publishing houses with few sales, missionaries with few donations. What do they place in *their* canoes?

Wealthy Christians

Here is a very difficult question. How do wealthy Christians protect millions of dollars in wealth? How do they get their wealth across to the other side of that river? Carry 100 thousand bills each in 1,000 dollar denominations? *Or* buy fifty million dollars in gold? Are there other options? (Yes, and many astute businessmen probably do not know them!)

These questions become even more complex when asking how a Christian or a Christian organization with one hundred million dollars gets across to the other side. There are answers.*

There are other questions.

Here is one: What about people living in high-rises! If civilization collapses, how do they survive?

All the material I have read seems to address people living in suburbs or in small towns. There are Christians living in 25-story buildings. (How to survive for three months in a high-rise void of heat, water, electricity, etc.? CF-Y2K has written on this. Again, this material is free.)

What of those who receive a monthly check from some investment—or a stock—which is their only source of income? Is there not an investment somewhere on this earth that is Y2K proof? Yes.

And what of those believers living on Social Security checks?

WHAT IS YOUR RESPONSIBILITY TO YOUR NEIGHBORS?

A lot has been said about: what does a Christian do when he

----

* *One Christian solved all his problems. He bought a gold mine!*

has food and his neighbors do not? This question has troubled all of us.

As of now, I have at least a partial answer.

I am going to sit on my front porch and count the houses I can see. These are my neighbors. I will give a copy of this book to *all* my neighbors. This is one thing I will do in order to answer to question, "What is my responsibility to my neighbors?" I will also be sending this to to my dearest and closest friends. With it a note: "You know me. I would never write a book like this unless I was certain this depression was going to happen." I hope this will get their attention.

To all of you I say again: Get a group started. And act on the guidelines printed here. And don't wait. Get there *ahead* of the panic. The only time to do this is to do it at once.

Christian Community

If it is a holocaust, if it turns out to be the end of American civilization, if it becomes an economic götterdämmerung, *community* is our only hope. Yet Christian community has been unknown to Christians for 1700 years. How does a small group of modern-day Christians go about rediscovering *community*? Is it possible, even when you know zero about it?

Some considerations: a water well, a diesel engine to supply electricity, the best kind of clothes, medical emergencies— perhaps without doctors *or* hospital. At the very least, there are questions to address, explore and resolve.

Get together with others and ask: "What are *our* resources? Where are the companies which can supply primitive non-electric tools? What do we buy now to survive living in a non-electric world?"

Again, all the above references are listed for you.

One reason there is a Y2K *Christian Forum* is because a great deal of helpful material you may wish to have at your fingertips is unbelievably expensive. Prices are a king's ransom.

CF-Y2K paid $100 for *one* book, and $290 for a newsletter, $25 for a tape, $115 for a set of 4 tapes, another $150 for a book set, and another book, $195. The price of resource material is ridiculous. CF-Y2K, which is non-profit, is run by volunteers who have gleaned all this information. All these source materials have been placed in one book. It is yours, *free*.

* * *

Let's not end our relationship here.

Let's stay in contact and up-to-date. Events will change. The situation with banks, will there be a run? The power grid, airlines, food scarcity, the situation with all of these will change every month.

Let's stay in touch.

Gold. I would like to tell you exactly when is the best time— or, at least, the last time—you can buy gold at a reasonable price.

So also the situation with silver. CF-Y2K will keep us both in touch on the situation, with answers to ever-changing questions.

And with how a group can develop *community*.

CF-Y2K has virtually all of this respective material available.

Beyond that, I have been made privy to ongoing research being done by one of the Fortune 500 companies. I hope to share this material as the landscape changes.

Further, you have questions to ask. Someone out there knows the answer. That is why *The Christian Forum* is called a *forum*. This forum is a place where all of us can go. . .go to share information and pool resources, a place where we can all contribute knowledge of things unique to our individual skills and knowledge.

The Forum will not only give you addresses on where to get storable food, but lists over 200 addresses of where to get every imaginable product you might want or need. Plus some none of us ever imagined existed!

Let's not end here.

Let's follow these events right up to New Year's Eve! Let's ask our questions, give our answers, stay abreast of new developments and *ahead* of the depression.

Write for the free information.

Buy silver.

Get cash.

Immediately get storable food.

* * *

I travel virtually every weekend speaking to house churches. If you would like to know my schedule, ask for it and it will be sent to you. I work with home churches; I plan to add an extra day to my schedule wherever I travel. The meetings, on that extra day, will be for you who are interested in getting together. Meetings will be very informal. Together we will sit down and discuss the exciting months which lie ahead.

My present schedule includes California, Washington, Minnesota, Texas, Denver, Philadelphia, Atlanta, Orlando, Jacksonville, and New York state.

Stay in touch.

CF-Y2K

Box 71323

Newnan, GA 30263

800-735-2857

Part VI

Part VI

14

The Day the Euro Kills the Dollar

A new currency is about to appear on this earth. One way or the other it is about to assassinate the dollar.

Today there is no nation on earth to compete with the United States in size, in wealth and in the production of goods. Nor the power of our currency. No other nation has so much money that it can be the "other" currency for international trading. This will change in December of 1999.

For the first time the dollar is about to be challenged as *the world's currency*. If this new challenger wins it will alter America's history, adversely, forever! This is the dollar's first competitor since about 1870. The new kid on the block is bigger than the mighty USA. When the smoke clears the dollar *will be* dethroned.

What will do this? The new euro, the currency of eleven European nations.

Estimates? I have read that the flight out of the dollar into the *euro* will be anywhere from 10% to 30% or 40%. In my judgement, if it goes to 25%, the dollar will be abandoned by the international market as *the* world's international currency.

And you are not sure you want to prepare for a depression? Better you prepare for an economic *Armageddon*!

In the 1870's the United States economy was three times larger than its closest rival, England. After World War II the dollar dominated the world. *No one* was in second place. Our government owned nearly 70% of all the gold owned by all the governments in the world. As for goods and services bought and sold, again, no one was in second place!

Some of that changed in the 1960's.

Discreetly, European countries were taking all the dollars we spent over there, brought those dollars back to America and exchanged megatons of dollars for tons of our gold. (Individuals could not do that. Nations could.) Half of our government's gold supply was gone by 1970. Our gold hoard had diminished radically. Our gold now filled the treasuries of Europe.

This was legal—and it was our policy. We imported too much and expected too little so that the nations of the world "took the difference" in gold. That gap almost destroyed us.

Still, there was no nation big enough and strong enough that could compete with the dollar as lord of international trade. The dollar was *the* currency for international buying and selling. All other hard currency countries were small by comparison.*

The loss of greatness

Today things have changed! Today, we Americans produce only about 20% of the world's goods, *not* one half. Nonetheless, 60% of all the international transactions made in this world still continue to be made in US dollars.

This is all out of proportion to our production and our real worth. But the nations of this world have had no choice. When the dollar was in trouble the world's monetary market could only flee to the Swiss franc (or later, the German mark). But there were so few units of those two currencies, everyone more or less sank with the dollar when it sank, or rose with the dollar when it was strong.

For sure, everyone on earth was stuck with the dollar. *When the American government inflated its currency, governments*

---

* *Since the Bretonwood conference in New England in 1944, the dollar had been the de-facto trading currency of the world. It still is.*

had to inflate their hard currencies. Even the stubborn (and wiser) Swiss had to do so too.

Then came the rise of Japan. At last, when the dollar got into trouble, the world's money markets fled to the yen. Now that haven has ended. The *yen* is in trouble. (At this writing, all of Japan's largest 19 banks are technically bankrupt. It is only a matter of time before *this technicality* becomes *reality*. That event will nail the coffin lid on the world's economy. When these banks falter it is economic Armageddon across the globe.)

Once more, everyone is stuck with the US dollar. Right now the dollar is very strong. No choice. It is us, or bust.

Can you imagine how the nations of the world *wish* there were some other big, strong currency to flee to?

They are about to get their wish. Big time!

A new nation is arising. *That* nation *outproduces* the United States! That nation *outsells* the United States! That nation has *less debt* than the United States! That nation has a larger population than we do! That nation will have a currency stronger than the almighty dollar! If that turns out to be true, banana republics watch out, here we come!

For the first time in this century, the United States of America has a competitor that is bigger than we are, and in a lot better shape.

For America, this competitor could not appear at a worse time. In fact, it is almost like God has designed these next three years to bring this nation to its knees.

The U.S. predicament

Look at us. The United States is $1.5 trillion in debt just to *overseas* lenders (plus about $5 trillion more that the government owes to you and me). The US has the world's largest *offshore* debt. The only reason those foreign countries bought our debt is that we had the only currency in the world which offered a stable deal. . .as currencies go.

But a nation is always open to a better deal.

At the end of World War II we had two-thirds of the world's gold. We now owe more money to non-Americans than any nation on earth, and the U.S. has 16% of the world's gold.

America is deeper in debt than anyone else on earth. Americans also save less money than any other industrialized nation. Just how much indebtedness is $24,000,000,000,000? For all we know, the entire North American continent may not be worth that much. (Never go into a bank expecting to get a loan if you are in debt proportionately that amount.)

Consider this:

In December of 1999 a new currency will make its debut on the stage of the world money market. The *euro*. From the moment the euro appears, it is going to be the *euro* versus the *dollar*.

For just one moment, let us pretend *there is no Y2K problem*.

Five years from now, what will be *the* currency used most on the international market? Will it still be the dollar? Five years from now (without the Y2K problem) the answer is almost certain to be *no*. When that happens, the value of the dollar is going to go through the floor. Those nations who loaned the US government money may have lined up at the door asking for their money back. Since we cannot possibly pay all of them back, we can only tempt them to keep their loans with us.

How?

By paying these creditor nations an interest that is astronomical.

If they keep their dollars, you and I will be paying our local banks 20% to borrow money.

Banana republics, here we come.

Businesses are going to be switching out of the dollar into the euro. The dollar, which has already lost over 90% of its purchasing power since 1941, is going to be the stepchild of the international market.

Remember all the above was a scenario *without* the Y2K problem.

What will happen to the dollar *and* the euro when you factor in the Y2K problem?

One way or another, the euro will kill the power of the dollar. Let's look at how the *euro* will damage the dollar when the Y2K bug is factored in.

If the euro enters successfully, the dollar goes through the floor. If the euro's debut is not successful, the dollar still goes through the floor. We are in a situation where the dollar is going to be hung if it does, and hung if it does not.

Let me explain.

Europe is busy getting ready to introduce the *euro*—Europe is *not* giving its attention to fixing the Y2K bug. In so doing, Europe is taking a terrible gamble.

If the eleven nations of Europe fail to get the euro off to a good start because of Y2K problems, the failure is going to wreak havoc with planet earth. If the *euro* is born while European mainframe computers are crashing, it will devastate the $200 trillion of international transactions. *Without* those transactions taking place, the world's marketplace freezes. The entire world dives into an unimaginable depression.

If the euro does not succeed (and our nation's leaders are praying that it will), Europe is going to be thrown into financial *ruin*. Europe will then drag the United States and Asia down with it. This whole world will go into an economic *apocalypse*.

If the euro does succeed? The euro replaces the dollar. We will still be in an economic apocalypse. Either way, the euro "funeralizes" the dollar. No one will ever again refer to it as "the almighty dollar."

What will be left? Probably it will be the Swiss franc. But the world cannot carry on business with a currency that sparse. What then?

Do you recall the question put to Albert Einstein: *"Sir, what will be the main weapon used in World War III?"* Einstein replied: *"I do not know. But in World War IV, it will be sticks and stones."*

With the euro and the dollar on the mat, the most recognized currencies will be *barter*, silver, gold, and food.

Again, in the name of economic sanity, get storable food, get silver and gold coins. Get cash. Get into community.

With the Y2K problem coming, with the introduction of the euro currency, with Asia, Russia, South America in deep depression, with Japan about to dive into an abyss, and with a nation called America teetering on the brink of financial ruin. . . there is no way this side of the intervention of the throne of God that this nation—and this world—is not headed for an economic Armageddon.

The equivalent of the sinking of the Titanic—the fall of the Roman Empire— the wreck of the Hesperus—the destruction of the Hindenburg blimp—as well as the fall of the Ottoman Empire awaits us.

Our confidence in our currency, and our confidence in computers, has caused us to do things financially that are nothing less than financial insanity. We have broken every law of creation's version of economics. *Poverty* awaits this entire planet.

Not many will act in time to prevent the loss of virtually everything.

* * *

We are now going to take a look at the probability of the breakdown of every segment of human society. We will bring the culprits to the bar and have them speak to you for themselves.

15

Interviews with More Mainframe Computers

The more you grasp the enormity of the Year 2000 crisis, the quicker and more decisively you will act.

But can the Y2K Bug actually bring down civilization? My answer is: the coming depression alone—apart from the Y2K problem—can bring down civilization. Every drop of blood in me calls out to you to take action to protect yourself from a horrendous depression which will come, and for which you *must* prepare or end up very, very impoverished.

The depression *will* happen. The Y2K problem may combine with the depression and make that depression even worse.

To prepare for the one—the depression—is to prepare for *both*.

Will the Y2K problem happen? Yes. Will it, single-handedly, bring down civilization? These next few chapters are written so that you may draw your own conclusions and make your decision. That decision—outside of your relationship to the Lord Jesus—will be the most telling decision of your life.

We will look at what will happen in the crucial segments of society when the Y2K Bug hits. It is difficult to believe this will be anything except calamitous. We will start with the IRS.

This most frightening interview with an IRS computer is, well, frightening.

The Frightening Interview
with an IRS Computer

"I have the bleakest story of just about anyone in our country!

"The entire Department of the Treasury received an 'F' from that same House subcommittee that gave the Department of Defense an 'F'. Let me be blunt. The IRS will not be able to put its computers back on-line for years! IRS computers will not be operative in time to handle the taxes for the new century. Sheer bedlam is going to follow. That is a fact admitted by everyone in IRS.

"No one that I know of who has looked at the situation believes the IRS or the Department of Treasury will be compliant in December of 1999. *Maybe* in 2005. That spells national catastrophe from any angle you look at it.

"We will not even come close to making the deadline. Not the IRS; not the entire Department of the Treasury.

"This means you may not be paying any taxes on April 15, 2000.* But it also means the government will have no money with which to operate. Of all the key agencies in government (or the private sector), the IRS is the most hopeless *and* most needed.

"Programmers have not been able to find any way to fix us IRS computers, nor to replace us! Not on time. Not even near on time.

"Further, the IRS's deadline is *not* December 31, 1999. Computers which serve the IRS begin getting year 2000 data *on June 1, 1999*.

"Without the Department of Treasury and the IRS, we will not see this country pull out of this economic pit for years.

"Imagine a nation with a government that does not have a penny. The shock of just *hearing* this fact will throw the entire world system into a black hole."

To resolve this crisis, the government may simply ask us to pay the same amount that we paid the previous year.

An Interview With
A Close-Mouthed Banking Computer

No mainframe computers from any bank would be interviewed. All refused.

The reason is very simple.

If the computers in the interlocking network of banks across America *and* around the world are not fully repaired on December 31, 1999 then the failure of that *one* sector of society will spell a depression of unimaginable proportion and, yes, perhaps an end of society as we know it.

A depression caused by closed banks could lead to a cataclysm. It would be the end of economics as we know it.

We did manage to get a private *off-the-record* talk with one of the mainframe computers. It so happens it was the one at *your* bank.

Mainly, this computer wanted to make a suggestion to everyone:

"On the morning of Friday, December 31, you must go to your bank and say to the teller, 'I would like to know exactly how much money I have in *all* my savings accounts and checking accounts.' Then ask the teller to place this information on a sheet of paper. Then have the teller sign the paper and date it.

"Do this so that you can walk back into your bank on Tuesday morning (January 4, 2000) and say to that teller, 'I understand your computers are down, and your financial records are lost. Well, I have here in my hand proof of how much money I have in this bank. This paper, signed by *you*, is *proof* of how much money I have in the bank.'

"In this way you will be able to prove to your bank the amount of your monetary wealth and *save* your savings."

At this point the mainframe paused. A look of sadness swept across its face.

"On second thought, *forget my suggestion.*

"Unfortunately, the teller will only know your balance as of Thursday, December 30, 1999 not on Friday, December 31. If you come back into the bank on Tuesday, January 4, with that signed sheet of paper, the teller is going to say to you: 'That information was good only up through *Thursday*, not Friday. As far as we know, you may have come back in here on Friday *afternoon* and checked out all your money.'"

The computer drooped his video screen, then added, "As best I can tell, there is no way for you—or anyone—to establish proof of how much money you have in the banks. *Or* with stock brokerages.

"There is no way to protect your money if it is in a bank.

"If the electrical power grid goes down during the holiday weekend, the bank *will not* be open on January 4.

"If there is a bank panic before December 31, then forget check books, Visa cards, ATM's, automatic deposits and withdrawals, paying bills, paying mortgages. All will have *ended*.

"And no one will be *receiving* payments.

"Maybe, on some propitious day, you should consider taking all your money out of the bank."

The Airlines

Let's interview a *mainframe* computer that controls all air traffic and all reservations here in the United States.

This computer schedules all airplane departures and arrivals, the buying and selling of all tickets, the making, tracking, confirming and consolidating of all reservations. It tells a plane when to take off and when to land, plots its routes while in flight, furnishes travel agencies with endless amounts of information, provides pilots with their critically needed information and prevents mid-air collisions.

The Interview

"Air Traffic Control computers are an array of some of the

most complicated systems on earth. We stretch across the globe. If it flies, we have something to do with it. We stay in direct contact with the personnel of other airlines all over the world. "And we are not going to make the Y2K deadline.

"You should know that in 1997 IBM officials informed the FAA that airline computers *cannot* be repaired. This means airports will be shut down the day after 12/31/99. Airline computers cannot read '2-0-0-0.'

"Luftansa Airlines announced it would *not* fly during the first days of the new century. Others will follow. If we do get repaired on time, there will be no time to test us.

"This is not the end of the story. If I *were* compliant—there are other mainframe computers of all kinds, varieties, makes, and languages that feed data to me from all over the world. *Most* of the world's mainframes are not compliant and will not be by December 31, 1999. These computers will corrupt me. We *will* go down.

"All countries *must* catch up with the rest of the world's computers. I must work out schedules and *then* exchange data with all the commercial airlines around the world. They talk to me; I talk to them. On January 1, there will be no talking.

"When will commercial airlines fly again—*safely?* No one on earth knows the answer to that question. I can only tell you there is going to be mass confusion and fear in the air transportation industry and among passengers, such as this world has never known.

"If I have anything to say, it is this:

Don't fly until all computers are corrected. Don't even fly then. Wait until all the defective embedded chips are found and replaced...and tested.

"One authority stated flat out: 'If the airlines are down one

month and nothing else happens, there will be a recession.'
Beyond that, ask me nothing. After all, I, and many other airline
computers, will soon be dead."

Transportation

Let us move across the tracks and speak with another
mainframe, one in the transportation sector. This one controls
the *railroads* of our nation.

"I am important. A good chunk of American civilization
will stop if I am not running the railroads of America after
December 31, 1999. Will I be out of commission? Yes!

"This fact is going to *change* your life profoundly.

"You have probably never realized how many different goods
and products the rails transport with my help. The triad of
telecommunications, banking and electricity all depend on me.

"Box cars are all told where to go by me. I tell them when to
go, when to wait, where to stay. Box cars cannot, and will not,
move without me. I also keep a record of what is in those box
cars. I tell engines where to go to pick the cars up and where to
send each and every different box car. The engineers are totally
dependent upon *computers*. So are you. Your very quality and
assurance of life *does* depend on me.

"The food which comes to your table depends on me. So
does oil and gasoline, as well as all the other fuels which are
absolutely necessary to drive the *electric generators* of America.
You will see gasoline shortages. Why? Because railroads cannot
make that deadline.

"I am not repaired, *most* mainframes in the rail industry are
not. Repeat: the deadline will not be made.

"That means your life *will* be adversely affected in many ways.

"To give just one illustration: If I fail, railroads fail. If railroads
fail, there will be little or no food in your supermarket within a
week! This will cause panic, probably *before* the shortage.

"I do not have to tell you that I (as the railroads) am also

tied in to Canada and Mexico. And the shipping ports. And the
entire trucking industry. As well as UPS and Federal Express.
"I will break down after December 31, 1999, a fact almost
everyone in authority agrees on. This breakdown could freeze
America's *everything*. With the rail industry paralyzed you could
see America thrown back to living the way your great-great
grandparents lived.

"Listen to one of the nation's leading railways speaking on
just the subject of the *switches* which throw the railway tracks:

> We no longer have a single switch in all our railways
> that is switched manually, that is, by hand! All
> switches are switched automatically by mainframe
> computers. We have no other way to switch them.

Dear reader, this is a small fraction of the information which
announces that our nation's transportation system is in jeopardy.
The clock ticks. We are seeing the rail industry fall far short of
its deadline.

An Interview With
An AT&T Computer

Now to a *telecommunications* mainframe. One which works
for AT&T.

Someone has said, "No dial tone, no civilization." Without
that dial tone: No satellites work, the nation's electricity stops,
the banking system ends, radio and telecommunications cease
to function, the internet goes down, rails stop, air flight ends.
Gasoline and all fuels do not move, sewerage stops, so does
water.

The telecommunications industry will not make the deadline.
Let's listen.

"I am not compliant. And it does not look like I am going to
be. I cannot begin to tell you what is going to happen if AT&T—
and all the telecommunication industry—does not meet its

deadline. AT&T is *most* of telecommunications, and it is 'behind the curve.' There is an excellent chance that you are not going to be making any phone calls on January 1, 2000, nor for a good long time thereafter. No dial tone may be the order of the day. The picture for all other kinds of communication that travel by *wire* looks pretty bleak. For you, for a nation, for the world.

"Ninety-nine percent of the generators which produce electricity for this country *cannot* operate without the telecommunication system working perfectly.

"The entire world depends on America's telecommunications. So do *all* international banking exchanges."

An Interview With
A Social Security Computer

We move on to a fearful interview with a Social Security Administration mainframe. Try to grasp the implications.

"The Social Security Administration has been at work repairing me (and all my computer friends in SSA) since 1991, which is *far* longer than *any other* government agency. Longer than just about anyone else on earth. Since 1991 all SSA mainframe computers have become 60% compliant. That means we are 60% compliant after *seven* years of repairs. Remember this: Social Security has one year left to finish the other 40% of the work! Some 60% in seven years, 40% must be done in one year. It cannot be done!

"If you receive Social Security checks each month, there is a chance mainframes may lose your records, even your *existence*. That means about 32 million people are not going to be receiving their Social Security checks. Do not even think about the chaos, confusion, anger, resentment and tragedy this is going to cause.

"Social Security observed that they would be receiving 20 million phone calls *per day* if Social Security checks do not go out.

"And if this breakdown continues for months? Very simply: This country will find itself in the greatest crisis since the Civil War!"

Are you beginning, dear Reader, to grasp the enormity of this crisis?

An Interview With
A Defense Department Computer

Some 40% of the government *is* the Defense Department. This includes our thermonuclear missiles. Will these missiles fire!?

"You have heard correctly; I will not be able to fire missiles in January, 2000. I will not be able to talk to aircraft carriers, freighters, destroyers or fighter planes. The entire national defense program stands a better chance of crashing on the last day of the last year of this century than it does of surviving.

"The Department of Defense did not properly program us for the new century. And the Defense Department waited *forever* to *begin* doing something about the Y2K problem. They have *begun* to do repairs, but they started too late.

"A House subcommittee gave the Department of Defense an 'F' in Y2K preparation. The Department of Defense is hopelessly behind in repairing me and scores of other mainframe computers. When will the Department of Defense be ready to operate again? When will it finish its *most* critical repairing?

"By their own estimate: *2019*.

"This involves even the Russians. They are very concerned about our vulnerability and theirs. Russia asked the American government to give them reassurances that these missiles can and will be back on line.

"By the way, there are an endless number of agencies in the military. *All* these agencies are far behind. This means 40% of the federal government may be totally nonfunctional on January 1, 2000."

An Interview With
A Hospital Computer

A VA hospital sent out letters to all the manufacturers of
their key equipment asking if it would work on January 1, 2000.
One manufacturer, who had sold fourteen x-ray machines at
$40,000 each, responded, telling the hospital that their machines
will not work in the new millennium. Further, the manufacturer
told the hospital that the radium in the machine must be removed,
at a cost of $14,000 per machine.

Now a grim interview with a hospital mainframe.

"I made headlines a few days ago!

*"Senator Christopher Dodd said the health industry was
headed for disaster.*

"There is exotic equipment in hospitals much of which will
not work on January 1, 2000. Because one computer can corrupt
another so easily, I fear there will be breakdowns during surgery.

"Most hospital mainframes are not compliant.

"Therefore I advise you to get your teeth repaired sometime
in 1999. If you must have an operation, better you have it *now!*
A great deal of dental equipment is date ignorant. Remember
that a great deal of crucial health equipment is not going to
function beyond the last day of this millennium.

"And do not forget, the health industry faces hundreds of
millions of dollars to be spent on replacing these machines."

An Interview With
An FBI Computer

Yes, an interview with an FBI mainframe computer. Law
enforcement is not usually considered in the Y2K problem, yet
our national security is at risk.

Let's learn why.

"What you have heard is true; I may lose all the fingerprint
records and criminal records that exist in my files. Parole officers

all over America may lose their data on parolees. Prisons may lose the records of their inmates, including such information as when the prisoner came in and when he is due to be released.

"Much of this will happen.

"There are lawyers, even now, revelling in the thought of bringing their clients into court saying, 'You cannot keep this man here beyond today because there are no *official* records proving he is a prisoner'.

"This same situation exists in state and county law agencies throughout America. Little is being done to turn this situation around. The civil and criminal justice system may find itself in shambles in the new century.

"How much has been done to rectify this problem? Very little. Much less than is necessary to meet the December 31, 1999 deadline."

An Interview With
A Food Distribution Computer

One of the most disturbing things we find in the Y2K crisis is to discover how unprepared the food distribution system is for the new century.

Let's find out.

"I am a mainframe handling one of the most complex movements of products on earth. I may be worth no more than junk very soon. This is true of most of the mainframes throughout this industry. The food distribution system moves by means of mainframe computers. Most of my fellow computers are still not Y2K compliant.

"What happens if we fail? Supermarkets will be out of food. So will wholesale markets all over the country. It looks bad. Very bad."

Do you want to hear the worst? Half a million families in America are *now* storing food. If that number grows? Shortages of food will begin showing up any day now. If that happens, and it looks like a certainty, there will be a food panic sometime in 1999. This will produce an international, economic, social disaster *long* before Y2K arrives!

* * *

If the triad of telecommunications, banks and electricity fails, we will be back to 1840, only we will not have the skills the people in 1840 had!

Before we leave mainframes there are a few other things to know about Y2K.

Cost

Fixing the Y2K problem will cost 600 billion dollars. That is the second most expensive event in human history; only World War II cost us more. Taking that much money out of the econmy on a nonproductive project will, by itself alone, cause an economic depression of the first order.

Programmers

There is a nationwide shortage of 700,000 programmers, and a worldwide shortage of over two million. These programmers are needed and necessary to repair mainframes, and they do not exist.

Repairs

For every 100 lines corrected, there will be eight new errors introduced into the software. "It has to be perfect, or it does not work" is a necessary goal that will take 20 years. But we have only 300 working days left.

Lawsuits

The gross national production of America is eight trillion dollars. Authorities estimate there will be two trillion dollars in Y2K lawsuits. That will destroy America's economy and bring down to a crawl the entire judicial system.

The International Situation

No country is as far along as the United States in dealing with the Millennium Bug. Europe is a year behind us. Asia, a year behind Europe. Both will miss the deadline, which very simply means international payments, exchanges and then commerce will collapse. The breadth of the scope of that collapse is beyond the understanding and imagination of anyone on this planet.

The rest of the world will become aware of all this before December 31, 1999. They will react in the same way we will: awareness, stress, uncertainty, fear, denial, panic and then action.

Section II

Part I

Dark Economics
versus
Economics in Harmony
with Creation

The following two chapters are among the most
important in this book.

16

The Billion Dollar Pine Tree

Wouldn't it be nice if gold were *money* instead of paper! We would *not* be having a depression. As it is, nothing can stop it, and the Y2K problem is about to throw us into something not far from a new dark age.

There was a time when all American money was gold! Not paper. *Gold.* The Constitution guaranteed that *gold* was America's money. How on earth did we lose so great a right? And how has that loss impacted our lives? *Your* life?

Here is the story.

From 1797 through 1932 gold was money. Inflation and deflation were unknown except in crises such as the Civil War and the end of World War I. In fact, it was the recession right after World War I that triggered a series of events that eventually caused all of us to lose *real* money. A war-induced recession followed by a boom. The boom was the legendary "roaring twenties."

Government allowed that boom to evolve into a great period of prosperity. *False* prosperity. This man-made, government-created boom went on until 1929. Gold was there, backing the paper currency, but government allowed more and more data-entry money into banks. The ratio of data-entry "money-in-the-bank's-records-but-nowhere-else" money grew all out of proportion to the gold which was backing the data-entry money.

That period of prosperity ended for *two* reasons: first, too much credit, too many loans, too much borrowing, too much "bank money" that is not money at all. And second, government began interfering in the market place. Any government which does this always destroys the market.

As is always true of a government-created boom, people get carried away, the banks making too many loans available, individuals, companies, and governments borrowing too much money.

The stock market, for instance, was so lucrative that people were going to their banks and borrowing money, then investing that money in *the never ending boom* on Wall Street.

There is a school of economics, called *natural* economics, which says that such a boom, built on loans and credit, *must* end in disaster. Natural economics understands the universal laws innate to creation. The boom *did* end in disaster. In fact, the amount of credit made available to the public increased by 60% in the months just before the crash. (Shades of 1998.) According to natural economics, a depression *must* follow.

In the last year of that boom easy credit got easier and the amount of money in the market almost doubled. It was an unheard of increase in credit expansion by banks and government. And the money was not really money. It was not gold; it was not even paper currency. It was *that* expanded. It was "money" added to the banks' ledgers, which is *not* money at all.

Every time more ledger money was introduced into the market place the gap between ledger-entry money and gold widened. America's currency and America's economy were doomed. President Hoover did not understand this. He saw no end to this great new prosperity. Nevertheless, this economy was naught but a house of cards.

As in the days of Hon Ts, the banks began issuing far, far more gold certificates and silver certificates than there was gold and silver to back it. Again, this "money" was merely *receipts* the teller hands you after you hand them a *check* and ask them to deposit the check into your account. The whole thing is movement of theoretical money. Neither the check nor the receipt is money. Not paper money, not gold money.

Ingredient Number One for an economic depression: credit, credit, and more credit. Today the amount of money available to loan and to borrow has never been so vast. The 1990's "credit available" dwarfs 1929 . . .and any other time in the history of North America.

America has never had so much credit as now. And the depression which will follow will be inversely as vast as has been the credit boom! That means we are headed for the greatest depression in history. The 300 years of the "central bank" philosophy and ledger-entry money are over. The consequences are unimaginable.

I beg you, dear reader, do not be one of the billions who are going from prosperity to poverty.

What brought down the 1929 "house of cards" economy? The inevitable! A *crisis* arose. (Actually, it was not the crisis, but *perception* that a crisis was coming.) That crisis revealed the economic *charade*, the surreal prosperity.

Here is what happened.

Lots of money, lots of spending, building, buying. The government wanted all the spending that Americans were doing to be spent on American-made goods, not foreign goods. Too much of that money was being spent on products made overseas. Government, therefore, decided to interfere in the market place.

(No power on earth can interfere with the *market place* with impunity. The market will eventually clobber interference. In the end, the market cannot be manipulated. It will eventually win out, to the destruction of the violators.)

Back in 1929 what caused the crash? Government decided to impose tarrifs on foreign goods. That brings us to Ingredient Number Two.

Out of this decision a major crisis arose.

As in the case of Hon Ts. . .it was not a crisis. . .but fear of a crisis which triggered the economic disaster. Also, as in the case of Hon Ts, the crisis revealed the fact that all that wonderful prosperity was nothing but a ledger-entry *illusion*. Everything you gain in an illusionary prosperity is *lost*, plus some.

Starting in 1999, we will begin to lose *all* the illusionary prosperity we have gained. Plus some. The loss is always greater than the gain.

The two ingredients are here with us. Credit gone wild. . .*and* a perception that a very big crisis is on its way. The crisis? Y2K!

In 1929 the perceived crisis was a proposed tariff—a *tax* on all incoming products manufactured overseas. Today, it is not a tariff. It is the possibility of a worldwide crash of mainframe computers. And billions of microchips going dead. Not to mention the euro, nor the drought.

Dear reader, take the illusionary prosperity we have, add to it the *fear* of a coming mammoth crisis, then add in the *reality* of that crisis. You have a catastrophe of apocalyptic proportions. . .unrivaled in all human history.

In the name of your Lord and mine, I implore you. . .prepare!!

In 1929 government announced it was *going* to pass tariffs. When this became known to the American people they did two things.

First, other nations announced they were going to pass tariffs against *our* American goods. America panicked.

Americans realized overseas trading was going to virtually stop. After all, if your company cannot sell goods overseas, your company will have to lay off some employees. Therefore Americans' *fear* of a drop in business, and *fear* of a declining stock market, caused America to act on their panic. So, secondly, they got out of the market and they went to the bank to get their gold.

That is what *wise* Americans did. Most did *nothing*. . .and lost everything.

As things got worse these same people developed a healthy fear of ledger-money! They wanted real money, not a receipt. They went to the bank and exercised their constitutional right to exchange all those receipts for actual, real (and legal) money. They checked out *gold*, en masse. This wise little group of people changed their ledger money into gold. How many? Perhaps no more than 2% of the population! This selling of stock, this switching out of bank ledger money into *monetary* gold all took place *before* those tariffs became law.

Perception of a coming crisis brought on *The Great Depression* of 1929. Not things real. Anticipation. A depression was in full swing *before* tariff laws. Shades of Hon Ts Yon and Kom Pu Ter.

And so it came to pass that—a little later—the rest of the American people went to their banks (and stood in long lines) to get out real money in order to exchange ledger receipts for gold. Banks took the receipts and handed people gold.

As long as they could.

The Achilles heel of banking was revealed. People were going into the banks with their ledger-entry *receipts*, taking out their gold and cash.

The bank killer: People were not putting it back in the bank! For the first time ever, people kept their gold and cash. That is fatal to all banks.

This is happening in Japan as I write. Right now, the nineteen largest banks in Japan have deposits that are only 1% greater than their loans. Legally, they must have deposits that are 8% greater. . .or the bank closes its doors.

Everyone is looking the other way. But when that 1% edge disappears, watch out! Why did the safety margin disappear? Two reasons. First, banks made bad loans: loans that were acceptable in present-day prosperity, but worthless in a downturn. Secondly: the Japanese people are losing confidence in their banking system. The *wise* are checking out cash, *and* they are buying gold. . .even as I write these words.

This same scene is about to happen here!

In 1929 banks began to collapse. When the banks ran out of gold and cash, they shut their doors forever. Seeing this, other people—a day late—lined up in front of the solvent banks to hand in their paper and get *their* gold. But there was no gold left. By 1933, 4,000 of the 8,000 banks in America closed *forever*. A lot of people were walking around with check books and receipts of deposits, but no cash or gold. All they had was worthless ledger-entry receipts which had *always* been worthless.

Dear reader, that is *all* that you have. . .little slips of paper called data-entry receipts, and a check book which records all those worthless electronic entries. And that, dear reader, is *nothing*.

A depression began. Sometimes it is called "a period of constriction of money" or deflation. It is also called "impoverishment of a people." It can also be called the result of government allowing the issue of too much ledger-entry money. But the best thing to call it is: *government confiscation of wealth*. This, or something similar, will happen to you; therefore, it is important that you grasp this scene.

In 1930, money of *any kind*, paper or gold, was scarce. (Unless you call ledger-entry receipts from nonexistent banks. . .*money!*) Those who had money clung to it. In the next years, while *everyone* else became poor, those people who *first* exercised their constitutional right to get their gold, and cash, out of banks. . .those people became America's *new rich*.

If you had cash, you could buy most anything for a song. Those who had only checkbooks had *absolutely nothing*.

Holdable, foldable cash was very hard to find. Hardly anyone had any kind of money. It was a *deflationary* economy. From a day with far too much money around (inflation, credit expansion) to a day of too little cash. And the banks which still existed were afraid to loan money to *anyone* (credit contraction). Very little money and very few loans. Things were bad.

But if you think that situation was bad, the worst was yet to come. At least a few people had real money (gold) and cash. Just a few months later no one in America had real money (gold) and suddenly there was way too much *cash*.

This dreadful state of affairs had its beginning with the election of November, 1932, the most crucial election of the twentieth century. Franklin Roosevelt was elected president. The Republicans went into virtual extinction. The only people in America who would admit to being Republicans were a handful of folks in Maine.

On March 5, 1933, Roosevelt took office. (When the Chief Justice asked Roosevelt if he would swear to uphold the constitution, Roosevelt said yes, but later admitted that he said under his breath, "but not the way *you* read the constitution.")

The very next day, March 6, Roosevelt dusted off an old act of Congress passed in 1917 called "The War Powers Act". He declared a national state of emergency. With that law as his justification, Roosevelt effectively became a virtual dictator in many areas of government.

On that very same day, Roosevelt ordered all monetized gold (coins) to be *illegal!* Gold, as money, *illegal!?* Such a thought is impossible, and absurd. Gold was money like air was breath. So it has been for all recorded history, among every tribe, culture, race and tongue. Gold as money is a virtual biological instinct of man. You cannot make breathing illegal.

But Roosevelt made gold. . .to be *not* money. Roosevelt confiscated all monetized gold from all the American people.

On that day America ended a 125-year policy of economics that was in harmony with the law of nature. *That* economic policy is the only trustable economic practice in existence. In its place we entered the era of Dark Economics, an economics that practices the slow theft of the wealth of all the American people. It is an economics that is "robbery by other means." Unfortunately, in so doing, government forced *dark economics* not only on us, but on all the other nations of the world.

It is difficult for any of us to grasp what really happened.

A semblance of organic economics—an economics in tune with creation—*ended.* An immoral economics took its place, one that must, by its very nature, fall. . .and leave us all in poverty.

From that day to this day, *you* have never owned money. *You. Never!* Real money has never been yours. You have owned an *illusion* instead of money. Wood pulp. And electronic sparks! Any economics built on that illusion *will* fail. And ours is built on such an illusion.

Since that sad day in 1933, you and I have been barred from actual money. It is illegal to enter the domain of gold as money.* Further, since that historic hour, your wealth has been under *confiscation.* You have never lived a single hour on this planet without your money slowly losing

---

On December 31, 1974, gold was allowed to be sold as a commodity on the commodity market. It is illegal to use this commodity as money! Folks, when a currency goes into the pits, gold does become money. All true value shifts out of currency into gold. It is a law of natural economics as certain as the rising of the sun.

its buying power. Every day you have lived you have had taken from you the fruit of your toil. Every day you contract *your* labor, *your* skills, *your* time, in return for a set amount of money, part of that money has been stolen from you. You have received less than what you contracted for. Government has stolen part of your toil, your skill, by causing your money to lose its purchasing power. This happens daily.

The story gets worse.

What I am about to tell you, I am embarrassed to recount. It is so bizarre it tests the bounds of belief.

The question is: How on earth could Roosevelt violate the Constitution? How could Roosevelt confiscate our money (gold)? That simply cannot be done. We are guaranteed, under the Constitution, that money *is* gold and silver. It is *in* the Constitution. How could he use the War Powers Act to end our right to gold as money? How could Roosevelt replace our gold with something as worthless as wood pulp?

"War Powers Act!" *There was no war.* There was no enemy. When the executive order was drawn up, an *enemy* had to be named.

Listen! Roosevelt resolved his dilemma by making *you and me* the enemy. In The War Powers Act, the American people were named as *the enemy of the State.*

It is true!

How so? *We* had committed the sin of *hoarding!* That made *the American people* an enemy of the federal government.

The American people, you and I, had exercised our right to exchange a bank's "ledger money" for real money—gold. But because in 1933 we kept our gold instead of going bankrupt like everyone else, we had committed the *not-a-sin* of hoarding. *That* made us *enemies* of the state.

All gold coins were returned to the state. If you were unwilling to give up gold in exchange for wood pulp, you faced a penalty of $10,000 and *10 years* in jail.

We lost our 154-year cumulative right to own gold as money. That "emergency" is *still in existence today!* It was—and still is—illegal to own gold as money.

No president since then has ever had the courage to rescind that act.

Folks, we are in a *real* emergency. Someone ought to suggest that the remedy might be found in rescinding that Act of March 6, 1933. Will we ever have a president with courage enough to let us have back the right to own gold as money. . .a right guaranteed in the Constitution?

What did we get in return?

Here is the scandal of the century.

When Roosevelt took office, there was very little cash. Gold money had disappeared. Nobody out there was turning loose their gold. It was their only wealth. To own gold was to *not* be impoverished. He who owned gold as cash was *not* poor. Everyone else was poor. Roosevelt wanted to remedy this lack of *cash*. His theory on how to end the depression was to end scarcity of cash. He decided to flood the nation with paper money. (This is exactly what is happening in Russia. Banks have frozen all accounts. *No banking, no cash.* The Russian government will soon be flooding Russia with cash, destroying the ruble in the process. And when you destroy a nation's currency, you destroy a nation. . .and you send its citizens into unimaginable poverty.)

To flood the nation with cash, Roosevelt *knew* gold had to go. If paper money is backed by gold, there can be no inflation. You cannot inflate and have gold backing the money. People will always ask for their gold in an inflation. And Roosevelt felt he *had* to inflate. So he had to get rid of gold! He outlawed gold. When you went into the bank and handed over your gold—in return you were given *newly printed* paper. To be exact, you got back twenty paper dollars and sixty-seven cents for every ounce of gold you turned in.

Paper in exchange for gold!

When Roosevelt finally had all our gold, he told the Treasury Department to turn on the printing presses. The banks also began loaning ledger-entry money. Both paper money and ledger money began losing their value. This is what happens to *any* nation's money when it is not backed by gold! Buying power of money nosedives. This continues until that paper money and data-entry money can buy *nothing*.

Here is a rule in Dark Economics: Government, unfettered by gold, will debase a people's currency until that currency is worthless. The result: poverty for everyone. That is a principle rivaling the law of gravity.

Few Americans realized our government had changed economic principles and practices.

On March 6, 1933 *the people of the United States got a new currency*.

New! Totally different. Utterly unlike the money of 1932. Money not backed by gold. Money backed by nothing. Money whose value *government* can utterly destroy!

From 1797 to 1932 we had one kind of currency, a *stable* one. From 1933 until today, we have had a *different currency*!! A currency that loses its value every day and, in so doing, *steals* from you. Robbery by slow means!

The economics we have had since 1933 is an economics founded on the practice of confiscation—confiscation of *your* wealth.

In the beginning (in 1933) this was a *slow* confiscation. As the years go on such confiscation accelerates. When a nation no longer backs its currency with gold, the value of that nation's money *will be* debased. Today there is not a nation on earth that backs its paper with gold. *Every* nation on earth has a currency that is constantly being debased. *Every* citizen on earth *is* having the purchasing power of his money confiscated. The sweat and toil of his being, daily stolen from him. This continues until mathematics can no longer be denied. The laws of physics finally declare the currency to have reached zero in value.

Dark economics steals the fruit of the labor of every man and woman on earth. So it is. So it will always be. *Until* gold is once again allowed to be money, this dark economics will repeat this immorality forever.

The 1933 American dollar finds its only value in the value of *wood pulp* and *perception*. It has no tangible value. How long will this *new (1933)* currency last? Not long. The end is inevitable and near.

The next time you pass a tree, pause in reverence. A tree with a 60-foot stand and a diameter of three feet is worth about 500 dollars. One ton of wood pulp sells for $3,500. Government can turn that pulp into paper, cover the paper with green ink, and declare that paper to be *one billion dollars*!

And you *thought* you had money? You *have* wood pulp—worth $3,500 a ton. Next time you get a chance, *weigh* 1000 one dollar bills. Then figure your "wealth" in wood pulp tonnage. You are not very wealthy are you?! Do you know how much it costs the government to print a *one thousand dollar* bill? It costs ten cents!

The most basic law in the universe concerning money not backed by gold is:

Some day, some how, a crisis, or a perceived crisis, will come and render such currency worthless.

That statement could have been written in 1933. This is a law written in the moral nature of creation.

And when a currency ends, it will end in the total confiscation of *your* wealth. You will be *poor*. You will lose all your monetary wealth. Why not! Your "wealth" is inherently attached to that currency, and that currency is paper. All your savings, everything, lost! This present dark economics, this new currency born in 1933* will end.

Your protection in such a time? Food. Real money. Items to barter. In this way, and only in this way, is poverty circumvented.

You must decide now if you intend that this confiscation of wealth *not* include you. It is your choice: impoverishment *or* action.

This new currency, this 1933-1999 dollar is not real enough to withstand the coming economic crisis! Do not try to save any money that is an entry in a ledger in a bank. It already has no worth. That fact will become evident. Instead, start by saving paper money. . .which will be powerful for a short time after the banks freeze assets. Then buy gold or silver. Be done with saving currency in any other form. Go for reality.

Gold can withstand any economic crisis. So also silver. So also food, especially storable food. The Roosevelt-created *ledger money* cannot withstand this crisis.

Just how fast can a currency not backed by gold accelerate in its loss of worth? In 1948 the government of the United States was 40 billion dollars in debt. Today, 50 years later, government is 24 trillion dollars in debt. How big is 24 trillion dollars? Definitely big enough for a bonfire!

At some point into this crisis, people will go to their banks and cash will flow out of these banks into people's pockets, safe deposit boxes and mattresses. . .and that money will not come back to those banks.

Then comes the götterdämmerung.

Government's Two Choices
In the middle of the ashes, government will have two choices as to how to get us out of this economic catastrophe.

One choice is to draw in the greenback and *issue a new currency*— probably ten greenback dollars in exchange for one blueback dollar. The issue of a new currency is the ultimate confiscation of your wealth.

The second choice is to do what Roosevelt did—flood the nation with more greenbacks. The result? A hamburger will be ten dollars. Gasoline will be eight dollars per gallon, and buying an old two bedroom, one bath house, will cost $750,000. And a third-hand Ford, $100,000.

Either way, we will all be poor. The end: the destruction of the value of the dollar and your wealth.

---

* Yes, the 1933 currency looked just like the 1932 currency, but they were totally different. One was worth 24.75 grains of gold! The other was worth nothing.

Economic Doomsday

These are government's *only* choices. Two, no more. Government will make that decision some time in the next few years. You had better be ready for that day. Only the wise will not be impoverished. A savings account in a bank in the age of an economic doomsday is insane. So is investment in the stock market. Forget *making* money. Think in terms of preserving what you have. (If you actually add to your wealth, thank your Lord, for you will be one of far less than one percent.)

You have read the past history of our currency. You see its future. What are you going to do to prevent *your* poverty? I have described two futures. Soon: deflation. After that: Wild inflation. Either. . and both. . . will destroy your wealth. Is there something which can protect you from both? Yes.

As I noted, one hundred trillion dollars in one dollar bills, stacked tightly on top of one another would reach around 6,400,000 miles into the sky. (That's six million, four hundred thousand miles!) But, in fact, our money is not a pile of bills, it is ledger-entry money and worthless.

Our ledger-entry money *is* worthless. Get out of it. This house of cards *must* fall. Move to intrinsic, tangible money. Or lose everything.

When this depression ends, voices across the world will call for more government and less freedom. They will tell us this will prevent future depressions. But it will only mean another currency not backed by gold, and a worldwide state of poverty. (A "one-world" banana republic!)

If enough people buy silver and gold coins, we can prevent this and force the return to gold as money. You, dear Christian, probably hold the key as to which way it goes!

You have a choice between trusting the natural stablility of gold. . . or the honesty and intelligence of men in government. With all due respect for those gentlemen, I advise you . . . vote for gold.

—*George Bernard Shaw*

17

The End Result of Dark Economics

Government takes your money from you in *five* ways. Learn these well.

You worked hard all day and received $100 in exchange for services rendered. That $100 is your hard-earned money which you earned by the sweat of your brow. But before the day ended, government took $50 of that $100 away from you. And you never knew it. (This has nothing to do with government taxes.)

On the same day you received your $100, government recorded in its ledger the existence of yet another $100. That should not affect you, should it? But it does. You earned yours, the other was created out of thin air. When government created $100 in ledger-entry money, your $100 became worth $50. The more currency there is per person, the less value that currency has.

When government issued their $100 dollars you did not realize you worked half a day *without* pay. You worked for *free* half a day. You worked without pay.

This was not your fault nor that of the man who hired you. Further, when government issued $200 out of thin air (which no one worked for), thereby again creating more currency per person, you made only $25 that day. If government issued 1,000 ledger dollars, government would so completely debase your dollar. . .so flood the market place with unearned money, it there would make money so cheap, so plentiful, that money would become near worthless. Then when you agreed on wages at $100 per day, you would get paid only one dollar. Put it another way: The spending power of your $100 would be down in value to one dollar. *This* is *debasement* of money. Only government can engage in such fine art of theft. Only government can steal on such a grand scale and not go to jail.

You hold in your hand 100 one dollar paper bills, all fast losing their buying power. You have lost 50% of your buying power through debasement of the dollar.

Taxes

Then. . . unbelievably . . .you have also been taxed 40% of the dollar by government. And remember, all taxes are collected against your will. . . that is, taxes are collected at the point of a gun. (Before the gun, taxes were collected at the point of a spear.) You think not? Then do *not* pay your taxes. Keep refusing. A gun will appear. That gun takes 40% of all you make.

You thought things were getting expensive. No, your dollars were just getting *worthless.*

You have now lost to government twice, debasement and taxes. *Theft* by other means.

It is hard for us to easily grasp that the hamburger you bought today, the same size as a year ago, is somehow worth more than it used to be. It is even harder to grasp that the currency in your pocket is worth less than last year. Made to be worth *less* by the action of today's philosophy and practice of economics, an economic philosophy based on the concept of invisible theft.

Over a period of *twenty* working years the practices of today's economics have *consistently* confiscated 64% of the worth of every dollar you ever earned or saved during those twenty years. (That does not include taxation.) This is *immoral* economics, the very essence of dishonesty.

It is also **our** own fault. We elected the people who, by invisible means, take away from us money earned for labor rendered.

All that John Q. Public really knows is that his wife had to go to work because *he* did not make enough. Someone accuses you of being materialistic and wanting too much of the world's goods because you both work. What John does not know is that his wife is a slave, a slave to government. His wife works *without* pay. She has two bosses: Mr. Debasement of Money (sometimes called by his vaguer name, *Inflation*) and Mr. Taxes. She works for both of them without compensation. John is the only one paid. He takes home about as much as his dad did, but his mother was able to stay home while John was growing up. Consequently, John grew up in a strong home environment. His children do not. That is because his wife is an indentured servant of government.

Your efforts at labor on this earth are being taken from you. *Invisibly.* Every day. The dollar you placed in the bank in 1945 is worth nine cents. The dollar you put in the bank in 1964 is worth 36 cents, *before taxes.* Further, when you withdraw that money, you will be taxed on the "profit" you made from interest.

You are, you assume, wealthier than you were in 1964. However, a man with $50,000 in 1964 was worth far more than you are with three times that amount. A man with $100,000 in 1946 would laugh at your millionaire status.

Devaluation

Government does not stop at debasement and taxes.

It also *devalues.*

On an average, every thirty years government devalues the dollar. If government devalues the dollar by 20%, that act has *reduced* all you have, all you earn, all you have saved, all your equity in anything and everything.

Roosevelt devalued "you" by 40% in 1935. Nixon devalued "you" by 20% in 1971.

The Ultimate Reality

The present economic practice, debasement of money, is not only theft by innovative means, it eventually *must* produce a form of slavery. You work and work hard. Your spouse works and works hard. Yet a large part of all your labor is taken from you by debasing your money.

No wonder your teenagers also had to get a part-time job in high school. It also explains why it will cost you $100,000—plus interest—to send *one* of your children to college. (My total college cost 1948 – 1951 was $4,000. Since then, learning Shakespeare has become very expensive. You figure it out.)

So far, government has taken your worth by debasement, taxes, and devaluation. It has two more means of procuring your wealth and thereby causing your spouse to have to work without pay.

Government forces you to borrow

You owe $80,000 right now. That is money the government borrowed *in your name.* Neither you nor the government can pay it back, but government makes sure you pay interest on that $80,000! How? Your taxes pay the interest. But the interest has grown so large, government cannot even pay the interest, so government is forced to borrow more money from you just in order to pay interest on the $80,000 it borrowed.

This tale is only going to get worse.

Government forces you to loan the government money

Government *forcing* you to lend it money? Do you ever remember such an act? It happens *every month.* Every month government takes money out of your paycheck for *Social Security.* You thought there was 11 trillion dollars in the Social Security fund? After all, it's *your* money! Well, you may not know this, but government has borrowed all 11 trillion dollars! From you and from me! How will government pay it back? Government has only one source for getting money. . .taxes. So, in order to pay back that 11 trillion to you, government must raise your taxes to pay you back.

Five ways government destroys your worth. Debasement. Taxing nearly half of all you make. Devaluation. Going in debt. Borrowing from you. One day the immorality ends. But when it does end, it also ends in your impoverishment.

Unless you are one of the wise.

The Cycle

The immovable laws of economics say that a money not backed by gold *must* ultimately be destroyed after becoming weaker and weaker. There is *no way* to prevent this process. Government will always destroy its nation's currency. . .unless that currency is redeemable in gold. All currency, 100% redeemable in gold. There are no other options. These things *must* be. On average, this cycle of destruction occurs about twice a century. (In Russia today, in Latin America in years past, it has happened as often as twice in ten years.) Any currency not backed by gold will rarely survive beyond 70 years. If it does survive, it is a banana republic currency where a hamburger could cost up to a six zero figure. (If you are ever in Greece, ask the price of a used car. It costs *billions* of drachma. The currency is a joke. The people are impoverished.)

The laws of economics say that when bank ledger money collapses, only a few people have cash. And because so many masses of people have little or no cash then you enter the *third* phase. Government must *print more cash.*

When that phase has finished its distribution of *cash,* the people have fled ledger-entry money *and* cash.

The *final* immovable law of economics tells us of the end result: the *impoverishment* of a nation. We *all* become poor.

We can add one more word. A few wise people will understand this, and will know there is a way out. Before it is too late, they will act to prevent impoverishment.

All this simply because we live in a world in which paper certificates are not backed by gold. And so it will always be when currency is not backed by gold.

This is the hour *you* are living in.

1999.

This economy is an economic concept based on services rendered *without* compensation. It is, by its nature, immoral. Stealing by any other name is still theft. You live in a time near the end of this cycle of economics. This economy must, this economy *will*, fall. Look up! A crisis is coming.

* * *

Is there a way to get out of this depression once we are in it? I mean a *way out* that breaks this cycle?

Lighting a Cigarette with a
One Thousand Dollar Bill

Have you ever seen a man light a cigarette with a bill equal to a thousand dollar bill? I have.

It was in southern California. I was working with South Vietnamese who had fled their homeland in the face of an invasion. Every day there were about a thousand new refugees coming into the camp at Pendleton. Those who had South Vietnamese paper money now had nothing. Nothing but confetti. North Vietnam's invasion had ended all value of South Vietnamese currency. South Vietnam, of course, had a "not-backed-by-gold" money.

The Money Lost Its Value Before The Invasion

The banks in South Vietnam closed *before* the enemy arrived, and no one was buying or selling with South Vietnamese money. The currency had collapsed before the invasion. The currency collapsed because of the *perception* of a crisis. Money was worthless *before* the enemy arrived. What did the people use for money? *Everyone was bartering!*

But here is the most interesting point.

One of the local banks from San Diego had pulled a mobile trailer right into the center of the refugee camp. On the side of the trailer were written two things, in English and Vietnamese: "Bank," and "Change your gold into American currency here."

Every morning at 9 o'clock the trailer opened its doors. And every morning between ten and twenty Vietnamese went in.

For every thousand refugees who came into Camp Pendleton, some nine hundred and ninety of them had placed their trust in *paper* currency. Then a crisis came (like the one Hon Ts Yon experienced). The invasion had exposed the always true fact that all modern paper currency is backed by nothing. Vietnamese money was, and *always* had been, *worthless*. Throughout all the years of South Vietnam, *perception* alone had made that paper currency of value. But in reality it *never* had intrinsic, tangible value.

One Percent Had Wisdom

There were a few Vietnamese who knew that paper was worthless.

They had exchanged their worthless paper for gold. They had placed gold in their "survival canoe". They had *paddled* across the Pacific to America just as we must "paddle" across from 1999 to 2001. When they landed here, they were perfect strangers in a strange land, knowing no one. Nonetheless, they arrived with their wealth *intact.* Ten out of every thousand.

Perfect strangers who did not know a single one of those Vietnamese, nor could they speak one word of Vietnamese, looked at the gold. . .and honored it as money.*

The man Kom Pu of Ter—like the North Vietnamese—is coming. Money, especially computer-recorded, electronic, ledger-entry money, will be held in deep suspicion *before* the arrival of the *insect.*

Be one of these ten out of a thousand.

---

*Government still says gold is not money. But these bankers knew better. Everyone on earth knows **gold** is money, government and laws be hanged!*

Part II

18

Why America Will Not Prepare
For This Depression

The last person a pastor would invite to his church to speak about this is a pastor who is in the middle of a building program.

—Ken Klein

Most Americans will not prepare for this depression, regardless of the signs of danger. Oh, they will act at the last moment when it is far too late. Why is this? The answer seems to be in human nature! Old Testament prophets batted zero trying to alert God's people to impending disaster. Human nature has not changed.

For an example: the Black Death that occurred in Europe during the 1300's, when half the people in Europe died of the plague. *No one fled!*

A village would know that the Black Death had struck a city *fifty* miles away. Then a town *forty* miles away. Then thirty, then twenty, then fifteen. Unbelievably, no one fled. Why? The Black Death was a thing so awesome that the human mind simply could not take it in. The people in the village simply would not, or could not, grasp its enormity. The fact that people stayed instead of fleeing was not an act of fatalism; it was an act of incomprehension.

So also today. When the Titanic was settling into the ocean, people refused to leave the ship and go into the lifeboats. They simply could not comprehend a tragedy so vast, even in the very midst of the disaster.

Can you imagine bread lines in the United States? Can you imagine no electricity anywhere in this nation? Permanently? Can you imagine America starving? Neither can I. Nonetheless it may be headed in that direction.

But let us step back. If 10% of the things explored in this book really happen, it will be told about a thousand years from now.

If you knew that Y2K held a fate as grave as the Black Death, would you act? Then ask yourself, why are you not taking action right now? You will find in your answer the same reason why no one fled the Black Death.

To my knowledge there is not a word in the English language which expresses the reason people do not get out of the way of virtually certain ruin. The coming depression *will* destroy your wealth and life style. An economic meltdown triggered by Y2K, a collapse of civilization because of the disappearance of electricity, could take your life. Explain to *yourself* why you are not taking action.

Life in America is about to change radically. Two generations of unbroken prosperity makes grasping an economic wasteland impossible. But that disbelief does not keep a civilization from collapsing. The people of America are sitting in denial of that possibility. This "thing" is coming. It *will be* written about a thousand years from now, yet only a small percent of the people in this nation, or any nation, are preparing for it.

If I could ask you to do nothing else, I would ask you to believe that there is going to be a very big depression. *Beginning* in 1999. Forget everything else, you have virtually no time left to prepare. You need cash, you need silver and/or gold, you need to store food.

Long-term storable food will become scarce in 1999. Scarcity of food will come about because a *few* Americans have stored food. The amount of surplus food in America is nil. Ironically, *computers* figure out how much food we Americans will eat each year. The computers then determine how much food to grow and cows, etc., to raise! Those computers *never* figure Americans may store food. Food is going to get scarce. There are people all over the world who depend on food grown here in America who are going to be without this supply.

I do not write this book for pleasure. I write to warn the entire Christian family that this depression is coming. And it will devastate.

I implore you, dear Christian reader, to act immediately to procure food, cash, some silver and gold, and, if possible, some Swiss francs. There is *much* more you *can* do, but if you can do *nothing else*, store *food*. If unemployment goes to 27%, as it did in the 1930's, you will be grateful you did. If the electrical grid goes down, unemployment may hit 50%. If the electrical grid *stays* down, unemployment could go *over* 90%! What do people do for employment when nothing moves and *very* few people have anything that is accepted as money?

Prepare now!

What can I do to make this so clear that you will get up, get out, and act!! I have but one possible thing I can do.

I am a conservative. I am not into prediction nor sensationalism. In fact, I recoil at such things. I do not believe in the "pre-trib" doctrine; I am not into a beast, horns, dragons teeth, anti-Christ, a sinister *one world government* plot to enslave mankind. I reject such teaching in toto and, again, recoil at such talk.

To write what I write, therefore, I do so to demonstrate to you that this present situation is grim. It is coming. You must act.

As I began to write this book, I realized that hedging my words to God's people with such phrases as "may," "might," "could," "perhaps," and "possibly," will *not* cause His people to take action. But to throw away "may" and "might," and to say to you "will," is risky. I decided to make it even more than risky. I would have you understand this is serious.

For your sake—to get you to act—I take away the "might." I state this unequivocably, flat-footed, unconditionally. We *will* have a depression. It begins in 1999. Period.*

The Lord Jesus said: "When you see. . .do not even take time to come down from the roof you are standing on (in order to see if Rome's army is coming your way). Rather, when you see, don't go back downstairs. Jump from roof to roof until you are out of danger."

Depression 1999.

You can *see* it.

May you "see," and may America's Christian institutions also "see." Right now, every Christian institution in the country is at risk. Grave risk. The depression of the 1930's set *missions* and Christian literature back decades. Nor did they fully recover until the late 1950's and early 1960's.

The Christian institutions *can* prepare. They can head off going out of existence. They can be the last ones into this depression and the *first* ones out of this depression.

To Christian institutions: Climb up on the roof; you *will* "see" this thing is approaching.

I implore you, in the name of your Lord and mine, because this thing is going to come. . .and because it will be big, bad and long, prepare for it!

In the words of Lincoln: "If I am right, no one will remember. If I am wrong, no one will forget." I know what I am risking in making an unequivocal prediction; nonetheless, my certainty is absolute.

If I dare to do what I have just done, then I implore you to believe this event is coming. As an individual: Act. As a bookstore: Act. As an orphanage: Act. As a mission board: Act. As a publisher: Act. As a member of Christ's body: Act.

It is coming. Why is it coming? Not because of a bug nor because of eschatology. Rather, because the laws of economics have been violated. This depression has nothing to do with Daniel, Ezekiel or Revelation. This depression is coming because of hard-headed, invariable laws of economics.

No nation can go through all the jerks, quirks, ups, downs, rumors, stress, loss of so many conveniences, so many brownouts, pressures, demands, accusations, assurances, and books and articles which we will be hearing and seeing in the coming months.

This crescendo *has* to destroy our economy.

* * *

Now, here is *the way out* of this depression and how to return to economic reality.

19

The Way Out
of the Coming Depression

Say it is 2003.

When that time comes there will be two forces seeking to bring us out of the impending economic catastrophe. One will be *government*. Its solution to a depression is, and always shall be, to issue a new currency or inflate the old. It is paper, backed by nothing.

The other force, a minority to say the least, will be seeking to cure the worldwide disaster.

This disaster has its roots as far back as March, 1933. The cry of this minority will be: "Return to gold as money. Cure the curse of 1933." If gold does *not* triumph, paper will win yet again. The result? The depression we will be in will be re-experienced by our children. Paper and ledger money will always lead to a depression, no matter how nice it is in between. The depression wipes out all "gains" made by paper. Your children will simply have to suffer through a *third* depression. Paper money and *ledger-entry* money, backed by nothing, will fail again. The cycle will go on.

Until gold returns, this cycle will continue until every nation and every future generation inhabiting this earth will be reduced to a banana republic.

(By then, none will know why all this poverty came into existence, and none will know *the way out*.)

This sad cycle need not happen. We are balanced between these two choices.

Preventing Reoccurring Depression

A new, golden, day can dawn out of this present tragedy we are entering. *The way out* is the soul of simplicity.

We need but pass a law, or an amendment if necessary, which states:

Gold and silver, by metric weight, shall be the only recognized currency of the United States. The price of all goods and services shall be stated in terms of the metric weight of gold.

Government shall derive its gold supply from one source only—taxation, and from no other source. Congress shall pass no laws debasing the value of gold nor of any gold or silver certificate. Such certificates must, at all times, be backed by a 100% storage of gold.

If we *really* want to put the *coup de grace* to insane economies, we can add one more:

Government shall not tax any individual, nor group of individuals more than 10% of their annual income, unless it be by a 2/3 vote of both houses of Congress or by a decreed emergency established by the president. Such acts shall be established either by Congress or president for a period not to exceed one year at a time. After the emergency has subsided, a return to a 10% taxation must be accomplished with all due haste.

Then shall we have returned to the inexorable and moral laws of economics.

Remember this when election year comes in 2003. . . as you bicycle to the polls!

20

The Cross of Paper!

Shall 2003 be the twin of 1933?

In 1929 our nation entered into the greatest economic depression of her history. Exactly seventy years later she enters into another depression as great or greater. In the Spring of the year 1933, the people of this nation had taken from them a right and sacred freedom, as sacred as that of freedom of the press—that is, the inalienable right to own real money.

Since that day, every man and woman who has lived within the boundaries of America has had taken away from them the fruits of their own labor. Onward from 1933, government has debased this nation's currency, and in so doing, government has *stolen* from its citizens. Not by taxes, but by slowly lowering the value of our savings, our homes, and of all else we have toiled for.

What will Depression II and 2003 hold for the citizens of this land? Shall we gain back that right, or lose even more rights because government— rather than the market place—is seeking to pull us out of this depression?

Politicians will be looking to the next election; statesmen will be looking to the next generation. Whoever sits in the White House and in the halls of Congress will be the men and women ordained to choose a currency unredeemable in gold—or one that is redeemable in gold! The future of America depends on that simple decision, and so also does the future quality of life for all the world.

Shall we break from this immorality, this invisible tyranny, this slow theft? Or shall this violation of man's inalienable right continue?

Is it possible that we might have a presidency, a legislative body, a court that will repudiate this unseeable sin and give back to the people of this nation a security which can never again be taken away? The end of *any* and all laws which allow government to debase money?

A Threefold Flaw In Our Fabric

This nation has had *three* great flaws in its history. The first was *slavery.* One hundred years had to pass, from this nation's birth until 1865, when at last the scourge of that terrible sin began to be removed from us.

The second was the loss of the right to life for those who have no voice nor defense of their own, *the unborn.*

The third great flaw in the fabric of this nation has been the loss of man's right simply to own *money.*

In 2003, what shall be government's solution to bring us out of this era of economic *poverty?* Shall we again, by the hands of lesser men, be handed a currency that government can daily reduce in value?

Or shall the peoples of this land rise up against this tyranny and say to our Congress, to our president, and to our Supreme Court that never again will we be denied this innate right: to own and keep those monies which we have fairly gained by means of our time, toil and skill.

If we do engage our nation in so bold an ethic we shall raise a standard in our land to which all other nations of this earth will soon repair.

Let this word go forth from the lips of all the people of America:

As we find a way out of this great economic disaster, perpetrated upon us by worthless ink and worthless pulp, we the people of the United States declare (and we call upon all the citizens of this planet to join with us in this declaration to the governing bodies of all the world):

Never again shall you crucify mankind upon a cross of paper.

Epilogue

21

A Beast Tail in Daniel, An Eyeball in Ezekiel, A Dragon Tooth in Revelation

Everytime there is a world crisis, someone gets labeled "the beast" or "666." It is a pattern: Crisis—nutty interpretations of Revelation. I wonder who it will be this time. The first person in modern history to get hung with the title "the beast" or "the man of sin" was Napoleon Bonaparte. The British had witnessed the American Revolution and were paralyzed with fear that the British Monarchy would be overthrown and a democracy set up. Hence, Napoleon must be *of the devil*, because the British Monarchy was *definitely* of God. Well, Napoleon did not make the grade.

Next came World War I, and Kaiser Wilhelm was called "the beast" and the "man of sin." Unfortunately, Wilhelm did not live up to this billing either.

During all this time not one single soul ever apologized for being wrong, *not one*.

For a while thereafter it was a contest between Lenin and Hitler as to who would be "the beast." Hitler won the contest. (But he failed "the prophecy.")

Now those were scary days indeed. Hitler was "the army from the North" and Mussolini was—for sure'nuff—"the beast." Mussolini, after all, had announced he was going to restore the entire original Roman Empire *and* proclaim himself emperor! He even set up giant images, in stone, in Rome, showing the borders of his new Roman Empire! In the meantime, someone figured out that the numerical equivalent of Hitler's name was 666. Folks, this was *it*.

It was at this time that predicting who the "man of sin" and who "the beast" was became a cottage industry. You could get rich writing these *insights*! All were wrong. No one apologized for being wrong, but rather rushed on to the next beast candidate.

After World War II, this school of sensational prophecy moved on to Russia and Moscow, with Kruchev thrown in for good measure.

With the birth of the United Nations came yet another ingredient: A one-world government and the conspiracy headed by the Rockefellers became popular themes. Or was it the Illuminate Society? Or the Trilateral Committee?

Zillions of books were sold and the authors became internationally known. Christians had their wits scared out of them. The United Nations turned out to be sterile, others passed off the scene, but no one apologized for being wrong in their interpretation of Revelation and the *last days*.

When the Soviet Union collapsed without a shot fired, did any of those prophets apologize for being wrong? Not one. Instead, they fled to predictions about melting icebergs, the ozone layer, Saddam Hussein, Desert Storm etc. Still not ever a hint of apology when all those predictions fell flat.

Today, yet another "one world government" conspiracy arises. The *European Economic Union*. (The others discarded. . .without a smidgen of an apology.)

Now comes Y2K. It turns out "the beast" is a computer! The Millennium Bug is a "one world government" conspiracy. "Terrible times are about us and the Lord is going to come and deliver us from the suffering."

A friend of mine made this observation: Twenty million people can die in China, and no one notices. Hundreds of thousands can die of starvation in Bangladesh, no one notices. A famine in Ethiopia, and no one in the West notices. But let the Dow drop in the United States, or England have a recession, and suddenly it is proof positive that the Lord is coming back.

I have money in my pockets that says when the Y2K problem is all over, once more, not one of these men who made predictions about the beast etc. will apologize for being wrong.

The Lord may come today. But computers are *not* what are going to bring Jesus Christ out of heaven. *Nor* is an economic depression.

If there is no depression I am committed to apologizing up one side of the street and down the other! In the meantime, as we stand on the threshold of a at least a dozen books on Y2K, with proclamations of a new world order, the curse of the beast, etc., etc. I would like to ask you a favor. If you ever meet one of these men, would you ask them if they plan to apologize for their predictions if what they say turns out to be false? Please do.

This anti-Christ, this beast-a-phobia, this secret plot to establish a one world government, and that teaching which says: "things are going to get so bad on earth that the Lord is going to come and rescue us," these are gloomy and pessimistic. This lady called ekklesia is as ready for Y2K as she has been for anything that has come along in 1900 years. Cheer up, dear reader, these are exciting times for the church.

* * *

We now come to Part III and the voice of authorities. Listen to them. These people are trying desperately to warn you into action.

CF-Y2K
Box 71323
Newnan, GA 30263
800-735-2857

Appendix

What Authorities, Experts and Analysts of Y2K have to say

Contents

I
International Situation

II
America

III
Federal government

IV
International Chain Reaction

Appendix
Part I

The
International
Situation

International Preparedness for Y2K
Is there any?

America is out in front of the curve when compared to our international counterparts.

—*Harris Miller*
President
Information Technology Association of America

On August 10, 1998, John Koskinen, the president's point man for Y2K, was interviewed on C-Span. He was optimistic about anything and anybody (except the Defense Department) that had to do with Y2K here in the United States. Mr. Koskinen went on to say that he was "very disconcerted" about *international* transactions, that Europe was behind us by a year and Asia even further behind.

What the average person watching C-Span missed is this: If we are perfect (we are not), a meltdown in international transfers of funds and currency means a meltdown in the world's economy.

If Asia is behind Europe by six months and Europe is behind us by a year, look at your calendar and figure it out. Neither Europe nor Asia will make the Y2K deadline!

Asia, right now teetering on economic oblivion, *must* be able to carry on international financial transfers in order to carry on international trade.

Nor does this address the fact that the *corrupted* data from the computers of these countries will corrupt our data when they try to do business with us. If they do not become compliant, 60% of all international trading *stops*!

Beyond that? Asia has been one of the largest purchasers of our debt. We are 1.5 trillion dollars in debt offshore with five trillion dollars in overseas commitments. (We co-signed other nation's debts!) Now Asia is in a severe recession, which some are *beginning* to refer to as a depression.

Japan and the rest of Asia are cutting way back on the purchase of U.S. treasury bonds. That strains America's solvency! The deeper Asia sinks into a recession, the less the people of Asia can purchase, including our *goods* and our *debt*. The United States depends on our selling a great deal of goods to Asia. When the amount of goods decreases, then U.S. companies all go to either (1) shutting down factories because they lost their Asian market, or (2) cutting deeply into their sales price to make it appealing for Asia to buy from us, or (3) laying off employees because of loss of sales, or (4) reducing employees' wages, or (5) all five! One thing is certain, our exports are going to suffer and, as a result, so are our citizens.

Capers Jones, author of *The Global Impact of the Year 2000 Software Problem,* points out the other dangers of a noncompliant Europe and Asia. He tells us that 78% of all the computers in the world are outside the United States. When our 22% of the world's computers are talking to their 78%, it is *impossible* for our computers to protect themselves from noncompliant computers.

Outside the electrical power grid going down, *this* international corruption of computer data may be the area of greatest damage. No matter how good we are at correcting our computers, our back door is open, and incoming gibberish is going to recorrupt our systems.

From the Reuter's News Service as reported by Robert Lau in Hong Kong:

> *It is our prediction that it will only take 5% -10% of the world's banks payments system to not work (just on that) one day to create a global-wide liquidity lock up.*

> *—Robert Lau*
> *Reuter's News Service*
> *Hong Kong*

Latin America

Latin America, as far as Y2K, is asleep.

In October, Jim Cassell of the Gartner Group spoke to a group of technological executives from South America. He learned firsthand just how unaware Latin America is of this problem *and* how few funds are available to fix it.

If you have traveled in Latin America you need not ask why the financial resources are so limited.

Chisel this in stone:

Asia and Latin America are *not* going to make the December 1999 deadline. Neither will the third world countries. This is going to cause international financial havoc. Throw in eastern Europe and a sizeable chunk of the medium-sized and small-sized companies throughout western Europe and (let's dream) 1% of American private companies and government agencies, plus brownouts and blackouts. . .you have all the ingredients you will ever need for a worldwide depression.

Britain

The uniqueness of Great Britain is that they are further behind than we are, but they are out in the open about how far behind that is. The Prime Minister himself speaks openly of the problem. The British like to tell about the computer in a meat packing company that ordered the destruction of tons of beef because the meat was over one hundred years old!

Asia

If Asian economies collapse, the western economies will follow. Asia is going to collapse. Of course, it is all relative. No nation, no economy, no industry is anywhere near compliant, but it is all the more obvious with Asia.

—The Australian

The recent Asian crisis has a little known footnote, as revealed by the World Gold Council Report, September 1997. A few people in Thailand Indonesia saw the crisis—and the inflation—coming. They bought gold *ahead* of the crisis. Thailand gold sales went up 30%, in Malaysia 16% and 10% in Indonesia. Later, inflation hit and the cost of gold soared as the value of the currency fell.

The Council's conclusion:

[It] highlighted, once again, gold's traditional role as a store of value and asset of last resort.

I recommend you consider the example of a few prudent people in Asia.

Japan

Japan, our number two partner, may see another nosedive in its markets. Its leadership is frozen. Japan is in no condition to rally its initiative to the Y2K problem.

Japan is set for a truly world-class banking crisis.

—Morris Goldstein
Institute for International Economics
Washington

For the record, I agree.

The Japanese at this moment are ignoring both their financial woes and the Y2K problem.

Keep an eye out for any mention of a Japanese bank called *The Long Term Loan Bank*. It is one of the world's largest. Japan is seeking to save it by some kind of a gimmick called "bridge banking." If Long Term goes, so does Japan's banking industry.

In 1998, two of the largest banks in the world, both Japanese, went defunct. This set off ripples all over Asia, and the Tokyo stock exchange plunged. The Korean currency lost 60% of its value in a matter of weeks. Indonesia went bankrupt; it took a massive bailout on the part of the International Monetary Fund to keep Indonesia afloat. Imagine the consequences if Long Term, or any other *third* bank, goes under.

There is a saying that when the economy of the United States sneezes, the rest of the world comes down with pneumonia. But you can turn that around: When Asia's economy gets the 'flu, America's economy will usually come down with a cold about eighteen months later.

(That eighteen months works out to be just about the same time when the Millennium Bug appears.)

The countries of Asia have been thrown into the greatest debt they have ever been in. (Of course, none of us are in debt quite as deep as the nation of Belgium, which is over 25% in debt.)

The International Monetary Fund has almost exhausted its resources in order to contain the economic crisis in Asia. That means that if the Millennium Bug sets off an economic crisis after December 31, 1999, the International Monetary Fund will be virtually impotent in its ability to help bail out any part of the world's economic system. The IMF recently came near its limits in a failed bailout of Russia.

The Gartner Group tells us the United States can expect 75% of its computers to be repaired by December 31, 1999. On the other hand, we are also told that half the countries of the world that belong to the United Nations do not have an initiative for the year 2000.

Japan has loaned 30% of its savings to the United States. The U.S.A. owes Japan a great deal of money. If Japan's economy gets much worse, they may ask us to pay back what they loaned to us.

Mexico

Mexico, our third largest partner, only recently appointed a task force to "look into the problem." In October of 1997!

Russia

Russia may pose the greatest threat to Y2K interfacing. Russia seems to have decided not to pursue dealing with the problems caused by the Y2K Bug. Keep in mind that Russia's very vulnerable nuclear power plants are run by outmoded, noncompliant mainframes. It is enough to make a person stop and wonder if he can think!

Canada

The Auditor General of Canada issued this report on the state of compliancy:

It may already be too late to avoid failures in some critical systems.

—*October 1997*

United States

On August 5,1998 the Federal government officially reported to the people of the United States that 50% of the government's mainframes will be repaired or replaced, or its mainframe *mission critical* programs will be repaired, in time for the new millennium.

We are *still* going to have a depression.

This planet does not work with half the nations on earth off-line and the rest with only 25% to 50% on-line!

The Euro

*The major central banks of this world now hold $1.4 trillion in
reserve in American dollars. The central banks will begin
switching to the euro as a second kind of currency reserve. If
that happens the strength of the dollar will begin to fade.*

—David Schectman
The Miles Franklin Quarterly
May 1998

The poor dollar! It is almost as though the Titanic is sinking and at
the same time is being hit by a huge meteorite. The Y2K problem has a
younger brother named *euro*. By late 1999 the euro will be the world's
strongest currency. The nations of this world will be avoiding the dollar en
masse. The value of the dollar will sink like the proverbial rock.

Not only that, but the greatest technological challenge in world history
is competing with the world's second greatest technological challenge. It
is sort of *Frankenstein Meets the Werewolf.*

Europe's New—Powerful—Currency

Eleven nations are about to give up their currencies. Every step that is
taken by the European Central Bank (ECB) will be to ensure that the
monetary policies of the euro will produce the world's *strongest* European
currency. The staggering complexity of doing so is lost to those of us who
are mere mortals. I have read documents about the euro changeover
explaining the complexity of what has to be done, and I find them almost
impossible to grasp. Changes must be accomplished on dozens of fronts—
all at the same time. The Europeans have been working on this new currency
for years. Starting January 1, 1999, the euro begins a three-year passage,
ending in 2002. This three year passage allows a gradual Europe-wide
changeover to this new currency.

Can the Millennium Bug and the new European currency coexist? It
is like World War II and the War of the Worlds happening at the same time
in the same place. The currency itself does not begin to appear until the
new century, but calculations of unbelievable dimension, all done on
computers (*most* not repaired), begin in 1999. This gargantuan project is

what is being referred to when you hear mention of the EMU (European Monetary Union).

It may end up being EMU. . .

Economic Murder for Us

Imagine every banker, every commodity broker, every stockbroker, and every manufacturer trying to calculate a new currency and doing so at the very same time that the world's mainframe computers are going haywire. Each nation, every company, every individual must take the ratio of their past currency and calculate it in euros. Or vice versa. While the people of Europe do that, they will also be trying to figure out their currency's relationship to other nations not yet using the euro.

In the meantime, we are over here trying to cope with our dollar problems, while Japan and Russia try to keep their noses above water. At the same time, North America and Japan will try to monitor the euro on hundreds of platforms even as the depression deepens, the banks teeter and the bug continues to chew.

As if banks will not be having enough problems, they will need to be doubling and tripling their calculations as they carry on business in the international market.

One of the nation's most astute financiers, an executive in one of the nation's largest international mutual funds, said to me, *"The Europeans are not going to let us know until one week ahead of the new century what the exchange rates are going to be for the euro and the U.S. dollar and all the other currencies of the world. One week before the new century. At that time we must calculate all of our European interest with the other currencies of this world. All in one week. We have stocks and bonds in hundreds of companies in Europe and all over the world which must be re-calculated."*

In addition, at the same time, try to establish ratio and forecast dozens of exchanges, figuring wealth, inflation, deflation, and local crises. . .etc., while, at the same time, wrestling with the transition crises into the new year! We have the last week in December blocked off to make changes in our computer data in a task that boggles our minds.

Try this scenario:

European tradition, dating back over two hundred years, of analyzing everything going on in Europe in the way of stocks, bonds, commodities, and insurances will change overnight, even as we face massive shutdowns in telecommunications. If that is not enough, each country in Europe has set a different timetable for moving into this new currency. The dates for conversion differ with *every* nation.

C. Fredbergsten, director of the Institute for International Economics and former Assistant Secretary of the Treasury for International Affairs, has made some very pointed predictions.

The United States has more than $4 trillion in external liabilities and a net foreign debt in excess of $1 trillion. . .which is rising by 15% - 20% each year. Obviously the other nations of the world are concerned about the huge debt and the stability of the dollar, and these countries are bound to shift some of their global holdings from dollars to euros. Such action will drive the value of the euro up and the value of the dollar down.

Long-range forecasts of the EMU between European countries and between Europe and the United States are going to break down. The Europeans seem to be sailing straight toward an iceberg in full view, without blinking an eye. I cannot help but wonder what politicians are going to be saying in the year 2003 to justify their profound blindness during 1998. Lawsuits are going to be piled as high as Mt. Everest.

Do you think, in the middle of all this, we will miss having a depression?

Appendix
Part II

America

The Power Grid

If it goes down, America's economy goes with it. If the grid stays down, it will be the greatest crisis in a 700-year history of civilization. Here is the situation.

There are 7,800 major electrical power generation plants in America, and 12,000 substations. They are all tied together in one behemoth system which is run automatically by mainframe computers. In the last 30 years, with none of us really noticing, every segment of society has worked itself into a gigantic network. At the heart of this network is the one which all society depends on: *the electrical power grid.*

If this grid goes down for a few weeks, it is the end of recognizable economics. Many believe it will go down. An alarming number believe it will stay down.

The chance of brownouts because of the Y2K bug? 100%. The possibility of blackouts lasting one or two weeks? 100%. The possibility of the entire grid going out? According to Senator Robert Bennett, 40%.

Chances of the grid staying down, 15% - 20%.

The purpose of this grid is to shift power from one place to another as needed. Unfortunately, each division of this grid has become interdependent on the rest of the grid. The Y2K bug threatens to bring down the *entire* supply of electricity coming from this grid. This means there is a possibility of a total shutdown of all electrical power. And over 99% of all electricity used in America comes from this grid. The jeopardy involved here is not small.

There are three things that could happen which could cause a permanent shutdown.

First: If the mainframe computers which run this grid *crash.* Many will.

Second: If the mainframe computers in the *gas* and *oil* and *rail* industry *also* shutdown as a result of having no electricity, or because their computers are defunct, there will be gridlock. This means no oil or gas to supply fuel to these enormous electrical generators.

Third: If, independent of all the above, the banks go under, no one will be able to buy and no one will be able to sell. The transportation industry, the telecommunications industry, the power supply industry mutually collapse.

Fourth: If the telecommunications industry stops working, the grid also stops working. All are in jeopardy because none have compliant mainframes.

Let us look at just how vulnerable this grid is to a total shutdown.

The main concern is not with large utilities like Southern Co., but with smaller ones on the grid. Smaller utilities could suffer outages that could cause a domino effect.

—Jim Jones
Information Management Forum
Atlanta, GA

How many of the 7,800 electrical power plants in the United States have repaired their computers? Here is the score:

Noncompliant Firms	*7,800*
Compliant Firms	*0*

Of 7,800 power-supplying *firms* in the U.S. *all* are non-compliant.

Congresswoman Constance Morella and Congressman Stephen Horn have been the most active members of the House of Representatives on Y2K. On May 14, Morella said, concerning the Y2K problem and *the power grid*:

If power shuts down, the rest of our society will shut down in its wake.

Then, there is this ominous fact: every time tests are run, the power company's mainframes crash. So far!

Every test I have seen done on an electrical power plant has caused it to shut down. Period. I know of no plant or facility investigated to this date (**May 13, 1998**) *that has passed without Y2K problems.*

—David Hall
an embedded-systems consultant
Cara Corporation

Hall added: *"You're going to have shortages because of panic."*

Honolulu did a "play-like" with its power grid. When 1/1/98 arrived, the entire power system shut down.

One electrical organization, Southern Company started mainframe repairs in 1995. They have 50 million lines of code to correct involving over 1,600 different computer programs.

Y2K is the single biggest nonconstruction project in the history of the Southern Company. Our company has already spent $86 million on the project involving hundreds of personnel and consultants.

—Pat Wylie
Mississippi Power spokesman

Ontario Hydro, a Canadian power company, has hired 500 programmers to get its system compliant. It is 40% finished. It has taken 36 months to get to this stage. They have 300 working days to finish the other 60%. *Then* must come *testing*, a two year project, at a minimum.

We have a lot of work to do and everyone wishes they had started sooner.

> —*Ted Clark*
> *Vice-President*
> *Ontario Hydro*
> *speaking to a Parliamentary committee*

Mr. Bellemare, of Canada's *industry committee*, said Y2K could make the ice storms that hammered eastern Ontario and Quebec last winter seem like a *walk in the park*.

The British are facing a similar crisis.

The British government is drawing up urgent plans to prevent a millennium nightmare in which the start of 2000 is marked by power failures, flight problems and hospital disasters triggered by mass computer failures.

> —*London Times*
> *Feb. 15, 1998*

These concerns have been echoed by the NHS Confederation, which represents health trusts and authorities.

Contingency plans require development to address a possible scenario of major cities being without heat, clean water or transport, as well as shortages resulting from failed distribution systems.

> —*the National Health System*
> *to the Commons Science Committee*
> *Great Britain*

Rick Cowles, at a conference attended by 5,000 electrical utility representatives, noted that few appeared to know anything about the Year 2000 problem. What he saw and learned at the DistribuTECH conference convinced him:

*There is a 100% chance that a **large part** of the domestic electrical infrastructure will be lost at the start of the year 2000.*

> —*Rick Cowles*
> *website: (http://www.euy2k.com)*

Try To Imagine

Water does not come to your home and sewerage does not leave your home without electricity. There will be two things that will cause you to lose those two precious modern conveniences: embedded chips that stop working and electricity from the power grid not coming to your home.

Try to imagine an entire nation without a sewerage system. If nothing else, it will cause rampant disease. In small towns and cities, the outhouse will return, but in cities filled with highrises, there is no such possibility. It need not be observed that the cities will suffer the quickest and the hardest. Imagine, for instance, a hospital without water for even 24 hours.

United States

A survey by two state representatives of Oklahoma found *one-third* of all utility companies had not started correcting the Y2K problem. Another third was severely behind.

The Microchip Problem

Besides mainframes which will *not* work beyond December 31, another reason all electric power utilities are at risk is the embedded chips. Many *are* going to fail, and no one knows which ones.

As stated earlier, the Gartner Group predicts more than 50 million embedded system devices will exhibit Year 2000 date anomalies. The electrical grid is rife with those embedded chip systems.

The Electric Power Research Institute (EPRI) report at their Y2K Embedded Systems Workshop: *Time is critical. The date for some failures has been identified as January 1, 1999.*

Nuclear Powered Generators

I have read a dozen reports to, from, and about how far along the Nuclear Power Industry is in resolving the Y2K programming problems. They have not named even one plant as being ready for Year 2000. Some 20% of the nation gets energy from nuclear-driven generators. Most electricity in New England has atomic power as its source.

Imagine such a major part of the power industry, the one industry that absolutely must stay in operation during the date change, yet so lackadaisical about plans to meet this crisis.

How Bad?

According to a survey made by Rick Cowles, most of America's power plants have not completed inventory of the problem which is Phase III and takes 1% of all the time needed to make computers compliant for Y2K. That leaves 98% of the job unfinished in a project averaging nine years to complete. Gentlemen, you have 300 working days left to pull off a bucketful of miracles.

If they do not? The grid *will* go down! How long to get it back on line? No one knows. That is why so many *survivalists* are purchasing diesel-primed generators and large diesel storage tanks!

How many are doing this? Enough to make small diesel generators scarce, and probably nonexistent very soon.

The Great Quebec Blackout

I once lived in Quebec. My daughter still does. When the world's largest hydroelectric plant shut down, and Montreal was freezing, it took 3,000 trucks from all over the North American continent, coming to the rescue, to bring supplies to repair Hydro-Quebec. The rescue was done in two weeks in freezing winter. Think, if all the grid goes down everywhere, even for a week or two, what that would mean.

* * *

What you have just read is only a fraction of the reports and statements about electrical power and the Y2K bug. I did not find a single encouraging word in any of it. Nor did I read a single "we will make it" comment from anyone closely familiar with the problem. For the power grid, there is not any such thing as this overworked phrase: "contingency plans." If the grid goes down, it goes down until it is repaired in total. In the meantime, what do we all do for electricity? And who, and what, and from where, will we pay the programmers to come fix the problem?

One analyst suggests, tongue in cheek, that the government arrest and jail all Cobol programmers so they can find them when the grid goes down.

Imagine

One week: no electricity. That means a standstill of everything that is electrical. Transportation, manufacturing, everything goes down as the grid does. Even with every other segment in society 100% ready for Y2K, if the electrical grid goes down for *one* week, that alone will create a depression.

* * *

Nor is it a matter of the embedded chip failing. It is also a matter of the embedded chip, the computer, the software, and the hardware, all spewing out erratic data. If no computer goes down, still the lives of every one of us is going to be altered radically. It is not just the dead chip nor the dead computer, but the embedded chip gone mad and the computer that has lost its mind which threaten to "do in" mankind's present-day society. There are 8,000 utility companies in America. All say they are repairing their systems. Statistically, over the last thirty years, on average of all the utility companies that have launched projects, 15% of those projects have come in late and 25% of them have been cancelled. The failure of all other systems can put our world back at least one hundred years; the failure of the power grid will be a matter of life and death. Some parts of the power grid may make it; some may think they will make it but do not. Some are going to be pulled off-line by authorities fulfilling the demands of the law.

—Rick Cowles
before a House Subcommittee

Just how much of the world needs to be compliant, ready for Y2K, in order to avoid the very worst, which is a "survival" scenario? The best estimates are that in Europe, so preoccupied by the new euro, some 24% of all European businesses will not have the problem corrected. Asia? Japan? Worse. Much worse.

Reach your own conclusions and act accordingly.

You can fully expect to be without electricity for at least one week. All America can. That has never happened in all the history of an electrically-driven America.

If the power grid in this country goes down and stays down, it does not matter what anyone else has done, we will be faced with something not much higher than a caveman society. We will be a nation full of large dark huts which were once called suburbia. We will live in them; nonetheless they will be huts. The largest huts in history, but still huts.

Forget the grid for a moment

Let's turn the coin over. Let's say the electrical grid performs perfectly—what will it take to avoid depression? Removing the electrical grid from the equation, what would it take to prevent a breakdown of society? Some estimate 85% of the world's computers must be working in 2000 as well as they did in 1999. Even then, we hit that unknown, invisible wall: the embedded computer chips! There is no human being on this earth who has the slightest idea how complex or difficult that problem is. Will it take sixty days, or will it take twenty years to find and fix embedded chips? On July 22, 1998, speaking on CNN, one authority who was being interviewed observed: "In order to check every embedded chip, we would have to examine 20 million chips per day from now until the end of 1999."

Some 24% of Europe's businesses will not meet the Y2K deadline. That alone is an invitation to disaster.

How many of the world's most essential computers must be working in order to avoid a depression (ignoring the power grid completely)? Probably 98%! It is a figure which can not be attained. Knowing this, the people of this planet will tense out. They will also see their friends buying extra food. They will hear that gold has reached insane heights after insane lows. Friends will tell nightmare stories. Hearts *will* sink. Confidence *will* falter. Economics, like currency, is good only if there is no reigning doubt. But doubt will reign. The depression will come.

Try to picture a strong, robust economy with brownouts and stalled airlines, no more! Just that! No, depression is inevitable.

Try this:

Imagine brownouts; then add only one other industry—just one—in major difficulty. Choose *any* industry. That alone will cause a depression.

Banking

A few days ago I wired money from Maine to California. The bank lost my wire transfer. The money was totally lost, no record of it in any direction, for two weeks. This created a problem on both sides of the continent. The worst part about it was that I never could get anyone to tell me the answer to this simple question. "If this money *stays* lost, who is accountable?" To my knowledge that question is never answered.

The FDIC transfers *trillions* of dollars per year (including the thousand dollars I sent). And its computers are not compliant. Further, the FDIC and *all* the major transfer agencies in this world *cannot* get through Y2K without major glitches. Add that to the world's international banking problems.

The unknown, the uncertain—simple apprehension—more than the breakdown of electronic machines, will be the father of Depression II.

> *The computers of the FDIC are not compliant. No Federal Reserve bank in America is presently compliant. The FDIC said that 88% of its banks are making "satisfactory progress in all key phases of the Year 2000 Project Management Process." And then added that 12% are unsatisfactory.*
>
> —The Reuter's Report
> June 1, 1998

The FDIC went on to say that the term *satisfactory* does not certify a bank as being ready for the new millennium!

If the 12% estimated failure comes true, the banking system will collapse.

On August 12, 1998, John Koskinen, the president's appointee to solve the Y2K problem, was interviewed on C-span. He divided banks into three sections, the last group being 5% in number. He felt those were on schedule and would make the deadline. Has anyone told Mr. Koskinen that a 5% closure of banks will bring the banking system down?!

Once more, we hear from the Gartner Group on this very subject.

> *Public confidence in electronic money (money that is not cash) is likely to be shaken. The question for politicians is what they*

*should do now to avoid loss of confidence in financial services
and markets.*

—*Andy Kyse*
Research Director, The Gartner Group
May 1998

The question is very simple. Will the bank system collapse in 1999?

Every estimate I have read, and there have been at least half a dozen, indicated that somewhere between 5% and 10% of the banks in America are going to fail.

There are 13,000 banks in the United States with a total of 60,000 branch offices. Let us use the lowest estimate of a five percent bank failure. It does not seem that there would be much damage from only a five percent failure—but that five percent translates into about 650 banks. There are 40 trillion dollars in those 13,000 banks. Five per cent of 40 trillion dollars is 2 trillion dollars. That is how much you, the American consumer, would lose from *only* a five per cent bank failure, with only 650 banks going under! That, and that alone, will cause a depression.

That 5% - 10% estimate was given based on the number of banks that would collapse because their computers were not prepared for the transition into the new millennium. This leaves out the psychological factor. How would you feel if five percent of the banks in the United States began to collapse? Your immediate instincts would be to make sure that *your* bank was not one of them, or to withdraw all your money out.

It does not matter that the FDIC will be telling you five times a day that deposits are insured up to $100,000. You will still want your money out of the bank.

If you should be one of those who trusts the FDIC, be aware that there are hundreds of thousands of people alive in America today who remember the collapse of the banks during the 1930's! They do *not* trust the FDIC, and *they* will take their money out. That *alone* can start a bank panic!

The FDIC has 40 *billion* dollars in insurance money to back their guarantee that *your* money is guaranteed up to $100,000. The FDIC needs between *600 billion* and *2 trillion* dollars in its coffers to insure a *mere* five percent closure of banks in this nation.

Do not remind the FDIC that half of the 8,000 banks closed between 1930-1933. If that happened again, that would mean the FDIC would need *20 trillion* dollars in their insurance slush fund to cover a 50% closure of banks.

Forget all the above. If lines begin to form outside your bank, the banks will close. The people in those lines want *cash*. The banks have only about 150 billion dollars in cash—versus 40 trillion dollars in electronic money! (You cannot hand people electronic money. Blips in a computer cannot be taken out of the computer. You have no place in your wallet that can hold money that exists as a blip in a computer!)

Add to that scene the rumors and innuendoes that will be flying. Add to that the price of gold having been pushed down to some ridiculously low price, suddenly soaring, and silver coins disappearing.

Try to imagine this scene. It is then up to you to decide whether or not you wish to take your money out of the bank, in cash, *early on.*

If someone says to you, "the government will print more paper money," is it possible? The paper used for printing *cash* is exotic. The printing presses are also unique. The entire process of printing paper money is unique. Every year the government takes paper money out of circulation because it is worn out. That alone keeps the presses busy. In order to replace soiled and worn out money, the presses at the United States Treasury run flat out 24 hours a day, seven days a week, 365 days a year. True, the Treasury keeps printed money in reserve. It now stands at 35 billion dollars.

The government is not prepared for a run on 40 trillion dollars worth of paper money. Or even one trillion.

But let's say the Treasury Department does print enough extra cash. Still, if as much as five percent of the American people were to withdraw paper money from banks, those banks would go under. Why? Because banks are required to maintain a deposit/loan ratio. Violate that ratio and a bank becomes insolvent. Loans beyond the ratio of money on deposit means insolvency. If the deposits decrease, and the loans outstanding remain the same, the bank is in default.

In a case like that, the banks have one choice: call in their loans. That is sure suicide. Do that and every customer switches their money to another bank. When that happens, you can know with absolute certainty there is going to be a nationwide panic. Banks are not supposed to call in loans. It is not considered nice.

The OCC looked at 24 of the nations largest banks to find out what their standards were for loans that started at $25 million. From now on, federal examiners are going to be looking very carefully at banks who loan money to organizations that are not working on the Y2K problem.

—*Eugene Ludwig*
Office of Controller of the Currency
To the Senate Banking Committee

Mr. Ludwig also made this statement, at a Risk Management seminar:

For banks, Y2K poses challenges of unprecedented urgency and complexity.

Mr. Ludwig went on to say that when he first heard about this problem he gave it little thought. Then added, "If anything, [it is] more serious than we had imagined. Too many of us continue to nourish illusions that the solution is right around the corner. Or that the real impact of the problem will be limited to a handful of businesses particularly susceptible to it."

In January of 1998, the Bank for International Settlements asked banks using their services, "Just where are you in dealing with Y2K?"

Listen to BIS's very reserved and conservative statement.

The year 2000 poses a significant problem for financial institutions. Many automated applications will cease to function normally as a result of the way that data fields have been handled historically.

That simply means banks and everything that has to do with finances are *not* going to be functioning normally. The BIS report went on to say:

If these problems are not addressed quickly it could cause banking institutions to experience operation problems or even bankruptcy.

Listen to these words in the report: It could also. . .

cause the disruption of financial markets. . .

What the BIS said was that the bankruptcies of financial institutions could bring down the financial market.

Now, these terrifying words:

It is our prediction that it will only take 5% – 10% of the world's bank payments systems to not work on that one day to create a global liquidity lockup. I do not think the markets have quite grasped the implications of what will happen if this entire system goes down.

—*Robert Lau*
Management Consultant
Hong Kong
October 6, 1997

The ability of international banks to operate effectively after the Year 2000 is, in our estimate, seriously in question.

—*Larry Martin*
Data Dimensions
before the Senate Banking Committee
July 10, 1997

If everything were absolutely perfect in America, a run on a bank in Germany, France, Japan, Italy—or anywhere—could bring dissolution to America's banking system.

In May of 1998, Susan Philips made a resignation speech from the Federal Reserve, in which she warned that there may be a recession because of the Millennium Bug, and then added:

If computer compliance is not fulfilled then it might even get worse.

She means by that more than a recession is likely. And if the international currency exchange organizations stumble, it becomes a certainty.

And the banks in Europe?

In June of 1998, Alan Greenspan said that it looked like American banks may be compliant in time, but it appears that the European banks are definitely not going to make it.

Then why not just unplug the noncompliant banks? No one has figured out how to do that without causing regional and worldwide chaos.

The Central Bank of Great Britain (which is simply called "the Bank of England") has been seriously considering asking the government and the banks of the United Kingdom to close on December 31, 1999 and not reopen until they have a handle on what to do next.

In Thailand, the Bank of Siam announced that three-fourths of its systems may not be able to operate beyond December 31 of 1999. Thailand started Asia's present recession...which many are now calling a *depression.* Thailand may also start the demise of Asia's banking system.

A decade ago, here in the United States, there was something called the S&L crisis, when less than 1% of the Savings and Loans in America went under. And yet lines began forming in front of solvent Savings and Loans all over America. The Fed stepped in. But there is no way that the Fed is going to be able to meet the crisis of the insolvency of even 5% of America's banks.

The Federal Reserve failed completely at its task in the 1930's when 4,000 of America's banks closed forever.

There may be a Y2K catastrophe in the early part of the year 2000, and there may *not* be. But as the American people, and the people of the world, become more acquainted with the information you are reading in this book, there is bound to come a panic. In 1999.

The Stock Market

You will not make a penny's profit by purchasing gold, but some portion of your wealth will survive—something which will *not* be the fate of most people. If today I had to chose between a million dollars in the stock market and one hundred thousand dollars in gold, I would have my answer before the question ended. If I had a hundred thousand dollars in gold I would end up with some money some day, somewhere. If I had a million dollars in stocks I may end up with some very impressive-looking pieces of paper certifying I own a great deal of worthless stock.

The best single piece of advice ever given to anyone in the stock market was given by J.P. Morgan. "I got rich by selling too soon." People seem to hate themselves for not getting out of the market at the very top. From my perspective, most people in the stock market today are going to get out of it at the bottom.

The computers which run the New York Stock Exchange are non-compliant. It may be "mission-critical" compliant by December of 1999. That, plus a nickel, will get you a five-cent candy bar. The stock exchanges of America all lead into markets all over this planet. These overseas stock markets will not be compliant on any level when December 1999 rolls around.

Bonds, treasury bills? Take a lesson from Russia. In August of 1998 long lines of panic-stricken people formed at banks all over Russia. The ruble was down by 34%. A few days later government announced it would *not* make good on government bonds or T-bills, while saying: "Don't worry, you'll get your paper money some day." The Russian stock market is in a free-fall. As newspapers all over the world reported: the Russian people were fighting to get money out of their banks so they could purchase gold! This same scene is almost certain to happen in America. When? No one knows. As early as now, or as late as November 1999.

Hong Kong's dollar and China's yuan are waiting in the wings to suffer Russia's fate. And South America, Venezuela, is devaluing its currency to try to save its banks. And Brazil, which is nearly 50% of South American production, makes a quarterly visit to the IMF to prevent insolvency. So also former Soviet block nations. The Asian tigers will follow. (Japan's greatest export right now is *deflation*.)

Telecommunication

*The Year 2000 issue is possibly the most critical problem we
have ever faced at AT&T...*

—John Pasqua
Program Management Vice President
AT&T Year 2000 Initiative

How bad is our communications problem in America? There is the
possibility of a *complete* communication collapse here in America. If AT&T
fails at its task, a large part of our communications system dies.

AT&T, the largest U.S. phone company, only began repairs in the fall
of 1996. AT&T is not Y2K compliant. It is spending one half of a billion
dollars on mainframe repair.

Others?

US West has spent the last 18 months trying to figure out what problem
the Y2K bug may cause. The most likely impact seems to be from telephone
switches, which are key components of the entire telecommunications
network. Many of these switches are "date ignorant" and *must* be replaced.

US West has stated:

*None of US West's switching system suppliers are compliant.
However, it is expected they will comply.*

This problem affects Britain as well.

From the chairman of Britain's Telecom Managers Association come
these words:

*Unless the Department of Trade addresses this issue
immediately. . .we will not be able to make calls outside of the
UK.*

> According to a survey by British Telecom, only 11% of its
> interconnect customers in Africa and the Middle East have even
> set up millennium projects to deal with Y2K.
>
> Just 23% of the major telecommunications companies in Asia
> have Year 2000 programs underway. That means 89% of
> telecommunications in Africa and the Middle East and 77% of
> telecommunications in Asia have 300 working days to do the
> impossible. Can the world's prosperity continue in such an
> atmosphere of unpreparedness?

Britain's Telecom is spending five hundred million dollars to repair its mainframes, but is making no effort to locate embedded chips. One of the members of the House of Lords said the only way to ensure Telecom will work after December 31 is to cut off *all* computer communications with the outside world.

South Africa's Telkon is spending 400 million dollars to update its mainframes and is still behind the curve.

If international telecommunications break down, international banking will collapse, as well as international trade. We will be in the greatest disaster since the Black Death and the fall of the Roman Empire.

On July 9, 1998 Peter de Jager told a story at a conference at the South San Francisco Convention Center that highlights the critical nature of this problem. De Jager said men in telecommunications came up to him and said: "Don't ask me my name or who I work for, but I want to tell you that on January 1, 1999 switches are not going to work."

Nor is this problem confined to North America and the U.K. The Australian telecom company, Telstra Australia, admitted:

> *There can be no assurance that this program will be successful, or that the date change from 1999 to 2000 will not materially affect Telstra's operations or financial results.*

Those are big words which imply: We are not going to make it.

And telecommunications is not just phones. There are also. . .

Satellites

A satellite called Galaxy 4 malfunctioned on May 19–20, 1998. Some 90% of all pagers in North America (20 million) *ceased* functioning. There are 149 such satellites in the sky. *All* of them may go out.

When just Galaxy 4 died, many ATM cards did not work. Satellites and banks could not talk to one another. People in the medical world could not communicate emergencies to the right people. Customers at gas stations could not "pay at the pump." All this *just* because *one* satellite went out.

About 300 working days from now it will be more than *one* satellite.

Some of the embedded chips, which cannot function beyond December 31, 1999, are in those satellites up there which we depend on every day!

The majority of the 140 communications satellites in the heavens may go out at midnight of December 31, 1999.

None of us understand how dependent we have become on tele-communications.

I recently learned that a compliant satellite was placed in orbit around the earth that is due to go into operation on September 9, 1999. That is 9/9/99. If you recall 9.9.9.9 was the way computer programmers used to say to a mainframe: "computer: stop." Does someone know something about noncompliant satellites that may shut down when they see 9/9/99? Is this new satellite a hoped-for cure to replace numerous old, soon-to-be-dead satellites?

The Internet?

In a recent conference Peter de Jager also mentioned that there may not be a dial tone on January 1, 2000 to which someone responded: "Oh, that's no problem. I'll just use the internet."

No dial tone, no internet.

You can add to that list: No dial tone, no banks, no electricity, no power grid, no stock market, no communications to anyone, by anyone, anywhere. It is *that* much of a crisis!

Banks, telecommunications, electricity—without them for very long—we have no modern civilization.

Will it get that bad? Maybe not, but knowing that it *can* get that bad will panic the public, and usher in a depression.

There is not one major telephone company in America that is compliant for Y2K. If they do become compliant? Then the behemoth telecommunications companies must talk to other mainframe computers all over the world. At least 50% of international phone lines will not be compliant. That will fry the mainframes, and stop most of the 200 trillion dollars of transactions in international trade.

Military, stock markets, every agency in government, all banks, all financial institutions of the world are dependent on wire and satellites in order to exist. Telecommunications companies worldwide are behind the curve.

Major disruptions *will* occur.

Why? Calendar-blind mainframes. Embedded chips. The chips are scattered out across absolutely everything and everywhere there is telecommunications.

The electrical power grid cannot survive without a near perfect telecommunications industry. So also banks.

Yet the electrical industry is behind the curve when it comes to embedded chips. It must make massive outlays of money; billions must be spent just so it can function in year 2000 as it did last year.

Civilization's Triad

The three most important systems required for our civilization to survive the Y2K computer crisis are (1) electrical power, provided by a continent-wide power grid, (2) the banking system, and (3) the telecommunications system. Again we can hear the refrain: If all of it does not work, none of it works.

Interestingly, the Federal Communications Commission, having full knowledge of the Y2K problem, is itself *not compliant!* The FCC has taken no action to ensure that local telephone companies or long distance networks are readying themselves for the year 2000.

The telecommunications system is Waterloo; the Federal government is Titanic; the electrical power grid is Pompeii!

If telecommunication networks, utility companies, or other large banks fail during the date change, the Federal Reserve's ability to process the nation's checks and distribute currency could be impaired.

—Edward Kelly Jr.
Federal Reserve Bank member
before a Senate subcommittee
*April 28, 1998.**

You have experienced your cable television's not working. You tried to call the cable company. You could not get through for days. Multiply that by several hundred million as everyone gets on the phone to complain or report a failure.

Telecommunications, electricity, transportation, water, Visa or Mastercard—anybody you owe money to—will experience billing errors because of a crippled telecommunication world. We are going to be living in one highly frustrated nation.

No nation can live under this much stress *and* keep a solvent economy. *It is utterly impossible!*

A depression anyone?

---

*Tech Web News

Transportation

Can America's transportation system actually collapse? Become frozen? Immovable? Not a train, a truck or a ship moving?

What does this nation's transportation system depend on? Two things. Fuel and computers. Electric failure can take away both. As goes the power grid, so goes American civilization. And right now, the power grid is moving at a snail's pace toward Y2K readiness.

A collapse of the electrical grid can take away *all* sources of energy.

Transportation is only slightly better off. Computer suicide on January 1, 2000 seems very likely.

Let's just see how unprepared we are for railroads to stop, and how unprepared we are to get them running again. We are again faced with *switches*, but this time it is those heavy steel rails which must be switched. Once they were switched manually, today they are switched by computers.

Rail

Many of these computers will die on January 1. Go back to manual switching? There are shopping centers sitting where the vast railway switching yards were once located! There is virtually no one left who knows how to manufacture, install, and operate manually these huge switching devices. It would take years to reinvent them. They were ripped out in the 1950s!

All rail switches are automatically computer switched. No national railroad has become Y2K prepared. When (not *if*) the rails stop delivering a good percentage of the products they ship, the psychological impact on America will be overwhelming.

> *The railroads are completely dependent on computers and the chips embedded in transportation equipment. Union Pacific is struggling to unwind its current mess, but is unlikely to. If they are not able to, then there will definitely be food problems in the year 2000.*
>
> —*Jerry Norton*
> *USA Today, November 12, 1997*

The likelihood of a severe impact is growing, when you consider just what is at stake in the railroad industry alone—farming, food, chemicals, petrochemicals, lumber, steel, seed, coal (for electricity), automobiles, military vessels, ocean shipping vessels, international trade.

There is great potential for food supply disasters when computers crash within the complex food processing and distribution system. The problem is very real

—*Geri Guedetti*
Non-hybrid Forum, November 1997

The following examples show what has already happened and what can happen in our very computerized transportation system. There is no evidence these things will not happen.

There is only a three-week supply of fuel available in America at any time. The whole transportation system moves this way: well to refineries, to pipe lines and on to storage facilities, then delivery trucks and trains to your service station. . .all this is utterly dependent on transportation which is dependent on mainframe computers.

The giant pipelines that distribute oil across this nation, as well as those that distribute natural gas, do not presently have compliant computers. The entire network might find itself stalled because of computers and embedded chips which simply do not know what to do as of January 1, 2000.

In 1996 in downtown Washington D.C. some traffic lights went into their weekend mode rather than their rush-hour mode. (The problem was caused by a new version of software installed in the central system.) The result was mile-long traffic jams. Imagine the entire transportation system in gridlock because of hundreds of mainframe failures and embedded chips not functioning.

Your supermarket has only three days of food. The restocking of the shelves is totally dependent on the regular flow of the transportation system.

Air

You already know that Lufthansa has announced that its planes will not fly on January 1 and the days following. Other airlines are considering the same action! Add that to this potpourri of transportation chaos.

Late in 1997 IBM sent a letter to the FAA stating flatly that the computer which runs the FAA, *and* the airlines of America, cannot be repaired. IBM did not mince words—the computers which run the entire airline system can*not* be repaired. The FAA has decided that the computers can be repaired. Which do you trust? I am not flying six months after December 31, 1999.

Trucks

All major truck lines are dependent upon computers in every area of their operations. (One trucking company has stated it has an average of 40,000 computer transactions each day!) There are dozens of such trucking companies. Are they working on the Y2K problem? There is little evidence that they are.

General Motors has two billion lines of computer code to search. The entire company's manufacturing facilities rely on the *immediate* and *timely delivery* of parts (JIT), to keep operations running smoothly. Just one supplier disrupted by the Millennium Bug could shut down GM's operations. And GM has over 85,000 suppliers!

Get a bicycle with sidesaddle and handle bar baskets. It is excellent exercise, and may be the best way to get water from the lake and then back home, not to mention a great way to haul a fifty pound sack of flour, for which you may have just paid a 1/8 ounce gold coin!

Will it come to this? A transportation system stalled, no access to processed foods? Maybe not. But when your neighbor hears this transportation freeze might happen, will he buy a bike and store food? I do not know, but this I know—sometime *before* December 31, 1999, America is going to panic. Whether or not the transportation system fails because of Y2K is almost irrelevant to the fact that the fear of a transportation crisis *will* induce a depression.

A bike and food will be nice to have in a depression, no *matter* what caused the depression. Understanding why a depression happened is secondary to preparing for it!

Testing

Once more we face the reality of the impossible. Virtually any comment such as, "we repaired our computers; we are compliant," does not include *testing* of the computers.

Trying to understand the world of testing is to tax the mind. You enter a whole new world. It is a world of almost insurmountable complexity. You do not just test. You must take a computer off-line. But you cannot do that first. You have to procure a computer to take its place. That means reprogramming the replacement computer. Then you must run another computer parallel to the computer being tested.

After the errors are diagnosed, you must go on to test the next mainframe in your company. (Remember, for every 100 lines corrected, 8 new errors appear!) Then the two mainframes must be tested against one another. On it goes, until all computers are tested and then tested against one another.

Then you must run a test with all the computers of *all* your suppliers. Ask yourself if that seems possible.

Yet, this is only the tip of the iceberg.

The Library of Congress observed the same: a problem unsolvable. (At least unsolvable with only 300 working days left.)

Testing is particularly laborious because the modified software must be tested in conjunction with all possible combinations of other software programs it interacts with. . . to ensure functioning has not changed.

—Library of Congress

None *of it works, until all of it works.*

—Comment by a computer analyst about the interconnectedness of computers

There are hundreds of thousands of computers which must individually be repaired and then tested and retested with all the computers they interact with.

The truth is that the doomsday date is not December 31, 1999, but somewhere between January 1, 1999 and August 1, 1999 because all these repairs must not only be made, they must be made perfectly. Look at your calendar.

How much more time is needed to test than to repair? Twice as much time, three times as much. Some experts have estimated four times as much time.

Let us say there are twenty different national banks. One through nine are all compliant and work perfectly and interact with one another. Bank eleven through twenty are compliant, work perfectly, and work perfectly with one another. But all of them must work with bank ten; and bank number ten is either not compliant or has errors. When that happens all twenty banks shut down.

Unfortunately, the year 1996 is the last year in which average *programmers working without sophisticated automation could have a reasonable chance of fixing the year 2000 problem.*

—Capers Jones
The Global Economic Impact

Here is yet another overlooked problem of testing.

You have just finished repairing your computer and now you need to test.

You have to test for near perfection on what the programmer has done and then you have to do another kind of test: to see if any new bugs were introduced in the process of putting in new information. Most companies, it seems, are simply ignoring the testing stage and especially this business of "regression" testing. . . looking for new problems that have come out as a by-product of repairing.

—*Bruce Caldwell*
Information Week
May 5, 1997

Caldwell made a strong case for testing's taking 60% of the entire repair time. He also pointed out yet another testing problem.

Tests will require access to comparable hardware platforms, but few companies are in a position to duplicate their tests, tests which can take days to complete.

In other words, you cannot cut off a computer and keep your business going; yet taking that computer off line is exactly what must be done in order to test. Either that, or a company must get a replacement computer while you test the original.

A litany of other detrimental factors, including technical factors (heterogeneous operating environments, missing source codes, new bugs, etc.) and management issues (competing priorities and lack of business focus) all compound our concerns.

—*Robin Tierney*
The Year 2000 Problem

Dear reader, here are the facts. Facts about only one aspect of the impending crisis. Do you believe the future looks rosy? Remember this is but one isolated slice of the crises we face throughout 1999 and the year following.

One more look. Social Security has done more to prepare for Y2K than any other agency in government. They *will* finish repairs on time. But what of testing?

Testing what they have done will take one or two years. But the SSA will not have time to test. Let's hope they are 100% perfect. The only testing will be "on the job." SSA failure—without a year or two of testing—seems assured. Will our economy survive, with Social Security mined in computer errors?

Normally, testing can be done in one month or year to verify that the new system will run, after testing, the following month or the following year.

But this testing during 1999 will not give a clear indication that the system will run during 2000. In fact, that is what we are testing for, whether the system will run in 2000. Simulation is not enough in order to test the system's capability to run in 2000...it actually has to be done in the year 2000.

For example, if a date has been overlooked in the code somewhere in the system, that potential glitch might not show up in testing in 1999, but only show up in true performance on January 1, 2000. Just one or two of these oversights could sabotage an entire system or even affect other systems.

You have to have two straight lines for them to be parallel. Either we have only have one line or else they are not straight.

We do not have two systems, even theoretically, where both will work at the same time. Even the whole idea of parallel testing does not work here.

—*Peter M. Logotti*

Four Stages of Testing

An organization called Mid Range Systems lays out four stages of testing.

Shock Assessment: "Probably the most basic test you can perform to test the impact on your system is to simply set the clock forward," said Allen Graham, VP of Comdisco's Continuity Services.

Unit Testing: "Individual programs need to be run as actual code conversion progresses," Graham says. "This can be done within the company's development environment."

Check-point Testing: Graham says, "You need to test your packages as a system. You want to be sure that everything is working in concert. You may be extending your date fields, but your software vendor may be using a windowing technique."

Validation Tests: A key part of this process is data exchange to other systems, outside vendors, business partners, and customers. That's the true validation that you are in fact going to get through the problem.

Here is another way of stating the problems of validation.

Dates are just so all-encompassing that when you start messing with them, every aspect of the system and all the inter-relationships between systems need to be tested.

CIO Magazine *March 1, 1998*
Albert Kern
Assistant Vice President of the Y2K project
Boston's Commercial Union Insurance

To add to the burden of making sure all systems are functional there is the necessity of documenting every step of the process.

"You cannot just run these tests," says Greg Pope, President of Azor, Inc. (A test tool supplier in Palo Alto, CA.)

You have got to have evidence that you have run the tests and gotten the correct results, because if you face litigation later, you need to be able to prove that you did the testing and were in good shape.

Testing Is Not The Last Step

One word describes the outlook of Y2K programmers as they speak out on *testing*. That word is *hopeless*.

I have more research material on testing than anything else referred to in this book. The conclusion, *sheer futility*.

Summary

To cut through the endless pages of computer jargon, here is a summary.

Every computer which retains its date must do parallel testing. Parallel testing and the discovery of the bug which it will uncover, takes longer than all else combined. Up to 60% of all compliant efforts is for testing.

All parallel testing must be done with a compatible computer running parallel with the repaired computer. Parallel testing, though absolutely necessary, must be done with another computer that has enough memory space to hold the entire repaired computer's software programs, *plus* have extra memory left over.

Virtually every organization claiming to be engaged in Y2K repair is setting aside 1999 for testing. *This* is not enough time.

Many date codes found in computers cannot be identified when you are looking straight at them.

Parallel testing is a futile act. Only when the year 2000 arrives and the computers are doing "real life" operations will you know if you have correctly repaired your computer's software.

(Perfect repair is impossible.)

No one is going to have their computer "fixed," no matter how many tests they do. *Real life* alone, done in 2000 A.D., will reveal the extent of the problems.

Even if there were enough time, testing cannot ever approach being parallel.

—*Peter Ligotti*
programmer
The Internet, January 5, 1998

There are four steps to testing: unit testing, check point testing, valid item testing, and vendor/supplier testing. When it is all done, it is inadequate. *Real life* alone is the only true and valid test that can reveal the undiscovered glitches not found in the repair process.

If you test, you are in the minority.

GIO Magazine
March 1, 1998
Greg Pope, President
Azor Inc.
Palo Alto, CA

Joseph Allegra, president of Princeton Software, noted that just creating a testing program takes a great deal of time *and* that testing must not wait until the end, but is done over and over again through *all* stages of repair from start to finish.

One programmer commented, *"Just getting to testing gives you celebrity status."*

Gary North, who takes the dimmest of all views concerning Y2K, and who is a man not known for diluting his words, stated;

> **Testing constitutes no less than 40% of every Y2K project. Some estimates place it as high as 75%. Few organizations have developed a testing plan. The conclusion is obvious: Y2K cannot be fixed.**

We are already looking at anywhere from three to seven years to get mainframe computers repaired. We might need time after that for testing the repairs. All that *before* we can use the repaired mainframes. Not a rosy picture for the world.

The Impossible

We need twenty more years to get ready for Y2K. Testing demands it. And without testing? Maybe *no* modern civilization.

Let us say you had one compliant computer and you were trying to make another one compliant. On a mainframe, running parallel programs until both computers can talk to one another perfectly could take two months to two years!

Both computers must be off-line while running parallel; yet most computers are being used 7 days a week, 24 hours a day, and are needed every minute of that time.

Making two zeros become four digits in every place where two zeros formerly appeared will automatically expand the program to a point beyond the computer's storage capacities. Some computer programmers are going to face the paradox of having repaired their computers, only to discover there is no storage space left in the computer.

Could Capers Jones, an authority of no small representation in this field, be correct when he declared in 1996 that an organization needs to finish with code repairs by the latter part of 1997? Well, when the end of 1997 came, only 20% of the nation's 500 largest corporations had *begun* repairs.

Or to put it another way, in order for us to rest easy on December 31, 1999, we would have needed to begin correcting the bug back in 1984. Most corrections on the bug were started in 1996 or 1997, with others not even having begun. Still others, *like my local bank,* are just now, *evaluating the situation.*

Nonetheless, it seems true that as complex as computer language is, and as subject to error as the repairing of billions upon billions of lines of code can be, the fact remains that incompliant computers must be enlarged from a two digit dating to a four digit dating. Then there is the absolute necessity of testing those repairs and *then* testing that computer's networking with all the other computers, each of which had to be tested prior to the networking test.

And then? The throwing of the switch that allows those computers to talk with computers in other businesses. Until everyone has tested and found all errors, only then can anyone say that they are ready for the new millennium.

This is not a small bug. Two little zeros stand a chance of sinking every aspect of civilization as we now know it.

The First Three Stages

Programmers themselves have estimated that *appraisal, investigation,* and *inventory* are only 1% to 5 % of the solution. Factor in the need of an estimated 750,000 more programmers—plus reading the code of perhaps a trillion lines of mainframe software—all of which is only 40% of the job. Testing has no room on the calendar. Compliance is impossible. Testing is also inadequate in solving the problem of finding errors. This old planet is in for rough sailing.

Look at the clock and the calendar.

All the steps below are inadequate, yet necessary.

1) Testing the computers and finding the errors,

2) Retesting to see if the errors are gone,

3) Testing with each of the other computers in the system which have also been corrected, and doing so, one computer at a time. . .not the whole system at once.

4) Finally, testing each and every one of the computers of suppliers and vendors which interface with your company's computer system, correcting every step of the way.

Capers Jones in a widely respected report, said:

Any organization not having begun its code repair by October, 1997 will not complete the project.

The Gartner Report has reported that less than 20% of the organizations listed in Fortune 500 had *begun* repairing their code as of October 1997. The rest of the nations of this world are even further behind than we are!

The facts presented in any one section of this appendix show a situation so grievous that any one of them can cause a depression. All of them at once?

I close with the following observations and statistics of experts.

We begin with an excerpt from a testimony given before the Senate Banking, Housing, and Urban Affairs Committee, Sub-Committee on Financial Services and Technology, July 10, 1997.

There is no silver bullet. . .there may be as many as five hundred different software languages in current use. . . automated corrective tools will not be developed for all these languages.

> —*Jeff Jinnett*
> *President*
> *Loeuf Computing Technologies*

The problem is far worse than even the pessimists believe.

The Gartner Group's much cited figure of 600 billion dollars to fix Y2K is misleading. If God and Bill Gates wrote out a check for the full amount. . .not much would change. The year 2000 problem is a people—and time—resource problem. Not just a financial one. You cannot buy the time [needed to fix this problem] at any price.

> —*Peter Keen*
> *Computer World*

Software developers have a reputation of being as far off from estimating costs for developing new software as the government is in its estimations. Only 16.2% of all corporate software-development projects are completed on time.

> —*The Standish Group International*
> *CHAOS*
> *1995*

YEAR 2000: GIVE UP, MOVE ON – NOW

—Computer World
July 16,1997

Here is a summary of what the Gartner Group said about testing.

. . .testing – or full compliance is somewhat improbable at this point. Management simply cannot get a job this complex done on time.

An excerpt from Jeff Jinnett's testimony given before the Senate Banking, Housing, and Urban Affairs Committee, Sub-Committee on Financial Services and Technology July 10, 1997, said it well:

We have run out of time.

Embedded Chips

The GIGA Information Group, a consulting firm located in Massachusetts, was quoted in *The Economist* as saying that 5% of all embedded chips would fail the calendar test after December 31, 1999.

Consider then, if the entire Y2K computer problem was solved by December 31, 1999, that success would be for naught. A depression will *still* begin in 1999. Because there are still two billion embedded chips out there which can still bring down this nation's economy.

There are enough dysfunctional mainframes in other nations to still sink the financial boat of the United States. A 100% cure rate of computers in America still gives us two formidable crises: (1) the failure of the rest of the world to correct its computers, and (2) the embedded chip.

There is a recession in Asia. Japan's finances are in grave peril, *and* with several of the world's most prestigious financial institutions on the brink of collapse, we are far from 2000. What Japan is going through is not an island. Every analyst in this country knows that if Japan's recession goes on much longer the United States will be dragged into very serious trouble. If Japan sinks much further, all the ships go down.

When I began writing this book Ed Yardeni set the chance of a recession at 40%. He now has it set at 70%. Another financial institute set the chances at 75%. By the most conservative analysis, a recession stands at the door of the United States economy, with Asia just off the stage, and Russia front and center. Add to this the tenfold greater stress the Y2K problem is going to create, and a depression is inevitable.

Programmers

Capers Jones, one of the nation's most vocal experts on the Y2K problem and software engineering expert, when asked if it were humanly possible to meet the Y2K deadline, replied:

If, at the beginning of 1998, we had assigned 85% of all the programmers in America to work on this job full-time, there might have been a theoretical possibility. But not more than 20% of the programmers in America are working on this problem. How much will programmers be able to get done on the Y2K problem? Estimates run from 65% to 75%.

This is not enough!

It *is* too late. Flat-footed, out-and-out, no hesitation, no conditions; it is impossible for America to meet this inevitable deadline. Beyond that deadline are grave economic implications.

It is estimated that the shortfall of programmers to get this job done by the Year 2000 is 30% worldwide just for Cobol alone.

—*Warren Reid*
Beyond Awareness
June 22, 1995.

In a year one programmer can review and repair 100,000 lines.

—*The National Institute of Standards and Technology*

The Gartner Group predicts that more than half of all organizations worldwide will not fully complete the Year 2000 effort.

—*William Rabin*
J P Morgan Securities Incorp.

This means that at least one-fourth of the organizations in the world are apt to not survive. (They may take down with them another two-thirds.) It takes healthy companies for other companies to survive.

Programmers Face Impossible Obstacle

Old language, old computer programs, and no manual left behind to even give some hints. This is what a programmer faces.

The people who drew up those original programs have retired. Those men were at the cutting edge of a new industry—flamboyant, fly-by-the-seat-of-your-pants pioneers. Many of them did not bother to leave even a hint of what they did, nor how they did it.

Today, younger programmers are trying to figure out what the original programmers did. The first thing they have to do is create a manual before they can even analyze the problem they face.

There is a dearth, a great shortage of experienced Cobol, C, etc. programmers.

Professor Howard Rubin, of Hunter College N.Y., has estimated that the United States will need an additional 500,000 to 700,000 experienced Cobol programmers between now and the year 2000.

Just recently the governor of New York ordered all state employed professors to lay aside all nonessential tasks and to concentrate exclusively on making the computers of the government of New York corrected for Y2K.

Worldwide estimates indicate at least another million programmers are needed. Such people do not exist; nonetheless, without them there is no fixing this problem.

In Great Britain, Robin Guernier observed;

Nationwide, private companies need 300,000 additional, experienced, full-time Cobol programmers.

—Rueter's Report
April 11, 1997

Apart from Cobol, another language often used in those old systems was RPG. There are also a few other mainframe computer languages commonly used, which are forgotten by today's generation of programmers, yet there are thousands of places where these languages are in use.

If these estimates are even remotely correct, then the Y2K problem cannot be fixed, and will not be fixed.

No standard about dates

Here is just one example of the many unique problems programmers face. It has to do with simply writing a date.

There are so many different ways to write January 1, 2000 and there is no standard. Would you write it 01/01/2000? Or would you write the new code 2000/01/01? There is one thing certain, programmers all over the world are repairing computers many ways. Because there is no standard, this must inevitably lead to chaos and shutdowns all over the earth.

Only 12% of the mainframe codes of this world are in the United States.

No matter what the programmers here at home do, they cannot save the *world's* economy. The interconnection problems between the USA and other nations on this planet mean that every compliant computer, as of January 1, 2000, will be threatened by data sent to it by noncompliant and compliant computers with different standards from all over the world.

A World Glimpse

The United States only has 22% of the world's computer codes. The other 78% need to be repaired just as well as ours do in order for our present society to continue operating properly.

There are 500,000 mainframe *programmers* working on the Y2K problem. The United States needs another 100,000—all experienced, all ready to go to work right now. Great Britain needs 300,000 *more* programmers working on this problem, right now. Every one of them needs to know several of the old languages including (but not exclusively) Cobol.

Where are repairs needed? In virtually every mainframe, mid-frame and personal computer. Think of spreadsheets such as Lotus 123, software on satellites, weapons systems, aircraft, hand-held devices, all these systems and much more which must run by the calendar and by the clock. Then there are the millions of switching systems on telephones and telecommunications, software that calculates pensions, Social Security, compound interest, mortgages, life insurance, it just goes on and on.

Things in your life that you never think about are being controlled by very powerful computers. City water, natural gas, mutual funds, your bank. Your city, state and national electrical power grid. The railways, the natural gas lines, x-ray equipment, prescriptions, blood banks, CAT scans, parole boards, every retail store in America. The FBI, state troopers, highway patrol, the police in your hometown, and 911.

Britain

According to Britain's manager of Telecom, the only thing that could possibly save the computers in Britain from outside corruption is to cut the United Kingdom off from the rest of the world.

He added:

Unless the Department of Trade gets suppliers to address this issue immediately, Telecom and its equipment could stop functioning on January 1, 2000, which would mean that we will not be able to make any calls outside the United Kingdom.

If the international phone system goes down, then international banking goes down, and international trade will also collapse.

While I was in England this spring, the government of England hired 20,000 programmers to go through Her Majesty's mainframe computers. Most of those programmers are young people who know little, if anything, about programming. The rest are older men and women who know the Cobol language and other early computer languages.

Mr. Tony Blair, the Prime Minister, launched this crusade in April, 1998.

Here is a genuine effort to stave off a national disaster. Nonetheless, Mr. Blair made this comment at the time he launched this program:

> *But regardless of what we do from this point on, it is still going to be a mess.*

That could be the watchword of everything about programmers' dash to the December 31, 1999, deadline.

Lawsuits

> *Through the eyes of lawyers the Y2K problem looks better than asbestos cigarettes!*
>
> —*Peter de Jager*
> *July 22, 1998*
> *So. San Francisco Conference Center*

Someone noted that the largest single profession represented at Y2K conferences is lawyers. The general description— "attorneys are salivating as they anticipate January 1, 2000."

> *Most decision makers are aware of the year 2000 bug, and doing nothing about it will not be a defense.*
>
> —*Warren Reid*
> *Y2K litigation expert*

The estimated amount of litigation to expect over the Millennium Bug is between 1.5 and 2 trillion dollars.

Yet, we are fortunate. In Britain there is something called "corporation manslaughter." If someone dies on the operating table because an embedded chip fails, then everyone in that room, the hospital that purchased the machine and the company that manufactured the chip can all be tried and convicted of manslaughter. Fail to correct Y2K in Britain and you find yourself being tried for manslaughter.

Let us hope that state and federal governments pass a *no-fault* Y2K law.

If not, our courts are going to grind to a halt, and in more than one way. After all, the entire federal judicial system is run on mainframes!

While we are on the subject of the judicial system, consider the impact Y2K will have on the criminal court system. Computers not working on bail and parole, prison door locks, electrical fences, criminal records of all kinds, and lawyers more than willing to say to a judge, "The people have no *official* records as to why this man is incarcerated."

The year 2000 problem is a litigation catastrophe waiting to happen.

—Vita Peraino
Attorney
Testifying before Congress, 1997

Mr. Peraino went on to say that banks which do not open on the first business day of the new century face the possibility of innumerable lawsuits. He added, "If *my* bank cannot open for several weeks [our law firm] is out of business."

So are most other companies.

If you recommend that your clients invest in companies which cannot ship or receive goods, make payroll or principle promised or mandated employee benefits because of the year 2000 defects, you may be liable for not performing due diligence.

—Warren Reid

Here we are, a world approaching potentially one of the greatest disasters of human history, and no one of national influence is breathing a word. Very soon people will be lining up to sue Wall Street, every brokerage firm, and every bank on earth, crying: "You knew. Why were we not warned!"

Enlarge that to hospitals and insurance companies and the list becomes endless. Nor can you blame them. Many CEO's see this coming, yet are trying to hide the inevitable.

The number of chief executive officers resigning in 1999 will be breathtaking. Captain Smith of the Titanic would have done no less if he had known what fate awaited him. These men know; hence, the lawsuits.

Admitting right now that your company is not going to be ready for the year 2000 is not a way to build a good image for your company, nor to please your stockholders. Admitting that you are not Y2K compliant can land you in court.

Litigation results from the year 2000 meltdown will be more costly than asbestos, breast implants and the Super Fund cleanup lawsuits combined.

—USA Today

As Y2K comes closer, you are going to see not only CEO's taking early retirement, but also people in the bureaucracies of government. In fact, there has been an inordinate number of people leaving the FDIC just in the last few days. The cost of doing repairs for Y2K is staggering, but the lawsuits that will come from it are going to dwarf even that figure. No matter which way you turn, the year 2000 looks like it is going to be chaotic, but no more so than in courts. If analysts are right, a flood of litigation like nothing this world has ever seen awaits 2000 A.D.

The United States of America has a GNP (the total output of America's economy) of $8 trillion a year. Lawsuits may take a fourth of that. *Without a depression!*

As a result, companies are going under. Do not forget that the person who finally pays for *everything* is *you*! All costs are going to be passed on to the consumer by manufacturers and suppliers in the form of price increases. In such a scenario, if by some miracle the economy is still afloat, *inflation* is inevitable.

Let us say only one-tenth of all those lawsuits happens, and only one-tenth of *everything* you have read in this book happens—there are still too many segments of society damaged deeply. Loss of optimism is inevitable. Too much will be happening to cause people to become discouraged. *These* are the ingredients which make up the *real* cause of an economic depression. Those who prepare have a chance at not only optimism, but a possibility of using these hours to advance the kingdom of God.

* * *

Cost

The true cost will certainly be even higher than current estimates.

—Robert Tierney
The Year 2000 Problem

The present cost of repairing the computers of this world is set between 600 million and two trillion dollars.

If you wish to believe the first number, don't! This figure has been often challenged as being too low. There is a great deal of under-guesstimates. Government and businesses are in denial about costs, just as they are about the problem itself.

For instance, on September 5, 1998, the federal government reported it had understated its Y2K cost by nearly 500 million dollars.

It will be the second most expensive event in human history.

Money is not the main problem. Time is the greatest problem, along with not having enough skilled people to make the repairs.

Notwithstanding, the cost is still great. With nothing to show for it when it's all over, expect some to say, "we are now where we were last year." No one wants to discuss so important an outlay of capital. After all, the outlay of money alone will cause an economic shutdown.

If God and Bill Gates write a check for the full amount, not much would change. . .[it] is a people and resource problem. You cannot buy the time at any price.

— *Peter Keen*
Computer World

There will be other costs most of us never imagined, such as traffic accidents.

The insurance services office in New York gave up trying to predict auto damage that might result from malfunctioning traffic lights.

The Chicago Tribune
August, 1998

Fixing computers to read **the Year 2000** *will become the single most expensive problem of all times.*

— *The Economist*
December, 1997

Despite this staggering outlay, the Gartner Group anticipates only 50% of the computers around the world will even get their *mission critical* systems prepared for January 1, 2000. Note: 50% of core repairs, not *total compliance.*

Because mission critical failures mean lost money means many companies will go out of business.

— *Smart Money*
"Countdown to 2000"
September, 1998

And some dare say Y2K—or the anticipation of it, will not cause a global depression! The final cost will not be known until 2020. How much? Some experts see 1999 - 2003 containing the most costly event in human history.

Water and Waste Treatment Facilities

*Interruptions of public and private services, business failures
. . .that is not the worst of it, because telephones and
transportation systems, water and sewerage treatment facilities,
chemical plants and oil refineries and even nuclear power
plants and weapon systems are at risk.*

—*Comlinks Magazine*
Feb 2, 1997

Sewer disposal plants and water purifying treatment centers are all
over America. The large ones are controlled strictly by electronics. There
is virtually nothing that is moved manually. Mark this: Computers and
embedded microprocessors are everywhere in this system.

Further, these treatment plants have been programmed to automatically
shut down in case of . . . a dozen things.

If any one national agency has addressed the problem of sewerage
disposal, I can find no records thereof. Here is a disaster, nationwide,
waiting to happen. There is a chance that there will be places in America
where, when you turn on the tap, the water pouring out will be contaminated.
Or there will be no water coming out at all.

Local water purification systems in small and medium-sized towns
seem to know nothing of their Y2K problem or, at least, have not addressed
it.

Small towns lack the money, the time, the resources and the
sophistication to repair their plants so that they operate after the new century
begins. Many large cities will also fall short of their December 31, 1999
deadline. We face a national emergency with backed up sewerage. We face
an equal one with the prospect of impure water. Reports I have read as to
American cities' preparedness in these two areas and the consequences of
failing to act are bone chilling. The consequence of failure would amount
to a massive calamity.

The non-compliant water and sewerage computers are but one more
straw on the back of a very overburdened camel which is about to collapse.

This nation cannot bear this much bad news *and* also prosper.

What is the population of your community? Divide that by four and
that is how many homes in your town your water department pumps water
to every day. All the valves within the system that pipes water to your

home are run automatically by computers—computers marked for repair or death.

If you had to make your choice, which would you rather not have coming into your home, *clean water or electricity*? You might make a poor decision if you said water. Both are indispensable to modern life.

Try to imagine a hospital operating for even 24 hours without water or with polluted water.

I would suggest you start saving up your large glass bottles. And while you are at it, buy several large metal garbage cans for water storage. They *must* be *round*. (It has to do with physics.) Fill them on December 31. If there is no lake, stream or pond within two to three miles of you (and there usually is almost any place in America) then by all means *move*.

Which brings up southern California.

Southern California, BEWARE.

There is very little water in southern California. Virtually all water comes from the north. If southern California were out of water for even one week, it would constitute one of the greatest disasters in American history. Yet, if it were left to me to try to prove to you this would *not* happen, I would be at a total loss to find any source of reassurance that water will keep running into your home in southern California. At this moment there is simply no such evidence.

What to do if you live in southern California?

Fill your garage with empty metal trash cans. Fill them with water in December of 1999. And wait. The worst thing that could happen to you if you do this is that you will have to pour the water out and give your friends new garbage cans. On the other hand, that water could save your life. When the water runs out? Leave southern California!

* * *

The White House is now mired in introspection and cannot effectively address the endless number of impending crises, nor marshal the moral resolution of a nation to face *the black hour* which lies ahead.

We may well be facing more than an economic depression, we may be facing the collapse of moral fortitude. Though the scene is bleak, pause and consider what a wondrous hour for a vital church that fears neither heights, nor depths, nor persecution, nor famine, nor things past, nor things to come. What an opportunity for the church to shine and to be salt in the coming hour.

That hour is upon us.

The world won't be disrupted by two small digits, but by pride in believing that we could create a technology-dependent world and not be mastered by it.

—*Gordon McDonald*
co-author
"What to Do When the Chips are Down"

The Death of Just-In-Time

Delay

There is no such thing as JIT without computers. Computers invented JIT. When JIT stops, two things happen: manufacturing gridlock and chain reaction shut downs. This shutdown spreads across the nation and across the world.   By using computer calculations a company has been able to order new parts at the very last moment. (A truck driver friend of mine tells of driving across America with parts which arrive only a few hours before the in-house parts are exhausted!)

This revolution has decreased warehouse size and expenses and labor costs. JIT has changed the shape of manufacturing, shipping, storage and production in dozens of ways.

Without computers JIT is unimaginable. Yet returning to the former way is even more unimaginable. One day's delay in delivery of *one* part can shut down an entire company. This is "chain-reaction" at its worst.

To illustrate:

In June of 1998 *one* GM plant struck. All of GM shut down, at the cost of 180,000 people idled. GM lost nearly 2 billion dollars. On and on go the result of that strike, including the major dip in the GNP because of the breakdown of JIT.

Getting parts and products to the right place *just in time is* American production. There is no place in the Y2K scene where you can be so certain as here: There are going to be breakdowns in deliveries and production. The results are going to be maddeningly frustrating.

One AT&T hub shut down because of a software glitch. In a chain reaction 43 other hubs cut off services to customers across the nation.

You *are* going to see this kind of mess all across America after December 31, 1999.

Strain, caution, fear, caused by this—and so many thousands of other breakdowns—are what is going to set off this millennia depression. Not the failure of those companies, not the lack of parts arriving on time, but profound uncertainty on the part of all 270,000,000 of us.

Try to imagine the days just before 2000. There will be rumors everywhere. There will be a few shutdowns because of delinquent computers. At the same time there will be predictions of failures of every sort and variety, across the board, in every segment of society. This is the first time in modern civilization every segment of society will be in jeopardy at the same time.

Dare we say this will *not cause* a depression?

A loss in production of only 2% in JIT arrivals will send cascades of shutdowns across North America.

That *alone* would cause a recession.

* * *

Manufacturing

The fall of JIT will almost certainly bring down a large number of companies.

You are compliant, it is the year 2000. You get on your computer and ask for certain products to arrive *just in time*. The supplier does not answer, his computer is down. Now you do not have the products you need. You turn to two or three other suppliers, their computers are down. Their warehousing information is gone. Soon you have to turn away *your* customers because you cannot assemble your product.

"I am sorry but the part did not arrive." "Sorry, but we are out of that product." "Sorry, it is the götterdämmerung."

Soon your company is out of business too.

Y2K is worse than we imagined because the imagination cannot take in so vast a convergence of so many problems all at once.

The PC's and the Internet

Bruce Hall, research director of Application Development Methods and Management appeared before the Congressional subcommittee on technology on March 20, 1997. He answered a question many are asking: "Won't the PC's see us out of this? Is not the mainframe a thing of the past?"

. . .the total number of large mainframe processors actually increased in 1996 by 20% and is projected to increase again in 1997 by another 20%.

Whereever you find our telecommunications, government agencies, banks, or any company that is complex and depends on electricity *and* computers—*there is where you will find the mainframes. In other words, the science fiction idea of the computers that took over the world was projected to take place four or five hundred years from now. Our mainframe computers, by a glitch made in the 1960's, may bring down civilization much sooner. The worst part about it is this:* so much that is being done in this world today can only be done by mainframes.

No matter how powerful the little PC claims to be, some of our latest PC's have 10 gigabytes of hard-drive, whereas a mainframe has thousands of times more storage than that. It uses 10 gigabytes just to sneeze.

PC's began coming out in the early 1980's. That seems only a few years ago. Have you ever noticed that your computer, when it comes on, knows what day it is? Some of these computers, when asked what happens right after December 31, 1999, may come to a rather strange conclusion: They are going to think that it was the year in which they were made! Most likely 1984. (Orwell was right after all).

Any pre-1997 PC chip may have an even greater problem. Only about 20% of the pre-1997 chips will be able to cross the millennium threshold and some of those are going to go berserk trying to figure how anything with two zeros could possibly have a leap year.

An article in Computer Weekly, May 22, 1997 written by Julia Vowler, said that you had only a 50/50 chance that you would buy a new computer that would work in the new millennium. (See your local computer service center.)

An article appeared in TechWire, May 29, 1997, by Doug Hayward, in which he quoted a consulting firm called Greenwich Meantime as saying that 2,500 out of 4,000 software packages tested had the Millennium Bug!

The Internet

Can the Internet save us? The entire network which the government spliced together years ago is driven by antique mainframes, of which none are Y2K compliant.

You want to communicate? There is only one *guaranteed* way to do so—become a ham operator and buy a ham receiver that derives its energy from a hand crank.

* * *

Healthcare Industry

The private sector of the Healthcare industry is as far behind as the federal government, which may produce an unimaginable catastrophe in human suffering and loss of life.

At the very best, there will be records lost or uncertainty of their accuracy. Insurance companies that pay health insurance claims will be in turmoil. Any serious need for surgery will be (like boarding an airplane) an act of courage.

There has been no study of the healthcare industry's preparation for the Y2K glitch.

I would think calling for that study is something we should look at.

—Senator Robert Bennett
Co-chairman
Senate committee on Y2K

A British government study stated there would be 600 to 1,500 Y2K-related deaths in the United Kingdom.

"A very conservative prediction," said Mike Smith, author of the Report, and professor of Medicine at the Royal London School of Medicine.

In the U.S. we have 6,000 hospitals, 50,000 nursing homes, and 700,000 doctors facing the need of repairing billions of lines of faulty codes.

The largest healthcare corporation in America—Columbia HCI—with 300 hospitals, has 400,000 medical devices and equipment to assess. [Inspect, discover, repair.]

During a visit to the Virginia Inora Fairfax Hospital we saw a $14,000 kidney dialysis machine two years old that could be junk in just 500 days because of the Y2K problem.

"I'm afraid it is too late," said Keith Ghezzi, Chief Operator, Officer for Inora Fairfax Hospital.

If there isn't more action, I'm afraid this Y2K problem could have this nation's health care system on a respirator come January 2000. And that is not hyperbole, it's deadly serious.
—Senator Christopher Dodd
co-chair of Senate special committee on Year 2000

Rural hospitals are in greatest jeopardy of defective equipment because they are the least able to purchase replacement equipment.
U.S.A. Today
July 22, 1998

As of mid-July 1998, 80% of hospitals are just now looking at the problem. Only 30% have made major progress!

And 90% of physicians are taking no action in their offices which involve computer updating and record protecting.

The healthcare industry will be like all other segments of society—behind in Y2K: vast outlays of money to repair or replace equipment, the hounding curse of trying to identify and replace embedded chips, grizzly headlines, law suits. Distrust and accusations will be everywhere.

There will be no *one* Y2K headline for newspapers in post-1999. The entire first page will be filled with headlines.

Agriculture

...the low level of Y2K preparation in America's farms could leave grocery store shelves bare come early January, 2000. Due to a very high lack of concern in the agricultural community, grain could end up rotting in silos and animals dying in their pens due to unremediated transportation and storage equipment.
—TechWeb
July 21, 1998

According to the United States Department of Agriculture about 25% of American farmers use computers as part of their farming operations.

When I was a kid, farmers sold their products. Today, that is the minority. The new market is located far from home. . .it is now global.

In just one growing season we will be in the new century. Keep in mind that the vast distribution system that gets food from the field to your table is in jeopardy. What if that system collapses? The large part of selling food will revert to being local. Unfortunately, most of the American population is not near "local farming."

There will be food shortages in 1999. Heaven alone knows what 2000 holds. Whether the shortages will be large or small we do not know. If it is large, such shortage could become calamitous.

I fear in the days leading up to January 1, 2000, consumers will panic and empty grocery shelves as word spreads about an impending food shortage producing long lines for limited commodities reminiscent of 1980's Russia.

—Congressman Richard Lugar
Agriculture Committee Chairman

Appendix
Part
III

Federal
Government

The Presidency

There is little to say about the Executive Board of government and the Y2K problem.

President Clinton has appointed John Koskinen, and three assistants, to take care of this Y2K problem. This was on February 4, 1998. In June of 1998, Vice President Gore spoke publicly for the first time.

This is one whale of a problem.

Before that? *Nothing.* Here is an editorial comment on Gore's silence.

When it comes to technology Vice President Gore never seems to be at a loss for words. But when it comes to the Year 2000 computer glitch, arguably the nation's most pressing technological problem, Gore has been strikingly silent.

—The Washington Post
May 28, 1998

Here is a worldwide problem of unlimited dimensions that needs an international effort equal to World War II, and the chief executive has *four* people taking care of the problem. To my knowledge no report or statement has come from Mr. Koskinen's office until August of 1998.

Immediately after his second inauguration, Bill Clinton set up a committee—composed of four people—to look into this (Y2K) problem. He did so by an Executive Order. That is the total amount of everything the executive branch of the Federal government has taken. On the other hand, if Clinton or Gore say anything with one word of pessimism in it, that will probably mark the quiet beginning of panic.

On February 4, 1998 the President issued his Y2K Executive Order. Mr. Koskinen then made a statement that could freeze an Eskimo:

The President will address the problem in the next few weeks. We are still reviewing what the appropriate way for (Mr. Clinton) to do that, in light of the state of knowledge and where we are. The question is what the appropriate forum is with (1) balancing the need to raise awareness without (2) unnecessarily causing people to think there is a problem out of control.

—May 21, 1998

Mr. Koskinen, you have 300 working days to remove the Himalayan mountains.

If the government tells us the truth, we are going to panic. If the government does not tell us the truth, we may end up living in caves!

Mr. John Koskinen appeared before the House Banking Committee on March 29, 1998. His first observation was, *"This is the first deadline Washington has ever faced which cannot be pushed back."*

I read the entire speech. What struck me was that everything he said was in reference to the *future*. There was not one sentence in his speech that stated what was *being* done now. *Everything* was a vague reference to what *should* be done.

Koskinen appeared again one month later before a Senate Committee. Again, virtually everything stated was *future*. The only sentence really worth quoting was, *"There is no doubt that the Year 2000 problem poses significant challenges to our government, our nation and the world."*

Koskinen noted it was going to be very tricky to both make the world aware of this problem and at the same time not cause a panic. He added, *"We need to help the public understand that despite our best efforts not every system will function effectively."* (Sir, what efforts?)

It gets worse:

"Some have described economic doomsday scenarios that could take place when we reach the year 2000. To ensure that does not happen, the Council will work to raise awareness and offer support to private sector firms." (I know of not one single penny that has been allocated to small businesses in America to help these firms meet their deadlines.)

He went on, *"Small and medium-sized businesses must be of special concern to us all because many of them do not have adequate financial resources to devote to fixing the problem. We are also reaching out to them."* (Again, for the government to have claimed to help anyone in the private sector or "reach out to them" it still has not allocated one dollar to anyone.)

The Casey Foundation, after a broad study of the Y2K problem, has begun pressing the Executive branch to begin taking leadership to prepare America for what is ahead.

Senator Christopher Dodd and Senator Robert Bennett continue the same theme. America's businesses and corporations and the American population need to be informed about the Y2K crisis.

I watched President Clinton's appointee in August on C-span. During the interview he sandwiched in this comment:

There will be electric brownouts and blackouts. . .some lasting a day, some two days, some a week or two weeks.

                                      —*John Koskinen*

(In making that simple statement Mr. Koskinen, wittingly or unwittingly, announced a depression in 2000.)

He also made this statement: "Some 40% of the U.S. government is the Defense Department." He went on to hint strongly to the American people that the Department of Defense will not be compliant by 2000.

It is not the probability that world communications will break down, nor the fact that the international banking system is teetering on the brink of destruction, nor that a feather could push it into an abyss. The problem you face is much simpler than that. The information you read in this book is information which will gradually become known in the months ahead. This will alert a small number of people to get their money out of stocks and banks, and turn that money into dollar bills. It will take no more than 1% or 2% of the American people doing that to ignite an economic crisis in America and the world.

The Executive branch of government really cannot act without causing a panic. It will probably be mired in scandal right up until Christmas!

Choose your course.

Federal Government

An Overview

The International Data Corporation was hired to do a study for the Federal government on Y2K. The IDC reported that 83% of the government's mainframes had an "average" to "high degree" of problems with Y2K. Only 3% of the government's mainframes had no such problems.

The United States Senate was given a report in January of 1997 which said they could expect the cost of repairs to the government's problems to be between about $4 billion and $30 billion.

The good news is that every Federal Government agency knows there is a problem. The bad news is that only a few of them have specific, realistic plans to solve the problem.
—Congressman Stephen Horn*

How is the Federal Government doing just on the *mission-critical* front? On, as they say, *triage*?

Some 21% of the government's *mission-critical* systems were reported to be compliant. With over 8,000 systems in all, that leaves over *7,000* of the Federal government's systems still needing to be replaced or repaired.

Over half of the government's 24 major agencies project they would be finished by late fall of 1999. Not including testing, a job which could take anywhere from a year to a decade. Yet 40% - 60% of solving the Y2K problem is taken up in testing. And remember these two facts as you consider *testing* worldwide: (1) for every 1,000 lines corrected, 18 new errors are introduced and (2) when programmers estimate completion dates; only 16% are completed in the time estimated.

Government is not going to be fully compliant until the year 2020!

Phase II, the assessment stage, some six of these twenty-four agencies did not make it. That includes the Treasury Department (which includes the IRS). The Department of Transportation did not make it. If that scares you, the Nuclear Regulatory Commission has not made it either!

The *assessment phase*, which comes right after the *awareness phase*, is exactly 1% of the job. Gentlemen, you have 300 working days to remove the Himalayan mountains.

Horn, of the House of Representatives, with Bennett and Dodd in the Senate have been the ones working hardest to alert both Washington and America to the dire situation the Federal Government is in as relates to Y2K.

There is a weird and ominous silence. . .the government is not
talking because the government does not want to know.
                                        —Bert Concklin
                                Professional Services Counsel
                                        Vienna, Virginia

Will This Be 2000?

Will there be a depression? Take a look just at government. Exclude
all other Y2K factors from your mind. Imagine eighteen months from
now.

No Social Security disability checks going out. Nothing going
out in the way of payments to disabled veterans. The IRS is in
absolute disarray. The Defense Department not sure of what its
missiles are doing, or can do, or *might* do. The Treasury Department
with a good portion of its records lost—or unreliable. The Army,
Navy, Air Force, Marines and Coast Guard—all facing chaotic
information interchange. The leaders at the Pentagon wandering
around the halls trying to figure out how to get down to the first
floor because the elevators do not work. The computers in the
Senate Office building and the House of Representatives office
building in a state of utter disarray. State police, county and city
police, highway patrol, parole boards and prisons: All trying to
work with errant information or no information at all.

And men debate the possibility of a depression?

Add two more scenes. Your bank cannot get the vault door to open.
The New York stock exchange "closed for repairs." Pagers inoperable.
Cellular phones do not work. The elevators in the office building stuck.
Airlines are not flying. Bank transfers overseas ended.

No, these horror scenes will not cause a depression. It will be the
anticipation of these events in 1999 which will cause the beginning of the
depression. That depression is as inevitable as are the finger pointing's of
blame.

Experts are concerned that many of our information systems
will not differentiate between dates in the twentieth and twenty-
first centuries. I want to assure the American people *that the*
Federal Government, in cooperation with state and local
governments and the private sector, is taking steps to prevent
any interruption of government services. We are determined
to see that it doesn't happen.
                                        —*President Clinton*

Horn's Congressional subcommittee reported fourteen of these Federal Agencies will not be prepared for December 31, 1999. Which one is furthest behind? The Department of Energy with expected compliance in 2019! That almost wraps up any hope of Americans having electricity in our homes in the early part of the new century.

The Department of Defense will not be compliant until the year 2012 with the Department of Transportation to be compliant in the year 2010. All of these speak of a royal foul-up. The Treasury Department (including the IRS) theoretically must be ready in 1999. It cannot be, yet it *has* to be. Nonetheless, the Treasury Department will not be compliant until 2004. And the one we are going to need the most, the *Federal Emergency Managememt Agency (FEMA)*. Expected compliance is in mid-2000.

Private Sector

Now the private sector.

Consider this: European computers are being repaired by one method. Britain's are being repaired by a different method and the United States has no less than *three* methods of repair! (I just received a report before this book went to print that over 70% of Europe's businesses have done *nothing* toward fixing their Y2K problems.)

Gentlemen, you now have less than 300 working days left.

Of course, there will be no depression!

* * *

Senator Robert Bennett stated to a Senate subcommittee in the spring of 1998 that there is *no way* everything in the government can be fixed and ready for Y2K.

In January of 1998 one analyst stated that at its present pace, 50% of the agencies of the United States will not make the December 31, 1999 deadline. When the public finally discovers this fact it will cause a major reaction.

There are presently 350,000 unfilled openings in this country for programmers. The Federal government cannot find enough of these programmers to repair these problems.

The Treasury Department, including the IRS, has not yet completed the assessment phase of the Y2K problem as of May of 1998. If the Treasury cannot send out checks and if taxes cannot be collected, how does government do anything except die? It will be a two-coffin funeral. Government and the entire financial system of America.

Three notable people have appeared before this Senate subcommittee

concerning Y2K. Mr. Alan Greenspan, Chairman of the FDIC. The governor of the FDIC, Mr. Edward Kelley, and Edward Yardeni, one of the world's most respected economist. All three have indicated in speeches to the subcommittee that America can expect some degree—yet undetermined—of economic problems.
(It will be called a depression.)

THE FDIC

The Federal Reserve and the FDIC are the guardians, keepers, sentinels and enforcers of bank solvency. They are also the *example* and the model to the banking industry. *The FDIC is not compliant.*

The FDIC handles 200 trillion dollars in transactions every year. Every deposit and withdrawal you make on Monday, goes to the Federal Reserve *that* night, and is then sent back to your bank the next morning! John Koskinen, Clinton's czar for Y2K, on August 12, 1998 told us all (on C-span) that there are going to be delays in these transactions come January. He admitted it in public, on television. And why not? Even the FDIC is not compliant.

Do you realize the chaos of the Federal Reserve's failure to keep a billion transfers running smoothly?

Further, the Federal Reserve is also a paper tiger. It has *no* power over bank. Its power is only by advice.

> *The FDIC is not prepared to predict whether any banking institutions may fail as a result of the Y2K problem...*
>
> —Andrew Hove, FDIC
> *(Federal Deposit Insurance Corporation)*
> *before a Senate Banking Committee*

The FDIC admitted it will see banks lose their records.

> *We already have arrangements in place to assist financial institutions in the event that they are unable to assist their own systems.*
>
> —Edward Kelley
> *member*
> *Federal Reserve Bank*
> *July 30, 1998*

This means that the FDIC knows that banks are going to open on Tuesday, January 4, 2000 to find that they have lost all their records.

Mr. Kelley then added:

Like our counterparts in the private sector, the Federal Reserve System still faces substantial challenges in achieving Y2K readiness.

Kelley admitted in that sentence that the FDIC is not compliant and is having difficulty getting there. Neither the FDIC nor the banks are compliant. If this is known to still be true by the summer of 1999, will *you* keep your money in a bank? Will anyone!

Mr. Kelley then listed some of those "challenges": The FDIC focus on trying to repair its own computers—a highly complex project, a multitude of interfaces with other organizations, "the readiness of vendor components" ensuring the readiness of applications and *testing,* as well as "establishing contingency plans."

This means the Federal Reserve is hoping to repair their *mission-critical* software and hardware, and hope that their "vendors"—the 13,000 banks!— do the same! The FDIC operating on "a mission-critical basis?" We are in very dangerous waters.

Cutting through the high-sounding language of the rest of his testimony Mr. Kelley said they were losing programmers whom they needed desperately (to work on the Y2K problem) because they are not paying those programmers as much as private companies.

Kelley's words:

"We [the FDIC] need to become compliant. All 13,000 banks need to become complian., The 60,000 branches need to become compliant."

The daily communication link between banks and the Federal Reserve is called the Fedline. The Fedline is also not compliant; that is, it has not been fully tested—under real conditions.

Buried deep inside the Federal Reserve is a regulatory body named the Federal Financial Institutions Examination Council. They sent out a report to America's banks on December 17, 1997. Essentially, this is what it said to America's banks:

Make contingency plans concerning the Y2K problem.

Most banks are working only on contingency plans and mission critical software.

The FFIEC sent American banks a statement about other possible courses of action. Allow me to condense:

". . .you have to interface with other banks and with all your vendors. Make sure that their computers don't start sending you corrupted data. In other words, any non-compliant bank that does business with your bank, can corrupt your bank's records."

To my knowledge, no one on this earth has come up with a contingency plan that would allow banks to continue operating if they have not reached total Y2K readiness.

In the months ahead, we are going to begin hearing more and more about these contingency plans of the world's financial system. Seeing these reports may be what causes the early uneasiness that leads to a panic.

The FFIEC gave American banks a most unique piece of advice. Again, condensing, it went like this:

"Be very careful about making loans to companies which are not Y2K compliant, as they may not survive financially. Be very careful about loaning money to companies that have fixed their computers, as they may have spent so much money in doing so, that they may not survive financially!"

This means if the company you work for does not fix its Y2K problem the bank won't lend you money. And if your company *does* fix its Y2K problem the bank may not loan you money.

An executive of Union Bank of California made this observation:

"We bankers have two problems; (1) We need to fix our mainframe computers. Union Bank of California is one of the 25 largest commercial banks in the nation with *22 million* lines of mainframe code to assess. (2) We also have to look at millions of other lines of code in our mid-range computers.

"We asked this question:

"Will the businesses that we loan money to have cash flow problems as a result of Y2K? What are some of the liabilities businesses face as a result of Y2K? Many that borrowed money from us are going to find themselves in very tight straits. Many simply are not going to be able to repay the loans which we have made to them."

This is the *chain reaction* the banking world is facing. Banks not compliant, companies not compliant. Companies in trouble, banks in trouble.

IRS

I have a contingency plan. I plan on taking up pottery in October of 1999 and moving to Montana.

—*Julie McCreary*
IRS Year 2000 Coordinator

The most compelling thing by far is fixing the (IRS) computers so they do not stop working on January 1, 2000. If we do not fix them, the whole financial system of the United States will come to a halt. It is very serious, it not only could happen, it will happen, if we do not fix it right.

—*Charles Rossitti*
IRS Commissioner
before a Congressional subcommittee

There has never been a year in my life that I have wanted to pay my federal income tax. But, I want to pay them in 1999. My taxes (and yours) are going to be due in April of 2000. What remains to be seen is whether or not the IRS will still be in existence to take my money. They have openly admitted that they will not have their computers fixed until the year *2019!* The reason: They started too late *and* they have perhaps the most complex computer inter-connectivity system on this planet.)

We are going to need a government in the year 2000 perhaps more than we ever have since the Civil War.

Each year the IRS collects one and a half trillion dollars from us. The Treasury Department is responsible for so many funds that are critical for keeping this nation going. Most of all, the Treasury Department has 300 billion dollars in annual interest it has to pay. . .or the nation goes bankrupt.

The IRS can hardly even get started on either repairing or replacing its present system. All IRS applications and databases are in danger of noncompliance.

Because of the unique situation that the IRS is in, that agency deserves *some* special attention.

The IRS' costs for becoming compliant are going to escalate as every year passes.

—*Susan Marshall*
Federal Sources
Inc. Federal Computer Week
June 27, 1997

The IRS has all of its information about you stored in a computer system called *master files*, located at IRS central storage facilities in Martinsburgh, West Virginia. There are 100,000 IRS employees, 1400 office locations, 800 mainframe computers, 1,000 midsize computers, 130,000 PC's, 88,000 software programs, 100 million lines of code, and a massive telecommunications system. There are ten regional centers. All ten centers feed information into the West Virginia complex every day. The flow of information is *staggering*. The complexity of the schematic is literally beyond *anyone's* comprehension.*

Those 800 mainframe computers (manufactured by many different companies) do not speak the same language, and *none* are anywhere near being compliant.

Over the years, an *enormous* maze has been jerry-rigged together to enable *all* of these computers to talk to one another, enabling the IRS to store, send, and receive information from your local IRS office.

Listen now to Arthur Gross, Chief Information Officer for the IRS.

These infrastructures are largely not "century-date" compliant.

To put it in other words, the computers *all* have the Millennium Bug and *still* will have it on Friday, December 31, 1999.

Mr. Gross went on to admit that the IRS could not (1) keep this incredibly complex jerry-rigging going and (2) also become compliant. He called it a "uniquely challenging" situation.

An incorrect entry in any line of code in a mainframe computer can shut down that operation. Now consider that the IRS has a 100 million lines of code with 50,000 applications that *must* be inspected, corrected, and then tested, computer by computer and then *all* tested against one another!

The IRS have 300 programmers working on the bug. Can the IRS finish in time?

Contrast that with the *fact* that the Social Security Administration has 30 million lines of code to correct, with 400 programmers working on the program since 1991. In 7 years of work, the SSA are only 60% compliant.

What chance does the IRS have of finishing? None!

The International Mess

There are over one hundred nations on this earth that collect taxes. The IRS is ahead of all of them, and the IRS is twenty *years* behind schedule.

---

* *You can request a copy of the schematic of the computer system nightmare from the IRS.*

All tax agencies of all governments on earth have 300 working days to fix their Millennium Bug.

To make matters more confusing, there are several ways to solve the Y2K problem. One method is called *windowing*—it allows the use of two digits (02 means 2001, etc.). It is cheaper and faster than a four digit revision, but it is a stop gap method that only temporarily solves the problem. The IRS has outlawed any computer with a *windowing* repair to talk to the IRS computers, which are being repaired on a four digit level. The IRS computers will only accept computers with the four digit cure. The IRS "standard" came too late for many companies. They had already spent fortunes using the window repair method. This is going to cause chaos and a loss of critical information.

April 15, of the year 2000 may prove to be very interesting. But so will April 15, 1999 the date the IRS goes into the "year 2000" mode. Watch that date.

We could be in the middle of a national crisis of unimaginable proportions, only to find that government does not have the means to tell us how much we owe, nor how much we are to receive back, because the IRS computers are not Y2K compliant.

Watch the IRS, as it may be the key that decides if our country goes into a Y2K crisis or just a depression.

By April 15, 1999 the government needs almost two trillion dollars from us and then must be fully ready to begin collecting our year 2000 taxes.

Recently, the challenges are far more over-reaching: To modernize functioning by aged systems which have been nearly irreparable. . . overlaid by an interfaced tangle of stovepipe distributed application systems and network infrastructure.

—Arthur Gross
Director
Internal Revenue Service
speaking to a government subcommittee

If I were a United States Congressman and had read the previous statements, I would suggest that the United States Senate immediately invent a whole new way to collect taxes; a way which does not need the computer system of the IRS.

Washington knows the IRS has the most complicated and outdated, "un-update-able" computer system in the government. They also know the IRS set has new records for slowness to begin remediation of the problem, only to conclude that they could do nothing with this vast labyrinth of computer networking.

The IRS computer system cannot be repaired. I leave you with these words by Mr. Gross:

> *The risk inherent in phase three [testing] may be nearly incalculable!*

Mr. Gross means the IRS could lose all of its data.

The IRS has brought in outside programmers to save the day—but they have no reliable manuals. Until a manual of some sort is re-created, the IRS and the private companies brought in to solve this gargantuan problem cannot even analyze the problems.

The IRS has 300 working days left to do it all. So do fifty states and thousands of counties. If today were April 15, 2000 not one of them could collect taxes.

There are 140 other nations with the same problem. They *also* have only 300 working days to solve their Y2K problems.

If 140 nations are going to have tax collecting problems, how, pray tell, can we *not* have a depression?

> *(The failure of the IRS) to achieve compliance by the year 2000 will jeopardize our way of living on this planet for some time to come.*
>
> —Craig Smith
> Swiss America

> *I don't mean that society is running out of time to fix this problem. Society has already run out of time.*
>
> —Gary North

> *The IRS has no fall back plan for failure. If its computer systems are unable to deal with the year 2000 it is not clear what the consequences will be.*
>
> —Tax Practice
> December 2, 1997

*   *   *

Department of Defense

They guard us. They keep us free. They are 40% of government.

A military with more departments and agencies any one man can explain. What effect will the Y2K have on the Department of Defense?

That department which defends our nation from all enemies and keeps a large part of this of this nation working will not have its *mission critical systems completely up and running until 2012!*

We should be out of the depression by then!

The Department of Defense and all other government agencies are utterly dependent upon the private sector. Our banks. Our financial institutions, our telephone wires, our utilities, our transportation, our telecommunications, and our electric power grid.

The Defense Department Logistics Agency reports that it alone has 35 different hardware platforms, 16 operating systems, 311 commercial software packages. *And* that agency is *not* compliant.

Emmett Paige, Assistant Secretary of Defense, speaking to one of the subcommittees in the House of Representatives, noted that the Department of Defense leans on computers more than anyone else. Yet, according to Congressman Horn, the Department of Defense will not have all its repairs completed for fourteen years!

The problems of the DOD seem infinite and complex, beyond the understanding of laymen. There are less than 300 working days to get all these jobs done.

Unless the Department of Defense works a miracle, all those missiles we have hidden down in silos will be inoperable. Along with thousands of separate agencies and entities.

The Military

The United States military is *not* compliant, having *begun* their computer repairs in late 1995. The military have almost 40 million lines of code to correct. These codes are in 77 different computer languages.

The military has already underestimated the amount of time and effort needed to (1) evaluate and (2) to do pilot testing. *In every case* where pilot tests of Y2K were done, glitches and obstacles have occurred.

In the book, *Diffusing the Millennium Timebomb,* by Braumberg, we are told a story of a corporation that was hired by the Department of Defense to do a study of the Y2K problem. *The organization could not find any inventory of military information systems,* consequently, they could not even figure out the total lines of code in the DOD's system.

Then there are the embedded chips. Everywhere. Including thousands of airplanes and helicopters. A plane might fly perfectly under normal conditions, but there are thousands of computer switches to be made under abnormal conditions. One malfunctioning chip could cause a pilot to eject and a plane to crash and burn, six months into the new century.

According to TECHWIRE, the Department of Defense now says it has nearly 14,000 systems and less than 10,000 are passed the 1% mark, with no more than 2,000 of those 14,000 systems actually in repair.

In August of 1997, the DOD played some military games in which they pretended it was the year 2000. Its global command system failed. This was reported in Government Computer News.

I wonder what terrorists are thinking about all this?

This matter of embedded chips in missiles and in ground control is being taken seriously by both the United States and Russia.

The following came out in a hearing on Capital Hill when the Assistant Secretary of Defense testified before a Senate subcommittee in June 1998.

> *There are currently discussions between the United States Defense Department and Russia (concerning the Y2K problem) as it relates to embedded chips sending out signals that say that the United States is under missile attack from Russia, and vice versa, as to what false signals they might get and how to respond to them.*

In June of 1998 the Air Force admitted that the F15 fighter jet's computer system will not be compliant. When December 31, 1999 turns to January 1, 2000 the Department of Defense will only be about 33% compliant just in the area of *mission critical* systems, which is about 25% of all they have to correct in the computer. This means that 25% of the Department of Defense will be 30% compliant!

Social Security

*The SSA faces a definite risk that incorrect data will be
introduced into its databases and that risk could be magnified
[if the SSA] does not develop contingency plans to ensure the
continuity of its critical systems and activities should systems
not be corrected in time.*

—*the General Accounting Office*

Let us give Social Security an "A" for courageous effort. They started
correcting the Y2K problem before anyone else in government. In 1991.
They are still hard after their goal. Keep in mind you are reading about the
knight-in-shining-armor. But if this is how far the best has come, where
does that leave government and the private sector!

In seven years the Social Security Administration has become *only
60%* compliant.

The Social Security Administration has less than 300 working days to
finish the other 40% of their re-coding. (That does *not* include the fact
that, after they finish, then SSA must test. Over again the word goes forth:
to do testing the way it must be done, will take longer than repairing does.)

Katherine Adams, head of the Social Security Administration, estimated
that if there is a one percent error in the SSA computer information at the
time of Y2K, the SSA will begin receiving somewhere between 43 and 50
million complaint calls *daily.*

Recently the SSA found an additional 33 million lines of overlooked
software code!

The SSA faces the possibility of major disruptions in their ability to
respond to claims by millions of individuals, if these "critical" lines are not
corrected in time.

The SSA must also exchange critical data with Federal and State
agencies which must be compliant at the same time.

The SSA also exchanges data with Darth Vader. . .the IRS, which
threw up its hands long ago and said, essentially: "The IRS is not going to
even come close to making the Y2K deadline." What will happen to the
hard work of the SSA when Goldilocks meets Godzilla?

The SSA is not the only agency which distributes funds to the elderly
and the disabled. Other federal, state, county and city governments do
likewise.

There are fifty states which also issue retirement checks and welfare checks. So does the Veterans Administration. There are also hundreds of thousands of insurance companies and other private institutions which issue retirement checks. All cannot possibly make the deadline. Probably a few will.

For the sake of millions, let us hope it sails safely into the new millennium. If not, a tragedy of unfathomable dimensions will sweep this nation.

At this time, not *one* government agency or private agency which issues retirement and welfare checks had announced that its computers were compliant with Y2K.

It is almost impossible for any human being to imagine that his own personal income will stop *completely*. The growing likelihood is that, unless the miraculous happens within the next 300 working days, not many retirement checks will go out beyond 1/1/2000.

Let us hope the SSA passes through the vortex of 12/31/99 to 1/1/2000 without a bubble. But if forty million Americans hear that the SSA may be in trouble, batten down the hatches, this country is in for a panic.

Veterans

The Veterans Administration found 20% of its medical equipment needs to be fixed or replaced. They sent out a letter to the manufacturers of their hospital equipment. After nearly a year of badgering these manufacturers they received approximately 800 replies. Here is what one company said:

"The seven radiation dosage machines which we sold you (radiation machines for cancer patients) at $400,000 a piece, are not Y2K compliant and cannot be made Y2K compliant. You are hereby put on notice to not use these machines beyond December 1, 1999. These machines must be decommissioned. This will cost $40,000 per machine because of the radiation material they contain."

"When faulty machines are found, where do they end up?" asked Senator Bennett.

Veterans Hospital Administration

One Veterans Hospital administrator has been quoted as saying, "I don't know how we are going to do this. I am 75% of my department's Y2K office, and I don't even know what I am doing."

National Debt

Can the national debt of 24 trillion dollars be paid off?

Let us say we only owed the 'on-budget' debt of about 6 trillion dollars, instead of the 'off-budget' debt of 17 trillion, or the total debt of about 23 trillion.

Let us say the federal budget got balanced today and stayed balanced. We owe 6 trillion dollars. Let us say the interest rate we paid on our debt was 5%. When would the 6 trillion be paid off?

Never.

Some 14 years from now the debt would be. . . not 6 trillion. . .but 12 trillion dollars. That is the curse of interest. . .at 5% The principle doubles every 14 years at 5% interest.

Do you understand what this means? The currency we presently have *must* collapse. That economic practice which was born in 1933 must also collapse.

This nation's economy is doomed.

Someday, somewhere, somehow, a crisis, or the perception of a crisis. . .

(Fourteen years from now can the U.S. find anyone to loan us 12 trillion dollars? Remember, that is with *no* inflation and with only 5% interest).

What if we returned to the gold standard? Ah, that would show all of us how little. . .how truly little. . .the dollar is worth. Keep in mind one ounce of gold has always been able to buy about 300 loaves of bread.

Let us see how truly worthless the dollar would be if we traded back the paper dollars and the ledger entry dollars for gold.

The government of the United States presently has 500 million ounces of gold. Let us say that tomorrow our government announced it would accept back all 100 trillion dollars and give us gold in return. Here is gold as money, once more! Remember, the government has 500 million ounces of gold to exchange for 100 trillion dollars! You and I go to the bank and turn in *all* our dollars. We would each get one ounce of gold for every $60,000 we turned in. That means that 300 loaves of bread would cost $160,000! One loaf of bread would cost over $50,000 per loaf. Yes, in the light of gold, paper money, actually ledger money, would be seen as worthless.

That, dear reader, gives you an idea of how void is the worth of the dollar. What is causing the dollar to be perceived as valuable is nothing but a very vivid imagination!

Right now, because of this vivid imagination, gold is selling at 300 worthless dollars per ounce. If you expect to preserve your present savings, get out of ledger dollars and get in to cash. And as we get close to 2000 convert some of your cash into gold.

Silver is selling at 5 worthless dollars per ounce. That makes silver an even better bargain.

Are you ready to take action?

The Gartner Report

The Gartner Group of Stanford, Connecticut, is an advisory organization on information technology. Here is some of the information they issued in the latter part of 1997 which came about through a global survey they conducted concerning Y2K. I found this to be perhaps the single most interesting statistic I have found.

Here is the most intriguing piece of information I have found. The Gartner Group discovered that 38% of 1,100 computer industry executives worldwide state that *they may withdraw their own personal assets from banks*—and from other investment companies—*before* the year 2000.

In this worldwide survey, it was found that 30% of companies surveyed have not begun addressing the Millennium Bug problem. Some 88% of that 30% were small companies with less than 2,000 employees. And 12% were large companies with over 2,000 employees.

The small companies, The Gartner Group went on to report, will be in very serious trouble on the first day of the new century.

In nations around the globe, government agencies were far behind in their efforts to come to compliance.

Many of these groups have made no progress whatsoever in the previous six months.

—*The New York Times*
September 25, 1997

The Gartner Group estimates as much as $600 billion will be needed to make mainframes compliant. (Other estimates are far larger. The closer we get to 1/1/2000 the higher the estimate.)

The Gartner Group surveyed executives of 2,300 companies in 17 different nations, including government agencies. The organizations which are trying hardest to reach compliance and which are the furthest along are those in the *financial industry!*

(It seems that the financial industry knows, within itself, that it is the most important industry of all. It bears the burden of being the most important industry of all to become compliant. They are trying hard. But for some reason this does *not* comfort me.)

Of companies with more than 20,000 employees, only 52% are in a position to make the deadline.

If you happen to find those statistics encouraging, then you should know something else that The Gartner Group observed.

These large companies are dependent on small suppliers. These small suppliers must *also* be compliant, yet they are the furthest behind.

To illustrate that point: A small company supplies parts to a very large company. If that small company cannot deliver its parts, it really does not matter if the large company is compliant or not. The fact is, the large company cannot produce its product without the parts of many, many small companies.

Imagine what that would do to General Motors, Ford Motor Company and Mercedes-Chrysler.

In the latter part of 1997 some 50% of our nation's largest banks were half way down the road in reprogramming their computers to the point that those computers will operate correctly in the year 2000.

Offset that by the fact that only 5% of the largest banking institutions in the rest of the world have reached that halfway mark. The Gartner Group estimates that organizations, worldwide, will spend between $300 - $600 billion on the Y2K problem.

Said Luke Carcoccio, Research Director of The Gartner Group:

"One of the big shocks of our survey is how little work has been done outside the United States."

Another finding of The Gartner Group revealed that many of the world's smaller banks have taken no action whatsoever.

If the banks of this world are not compliant by the year 2000 there is a potential for a financial chain reaction across the globe.

This is because banks are interconnected by computer networks through which billions of dollars are transferred every day. (This does not mean that the dollars were actually transferred, it simply means that a great deal of electronic information flowed across that network in thousands of different directions making *theoretical* transfers).

And just how much money is transferred each day over this interlocking network? Approximately $1 trillion per day, all in electronic transfers, not a single dollar bill moves anywhere. Neither does any other currency. Everything is a *computer entry*. Some $5 trillion in electronic transfers per week, all done by *non*-compliant computers.

Try to imagine how messed up government would be if only its fax machines do not work.

The Feds and the IMF(International Monetary Fund) paralyzed because they are facing outside computers that are not working. Bank notes are being called in, as are mortgages, no one at the other end of the telephone, prison doors not opening or closing as commanded. Gasoline pumps which will not pump, no Visa or Mastercard or American Express cards being accepted, traveler's checks are being refused, a world sits in disbelief.

No one has been able to build a model that says this scenerio will not happen.

Yes, there will be a depression. Big. Bad. And maybe very long.

Those people who have cash and food may be the most fortunate people on earth.

Someone commented to me, "We are facing the greatest shift in the ownership of wealth in the history of mankind." Having cash and food (and real money) may not sound like a great deal. But there is an old saying, "In the land of the blind, a one eyed man is king."

Also keep in mind that no one will say to you in the next two years; "Oh, all you have is gold and silver. You are so poor. I have paper and ledger money."

Part
IV

An
International
Overview

The International Chain Reaction

Even if all of us around the world managed to complete our work on time, we risk creating an electronic 'Tower of Babel' if we do not agree on standards and then test our systems against one another.

—*Tony Keyes*
author and radio commentator

If, by some miracle, 95% of the nations of this world become compliant in everything, and the United States was 99% compliant in absolutely everything by December 31, 1999, its that small percentage remaining that can *still* sweep around the world, doing incalculable damage.

The words used to describe this phenomena are: a *cascade*, the *domino effect*, the *ripple effect*.

There are banks in South America and Asia and in most of eastern Europe, and even banks in western Europe, which have barely started dealing with this problem at all. Any company operating with these countries faces a high risk that the banks which that company is doing business with, will have a computer failure that could knock the banks out.

— *James Leach*
Congressman
Ohio

Proof of the effect the Y2K bug can have on the global economy lies in the effect of the recent breakdown in the Hong Kong stock exchange. It caused a breathtaking swing downward in the entire global marketplace. And when the history of this Depression II is written, it will be noted that it began in the obscure stock market and banking industry of Thailand in 1997.

The USA is ahead of most countries by six to eighteen months, but every nation's computers are experiencing their repairs differently. There may be no global interfacing because there is no international model nor universal standard on *how* to repair mainframes.

A friend of mine, and an advisor to one of the nation's largest financial institutions, who receives daily briefings on the Y2K crisis from around the world shared a few insights with me about Europe and the Y2K.

European banks are ignoring the Millennium Bug. They know they cannot solve it in the time left to them. Right now, they are totally consumed by the EMU problem.

Since May of 1998 European nations have been invited in to this 'one-currency' union. Eleven nations are surrendering their own national currency. Each nation will receive *euros* in exchange for national currency. The ratio of exchange is different for each nation. [To give an inaccurate illustration it could take 2 German marks to receive 1 euro. Italy, in turn, would surrender 1,500 lira for 1 euro.]

All of this negotiation and agreement must be done by November of 1999. Europe simply has no time to worry about the Y2K bug.

Europe has moved from a strategy of '*repair*' to a strategy of '*prepare*.' European leaders plan to admit the problem; then tell European citizens they must each and all *prepare* for 1/1/2000 on their own!

European leaders have resigned themselves to preparing Europe for the bug, and then dealing with it *after* the new century begins.

What kind of problems or disasters this will cause, no one knows.

I asked my friend if he thought our government would attempt such a policy. . .a policy of *let America know so that we, as individuals, can make our own preparations to survive the transition into a new century.*

You can guess his response. (It is probably yours). "No, I cannot see Washington being that practical. We will go into the new millennium blind, unprepared and innocent."

One of the reasons I chose to write this book was so that the Christian community would become *aware*, so that *you* could then choose on what level to *prepare*.

My friend then added one other interesting insight about the international company he works for. "We do business with all these European nations. Every week we do hundreds of millions of dollars worth of business with European financial institutions, so we have to understand the ratio of exchange each nation will have as they switch to euros. We call this *our EMU crisis*. They will not give us this information until just before 1999 ends. We have *one weekend* to change all our records to match the new exchange rate. *"And the very next week we face the onset of the Millennium Bug!"*

Not only can Europe not juggle two crises at once, they are causing many Americans to face a minor inconvenience (the EMU) while also trying to survive a major crisis. Others have given up and are focusing on the transition to a 'one currency' Europe.

We all started too late, and resolving this crisis before 12/31/99 seems more and more impossible with each passing day. Is this world headed for a worldwide Waterloo?

The European model is: *prepare for the future.* The American model is: *fix it.* Try to imagine this on a truly grand scale—glitches in the airlines, glitches in the power grid, glitches in the telecommunications, glitches in railways, glitches in the trucking industry, glitches in the universities and colleges, glitches in the stock market and the banking system, subways not moving, elevators stuck, and cell phones not working—each affecting the other and knocking down more dominoes than anyone could dream of all across Europe.

> *Should a shop floor system snafu be allowed to go undetected until it is too late? Not only is the company that caused the trouble at risk, but so are its dependent business partners.*
> —Industry Week
> January 5, 1998

The effect would be felt all over the rest of the world. Once more, this in itself, will cause a worldwide depression. There are simply too many problems happening at once, too many uncertainties. Economy *does not* stand that much stress.

Interrelated? Chain reaction? Read this:

> *Consider the tangled web of business interrelationships that exist among organizations. First there are the customers, next, suppliers, vendors, financial service providers, insurance carriers, federal, state and local government agencies, electric utilities, telecommunication networks, and even computers. If the performance or dependability of one falters, the survival of your company can be at risk.*
>
> *The problem is that none of these external dependencies shows up in the millions of lines of codes that your companies inventories, scans, fixes, or tests. That even one dependency gone awry can jeopardize the stability of your firm.*
> —Datamation
> January 1998

> *Time is running out fast. . .and for some it might already be too late. One faulty link can weaken the whole chain and break it. Montreal based BCE will tear up contracts with any of its 15,000 suppliers if they have not routed out their millennium bugs. By the middle of next year we will be looking for other suppliers...*
> —Jean Monte
> President
> BCE (a telecommunication firm)
> Toronto Star
> February 8, 1998

Can future international trade exist under the conditions as described here?

If so, how? If not, what are the implications? To the world? To you?

The Laws of Economics
What happens when a currency is not backed by gold

Someday, somewhere, somehow, money that is not backed by silver and gold, (paper money—ledger-entry money—not backed by anything,) will become utterly, totally worthless. The currency's final demise is usually caused by an *unexpected* crisis or by the *perception* that a crisis is coming!

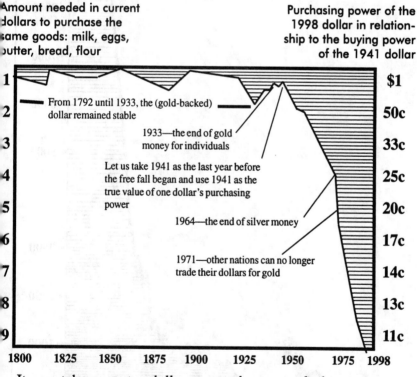

Amount needed in current dollars to purchase the same goods: milk, eggs, butter, bread, flour

Purchasing power of the 1998 dollar in relationship to the buying power of the 1941 dollar

From 1792 until 1933, the (gold-backed) dollar remained stable

1933—the end of gold money for individuals

Let us take 1941 as the last year before the free fall began and use 1941 as the true value of one dollar's purchasing power

1964—the end of silver money

1971—other nations can no longer trade their dollars for gold

1	$1
2	50c
3	33c
4	25c
5	20c
6	17c
7	14c
8	13c
9	11c

1800 1825 1850 1875 1900 1925 1950 1975 1998

It now takes over ten dollars to purchase *exactly* the same goods which you could buy for one dollar in 1941.

You need only look at the last ten years to understand why there is going to be a depression. There is too much credit. This is a fake boom.

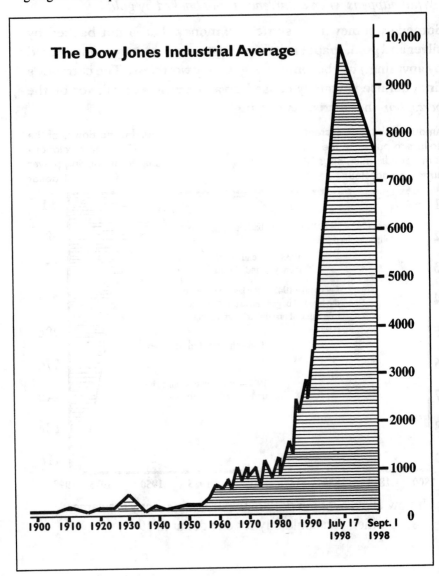

How much will repairing the Y2K problem cost? It is
the Second Most Expensive Event in Human History

EVENT	ESTIMATED COST
World War II	$4 Trillion
⇒ **Millennium Challenge**	$600 Billion*
Vietnam Conflict	$500 Billion
Kobe Earthquake	$100 Billion
Los Angeles Earthquake	$60 Billion
Desert Storm	$53 Billion

For America only. Worldwide: 2 trillion dollars.

The withdrawal of that much capital on a project that nets *nothing*
new, *must* adversely affect the world's economy.

The Purchasing Power of Gold vs. the Purchasing Power of Paper Money Over a 79 Year Period.

If you *had* to be in paper money, note which currency is safest. (It is the only currency on earth *strongly* backed by gold.)

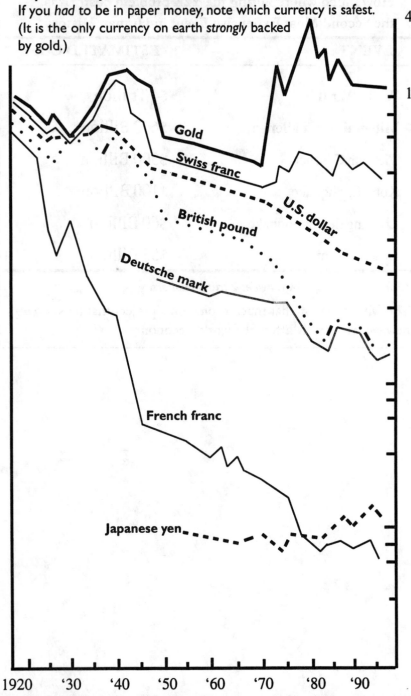

4

1

Gold

Swiss franc

U.S. dollar

British pound

Deutsche mark

French franc

Japanese yen

1920   '30   '40   '50   '60   '70   '80   '90

None of the organizations listed below are compliant for Y2K and are unlikely to be by December 31, 1999! Yet errors of only $\frac{1}{10}$ of one percent would bring the world's financial institutions into utter chaos.

Fedwire Securities Transfers

- 8,000 Depository Institutions
- 13 million transferred
- $650 billion in average total *daily* value
- $160 trillion transferred per year

Automated Clearing House (ACH)

- 14,000 Financial Institutions
- 400,000 companies
- 50 million customers
- 4 billion transactions processed in 1996
- 12 trillion dollars transferred per year

Fed Funds Wire Transfer

- 10,000 Depository Institutions
- 86 million payments
- 1.1 trillion total average daily value
- 280 trillion dollars transferred per year   ⟵

Question: How much does the Federal government owe?	
"On Budget" debt only	
1932	**22 BILLION DOLLARS**
1940	**400 BILLION DOLLARS**
1980	**800 BILLION DOLLARS**
1981	**1 TRILLION DOLLARS**
1998	**6 TRILLION DOLLARS***

*This 6 trillion dollars is "On-budget." There is an"Off-budget" debt of 18 trillion dollars, which means the Federal government is approximately 24 trillion dollars in debt—an amount so astronomical in size it cannot be paid back nor can it be serviced indefinately. This debt is greater than the total value of the United States.

Answer: 24 trillion dollars!

Purchasing Power of Gold and of the U.S.Dollar

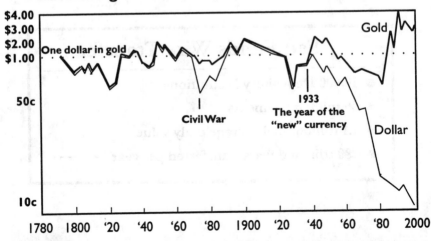

The three main payment systems used in the American economy

None of these institutions have compliant computers. Think of what *one* glitch could do!

	Fed Funds Wire Transfer	Fedwire Securities Transfers	Automated Clearing House (ACH)
Purpose	*Real-time credit transfer system used primarily for payments related to interbank funds transfers.	*Supports the safekeeping, clearing, and settlement of U.S. government securities in both the primary and secondary markets.	*Electronic payment service that supports both credit and debit transactions.
Used By	*10,000 Institutions	*8,000 Institutions	*14,000 Financial Institutions *$400,000 companies *50 million consumers

Transaction Volume	*80 million payments
	
	*$280 trillion
	
	*$1.1 trillion total average total *daily* volume
		*13 million securities transferred
		
		*$160 trillion
		
		*$650 billion in average total value *daily*
			*4 billion transactions, 1996
			    *625 million payments by the Federal government
			    *3.3 billion payments commercial
			    *$12 trillion

Federal Reserve, Board of Governors

The Crash of '99?
—Newsweek
Oct. 12, 1998

The U.S. economy suddenly looks weaker than almost anyone expected. The conventional wisdom still says we won't be pulled down by global economic woes. Don't bet on it.

Sorry, folks: it looks like a recession.

—*Newsweek*

*Sorry, Newsweek: it **is** a depression.*

—*the author*